THE
REFERENCE
SHELF

SOUTH AFRICA: APARTHEID AND DIVESTITURE

edited by STEVEN ANZOVIN

THE REFERENCE SHELF

Volume 59 Number 1

THE H. W. WILSON COMPANY

New York   1987

THE REFERENCE SHELF

The books in this series contain reprints of articles, excerpts from books, and addresses on current issues and social trends in the United States and other countries. There are six separately bound numbers in each volume, all of which are generally published in the same calendar year. One number is a collection of recent speeches; each of the others is devoted to a single subject and gives background information and discussion from various points of view, concluding with a comprehensive bibliography. Books in the series may be purchased individually or on subscription.

Library of Congress Cataloging in Publication Data

Main entry under title:

South Africa : apartheid and divestiture

    (The Reference shelf ; v. 59, no. 1)
    Bibliography: p.
    1. South Africa—Race relations. 2. Apartheid—South Africa. 3. South Africa—Foreign economic relations—United States. 4. United States—Foreign economic relations—South Africa. I. Anzovin, Steven. II. Series.
DT763.5.S584   1987   305.8'00968   87-2028
ISBN 0-8242-0749-1

Printed in the United States of America

CONTENTS

PREFACE

South Africa is a land of contradictions. The most western-ized country in Africa, it lacks many of the freedoms taken for granted by the western democracies, such as a free press, a free judiciary, free elections, and the right of free association and free speech. Its army, one of the world's best, is engaged in a low-level, sporadic civil war that has no obvious military solution. Though South Africa is the continent's richest and most powerful nation, the majority of its citizens are poor, with little immediate hope of betterment. Firmly allied with and of great strategic impor-tance to the West, South Africa is increasingly shunned by its al-lies as unfit to consort with civilized nations.

All these contradictions stem from one basic fact: In South Africa a white minority uses its overwhelming political, econom-ic, and military power to oppress a disenfranchised black majori-ty. This condition, formalized under the complex legal/social/political system of racial discrimination and separation known as apartheid, has earned South Africa the condemnation of much of the world since apartheid's official inception in 1948. Most outsiders appear to agree with Helen Suzman, for years the only member of the South African Parliament to oppose apartheid, who called the system "an affront to people concerned with civi-lized values."

Within South Africa, the situation is balanced on a knife-edge. The whites belong to two main groups, the Afrikaners (of Dutch ancestry) and the English. The Afrikaners especially are committed to preserving their racial, economic, and political privileges. This requires the maintenance of apartheid in some form, by whatever name. The whites as a whole have therefore resisted major reform of apartheid, offering instead mainly cos-metic changes. Blacks, coloreds (of mixed descent), and Indians, who together comprise about 85 percent of the population, want to share power and prosperity with the whites and want institu-tionalized discrimination to end. Some blacks, especially among young people, seek to eliminate the hated whites altogether and use terrorist methods to achieve that goal. It is this group that the white government in Pretoria refers to when it claims that an im-mediate switch to majority rule will lead to a bloodbath in which whites will be "driven to the sea," leaving the country in ruins.

5

Since late 1983 black pressure for change has grown rapidly, yet there seems to be no real chance that South Africa's unarmed and loosely organized blacks can force major change (much less prevail in a military encounter) in the face of Pretoria's superior strength. But South Africa does not exist in a vacuum. Its neighbors to the north, black nations dependent on South Africa for trade and services, support and shelter the leaders of the black opposition movement. That movement is armed and encouraged by the Soviet Union. The United States, after seeking in vain to persuade Pretoria to relax its apartheid rules, has imposed economic sanctions on South Africa. American companies are abandoning their South African operations. Hanging over all is the question of where South Africa can go from here. With the irresistible force of black aspirations facing the immovable object of white stubbornness and fear, the prospects for a peaceful future in South Africa are at best uncertain.

Several major aspects of the plight of South Africa are discussed in this compilation of articles, essays, and speeches. The first section outlines the history and present structure of the system of apartheid and provides some insight into the attitudes of the chief beneficiaries of the system, the Afrikaners. Section two deals with the black townships, the sites of frequent white-on-black and black-on-black violence. Section three reviews the prospect for peaceful change in South Africa, a process in which religious leaders may play a crucial part. The last section discusses the strategic, economic, and moral relationship between South Africa and the United States.

The editor thanks the authors and publishers who kindly granted permission to reprint the material in this collection. Special thanks are also due to the staffs of the public libraries of Englewood and Teaneck, New Jersey, and to Diane Podell of the B. Davis Schwartz Memorial Library, C. W. Post Center, Long Island University.

STEVEN ANZOVIN

February 1987

I. AFRICANS AND AFRIKANERS

EDITOR'S INTRODUCTION

The present situation in South Africa is a product of the country's unique history. Racial discrimination was not suddenly invented by South African whites in the late 1940s; it has been a feature of South African society ever since Dutch settlers landed on the southern tip of Africa in the mid-17th century, enslaving native blacks and imposing the first restrictions on interracial contact. The descendants of these Dutch settlers, who call themselves Afrikaners and who speak a variety of Dutch called Afrikaans, are now the major white group in South Africa. It was Afrikaners who, as a part of their drive to create an independent state of South Africa in the 1930s and 40s, devised the system of apartheid as it now stands.

But what exactly is apartheid, and how does it affect South Africans? In the first two selections, chapters reprinted from Roger Omond's *The Apartheid Handbook,* the South African journalist relates the history of apartheid and answers some questions about apartheid's fundamental tenet: the classification of every South African into a legally defined racial category. Rob Turrell's article from *History Today* on diamond mining and migrant labor in turn-of-the-century South Africa demonstrates that apartheid has its roots deep in economic practices that were in place long before the development of "apartheid theory" by Afrikaner intellectuals in the 1930s.

And who are the Afrikaners? Many Westerners see them as brutal oppressors, an image drawn from television news footage of white police beating and killing black protesters. But, as novelist J. M. Coetzee argues in a piece reprinted from *New York Times Magazine,* the reality is more complex. The Afrikaners he interviews are much like middle-class American moderates—with the crucial difference that they fail to understand their precarious situation "perched on the lip of a volcano."

SOUTH AFRICA AND APARTHEID:
A SHORT HISTORY[1]

The origins of apartheid are linked to a dispute on who arrived where and when in South Africa. White mythology is that Europeans and Africans arrived roughly at the same time: this leads some whites to claim that territorial segregation, one of the main planks of latter-day apartheid, is justified. In reality, the Africans arrived in South Africa much earlier than the first Dutch settlers, who reached Cape Town in 1652. Radiocarbon dating, says the liberal historian T. R. H. Davenport, "has produced evidence of negroid iron age settlement in the trans-Vaal as early as the fifth century AD."

When the Dutch settled at the Cape they did not encounter any Africans. They did, however, come across earlier settlers: the Khoi-khoi (Hottentots) and San (Bushmen). Often competing for the same natural resources as the whites, many died, killed by white hunting parties, in wars, and by smallpox. The Khoi-khoi, particularly, lost their identity and inter-married with slaves from the East Indies and East Africa to form the basis of what today is called the Coloured community.

The Coloureds—the term is often resented but there is no other generally accepted name and it is enshrined in law—also have white blood. Just how much is a matter of acrimonious dispute. The leader of the right-wing Conservative Party, Dr. Andries Treurnicht, contends that any 'white' blood among the Coloureds came from visiting sailors and that "never since the establishment of the [Afrikaner] nation were the Coloured groups allowed into the Afrikaner ranks or accepted as part of the white community."

However, historical evidence does point to a problem. The first "Immorality Act" curtailing sexual liaison across the colour line came in 1685, when marriage between whites and full-blooded blacks was forbidden, although marriage between whites and half-castes was still allowed. The Coloured poet-philosopher Adam Small said recently: "We have blackness and whiteness in

[1]From *The Apartheid Handbook* by Roger Omond, chief sub-editor in the foreign department of the *Guardian*. Penguin Books Ltd. '85. Copyright 1985, 1986 by Roger Omond. Reprinted by permission of Penguin Books Ltd.

our families. There are some of us who are as black as pitch and some as white as snow. That is what being Coloured is all about. We are the past and the future of South Africa."

The white community soon began to move away from Cape Town. Known as the *Trekboers* and described by the novelist André Brink as "a ruggedly independent race of individuals," they were stock farmers. Restlessly in search of new grazing, they moved north and east, encountering the Khoi-khoi, then the San, and then Africans—all competing for land.

By the end of the eighteenth century many of the Boers were in what is now called the Eastern Cape. They were pushing east, the Africans west. Into this conflict came the British government, whose permanent occupation of the Cape began in 1806. London, or its local administrators, felt the only way to maintain control in the colony was through large-scale immigration. In 1820 just over 5,000 Britons came to farm around Grahamstown. With these settlers came a more efficient system of government and some liberal thinking. Ordinance 50 of 1828 repealed the pass laws and established the principle of equality with whites of "all persons of colour." Slavery was abolished in 1834. Missionaries from London cast what the Boers called "unjustifiable odium" on their treatment of blacks. In addition, an attempt was made to suppress the Dutch language. A new war with the Africans broke out and land became scarcer.

The Boers responded to these pressures by moving on again: the Great Trek—a "major intimation of national unity," as Brink calls it—had begun. The Trek has been important in Afrikaner folklore: the centenary re-enactment, in which wagons from many parts of the country converged on Pretoria, gave some impetus to the rise of the National Party and its election victory in May 1948.

The first Trekkers went initially to Natal around 1836, leaving again after a series of bloody wars with the Zulus and when, more importantly, the British followed them there. Their next havens were the Transvaal (called the South African Republic) and the Orange Free State. In these two republics the Boers enshrined the principle of "no equality in church or state," a theme that, according to critics, was to form the basis of *baasskap* apartheid legislation nearly a century later.

The self-governing Cape Colony, largely controlled by the descendants of the 1820 settlers, began on a different political path. In Cecil Rhodes's phrase, the policy was "equal rights for all civilized men." In the Cape there was a non-racial qualified franchise from 1853 for all Her Majesty's subjects, "without distinction to class or colour." In the 1870s, however, Rhodes raised the franchise qualifications to exclude 'red blanket' Africans—unwesternized peasants.

The political development of Natal, very much an English colony with fewer Afrikaners than the Cape, was different again. After 1860 it saw an influx of Indians imported as indentured labourers to work on the sugar plantations. This became a political issue among the white voters of Natal, which supposedly also had a non-racial franchise, and a law was passed denying the vote to anybody whose country of origin did not have "representative institutions founded on the parliamentary franchise." In 1896 India, of course, did not have these; and the measure also disqualified the Africans.

The four states of South Africa—the Cape, Natal, the South African Republic and the Orange Free State—co-existed uneasily for decades. All attempts at national unity were aborted. However, when diamonds and then gold were discovered, the economy began to move away from its old agricultural base. Led by people like Rhodes, the British began to enter the South African Republic in greater numbers with the twin aims of making money and extending the Empire. What the Afrikaners (as they were calling themselves) thought of as their freedom from British rule came to an end with their defeat in the Anglo-Boer War of 1899–1902.

After the war, talk of unity revived. In 1910 the Union of South Africa was formed from the four colonies. Their different racial policies nearly sank the union before it was established; only a compromise averted the collapse of the National Convention of the colonies which set up the Union.

The compromise involved accepting all four colonies' franchise policies, rather than imposing a general system over the country. Blacks were therefore permanently barred from voting in the Transvaal (as it had reverted to being called) and the Orange Free State. The Cape's non-racial franchise was allowed to continue. By that stage 15 per cent of the electorate was black, with two Coloureds for every African. Natal's token non-racialism, with less than one per cent of the voters' roll black, also continued. Parliamentary seats in the new House of Assembly and Senate were, however, reserved exclusively for whites.

It was the Afrikaners of the two northern provinces, rather than liberals from the Cape, who provided the country's leadership for the next 38 years. Three Boer War generals—Botha, Hertzog and Smuts—were the only three prime ministers until a new generation of more conservative Afrikaners, under D. F. Malan, took over in 1948.

From 1910 racial discrimination began to be institutionalized. The 1913 Natives Land Act forced hundreds of thousands of Africans off farms they had either bought or were squatting on in the Transvaal and Free State. As part compensation, the African "reserves"—today forming the basis for the self-governing and "independent" homelands—were to be for Africans only. The legal reservation of jobs for certain races was implemented in the Mines and Works Act and strikes by contract workers forbidden. Some years later the beginnings of separate political institutions for Africans were shaped.

The institutionalization of the discriminatory franchise in the Act of Union led to the formation of what was to become the African National Congress (ANC). At first it was composed largely of African intellectuals who wanted amelioration of their people's economic plight and the extension of political rights. But the current was running against them. In 1936 the Cape Africans— the only ones allowed to vote—were taken off the common roll, put on a separate one, and given the right to elect three white MPs and four senators. In return, more land was promised to the "reserves." At no stage has that area of land risen beyond 13 per cent of South Africa.

The rise of African political consciousness coincided with the growth of the National Party, whose original impetus was not, however, anti-black racism but the urgent desire to uplift the white *volk* from poverty. By the 1930s a total of 300,000 Afrikaners—17.5 per cent—were living in penury, many of them in the cities, displaced from their farms. In this period were launched campaigns for self-help for the "poor whites" which eventually led to the growth of a large Afrikaner industrial and commercial empire. The same decade also saw the re-enactment of the Great Trek, increased national confidence which demanded equal status with English for the Afrikaans language, and the "theologizing" of apartheid. All these elements were blended into what the Afrikaner intellectual W. A. de Klerk calls a "resentful nationalism," in reaction against the condescension of the more

affluent English and, again in De Klerk's words, "the newly appre-
hended threat of a black proletariat."

The National Party's 1948 election victory, which surprised
many, including its leaders, gave the opportunity for apartheid
to be put on the statute books. Movement in this direction was accelerated when Dr. Hendrik Verwoerd, one of the main theolo-
gizers of apartheid, became Minister of Native Affairs and then
Prime Minister. Three legislative pillars of apartheid were passed
rapidly: the Population Registration Act, the Mixed Marriages
Act and the Group Areas Act.

Legislation like this pushed the ANC towards a more militant
stand. The result was the 1952 Defiance Campaign in protest
against a number of racist laws, which was launched just as white
South Africa was celebrating what it called three centuries of
"white civilization" in the country. The Defiance Campaign led
in turn to the introduction of stricter "security" laws; thousands
of Africans were arrested and within a few months 52 ANC leaders had been banned under new legislation. The implementation
of apartheid also led to greater unity among those at the receiving end, and the Congress Alliance was formed of the ANC, the
South African Indian Congress (started after Gandhi began to
put into practice the philosophy of *satyagraha*—'soul force' and
passive resistance—in the 1890s in South Africa) and the white
Congress of Democrats. This sometimes uneasy unity was to lead
to the drawing-up in 1955 of the Freedom Charter—today still
the basis of the ANC's political demands and philosophy.

The parliamentary stage during the early and mid 1950s was
dominated by the government's determination to impose political apartheid on the Coloureds. Until then, Coloured men (but
not women) were still on the common voters' roll in the Cape and
were registered in sufficient numbers to be able to swing the balance in half a dozen or more constituencies. Most voted for the
United Party, which had lost power to the Nationalists in 1948.
One of the movers behind the legislation which stripped Coloureds of their common-roll franchise was P. W. Botha, who was
later, as Prime Minister, to bring in the new constitution giving
them a separate parliament of their own.

A bill removing the Coloureds from the common roll was
passed in the early 1950s by a simple majority in Parliament. It
was then challenged in the courts on the grounds that the constitution demanded a two-thirds majority for any change in voting

rights. This the National Party did not yet have. Parliament then passed a bill reconstituting itself as a High Court with power to review legislation declared invalid by the Appeal Court. The High Court of Parliament solemnly sat and set aside the earlier court decision. This was again taken to court and the High Court of Parliament itself declared invalid. There, in 1952, the matter rested.

In 1954 the fiery J. G. Strijdom took over the premiership from the gentler and older D. F. Malan and the next stage began. First the Appeal Court was reformed to increase its membership to eleven, with a full quorum required to hear constitutional appeals. Next the Senate was enlarged so that the Nationalists would get their required two-thirds majority at a joint sitting with the House of Assembly. Both the Appeal Court and Senate were packed with government supporters. Finally, the bill to put the Coloureds on a separate roll was introduced, passed by the new parliamentary majority, and validated by the new majority of Appeal Court judges. In compensation, Coloureds, again in the Cape only, were given the right to vote for four white MPs. The government would also nominate at least four senators who were to be "thoroughly acquainted . . . with the interests of the Coloured population." All were Nationalists.

Shortly afterwards the government moved to end the limited franchise of the Cape Africans. Their power to elect three white MPs and four senators under the legislation of 1936 was abolished by the Promotion of Bantu Self-Government Act of 1959, which laid the legislative foundations for self-governing and "independent" homelands.

In the late 1960s government attention turned again to the Coloureds when they showed signs of leaving the United Party for the Progressive Party, an offshoot of the UP that took a stronger stand against apartheid. The Prohibition of Political Interference Act was passed, limiting membership of parties to one race only. At about the same time Coloured representation in the House of Assembly and Senate was abolished. In its place came the Coloured Representative Council (CRC), on which nominated members tipped the balance for the pro-apartheid Federal Party against the anti-apartheid Labour Party after the first elections in September 1969. The CRC was eventually scrapped in 1980.

Amid all this legislating for apartheid, the National Party had steadily increased its parliamentary representation at successive elections. In the 1948 election it and its short-lived ally, the Afrikaner Party, which it soon absorbed, had a majority of only five seats over the United Party and others on the opposition benches. By 1966 the Nationalists had an unassailable majority: 126 seats against the UP's 39 and the Progressive Party's one (occupied by Mrs. Helen Suzman, who spent from 1961 to 1974 as her party's sole MP).

As well as gaining increased representation in the Assembly, the Nationalists ensured that many senior jobs went to like-minded *volk*. Afrikaners climbed up the rungs of the Civil Service or were imposed (notably in the Defence Force and broadcasting) over the heads of senior officials. To cope with the need to administer apartheid, as well as to provide employment for many of its supporters, the Civil Service was expanded: by 1984 there was one civil servant for every 25 people in South Africa—a total of 998,124 at an annual cost of R8.4 billions (£4.2 billion),[*] representing just under 40 per cent of the country's budget. Despite efforts by the government, faced with a worsening economic crisis caused in part by loss of international confidence in the wake of widespread unrest, to curb the growth of the state, the Civil Service continued to grow. The state's wage bill for the second quarter of 1985 was R2,555 million—more than R10.5 billion (£5.25 billion) for the whole year. The number of public servants, excluding postal and transport workers, was more than one million, according to an estimate by the Central Statistical Service. Afrikaner capitalism took off, too, while parastate organizations flourished.

This same period saw a decline in white opposition. The United Party seems never to have recovered from the psychological blow of losing the 1948 election. It compromised and changed in efforts to regain support; instead it lost votes and MPs at all but one election after 1948. Finally, in a last desperate bid for survival, it changed its name to the New Republic Party and so lost its identity and identifiability. Today it has five seats in the white chamber.

A number of the many MPs who left the United Party during its years in the wilderness came together to form the Progressive

---

[*]At conversion rate of R2 to £1. The rand later fell lower.

Party in 1959. Having absorbed more breakaway groups from the UP it was re-named the Progressive Federal Party, and is now, with 27 seats, the official opposition in the white chamber. The PFP got 18.17 per cent of the votes cast at the last white election in 1981. Yet when it actively canvassed a "no" vote in the 1983 referendum on the new constitution, it could not hold much of that support and Mr. Botha got the backing of two thirds of those whites who voted in the referendum—with much of the opposition coming from a completely different quarter.

The PFP found itself advocating a "no" vote with the Conservative Party, a right-wing breakaway group from the National Party, and the even more rigid Herstigte Nasionale Party. The PFP was saying that the new constitution's exclusion of Africans from any voice in central government meant that it could not solve South Africa's problems; the CP and the HNP, on the other hand, saw any power-sharing, however limited, with Coloureds and Indians as the thin end of the wedge and the probable downfall of "white civilization." Today the Conservative Party has 18 seats in the white Parliament; it has scored some notable by-election successes and near-misses, and is a constant right-wing factor among the *volk* that Mr. Botha feels he has to take into account. This feeling was reinforced at the end of October 1985 when the HNP scored its first parliamentary win since its formation in 1969. With Conservative Party support, the HNP won the Sasolburg constituency in the Orange Free State, overturning the National Party's majority of 2,619 in 1981 to win by 367 votes. This result, plus strong showings by the Conservative Party in several other seats, was widely interpreted as a setback for the government's reform programme, and even Mr. Botha said that he would have to "take cognizance" of the by-elections. The National Party's majority is still large, however: 127 seats against all the opposition parties' 50.

To compensate for the withdrawal of support on the right wing of Afrikanerdom, Mr. Botha and his predecessor, B. J. Vorster, have turned more to the English-speaking voters. Several English-speakers have been in the Cabinet since the 1960s, and in the referendum on the constitution many English-speakers voted "yes." One survey showed that, of the supporters of the predominantly English-speaking PFP, seven voted "yes" for every five who voted "no." The mainly English-speaking areas of Natal and the Border had the largest "yes" majorities.

Much of this white parliamentary activity has, however, been overshadowed by black extra-parliamentary action. The pattern of protests against apartheid, government reaction, sporadic violence and the arrest and/or banning of individuals continued throughout the 1950s, culminating in the events at Sharpeville in 1960. What protesters said began as a peaceful demonstration against pass laws ended in the police shooting dead 69 people. A state of emergency followed; the ANC and an offshoot, the Pan-Africanist Congress (PAC), were banned and thousands of people detained without trial.

At this stage the ANC and PAC went underground and resolved that the era of non-violent protest had passed. Umkhonto we Sizwe, the military wing of the ANC, and Poqo, military wing of the PAC, began the armed struggle that they are still pursuing. After some successful sabotage in the early 1960s, both appeared to be crushed by the increasing powers and efficiency of the Special Branch and the tendency of the courts to hand down heavy sentences.

After nearly a decade of sullen acquiescence, the Black Consciousness movement led by Steve Biko developed in the late 1960s and the 1970s. W. A. de Klerk has pointed out similarities between the birth of Black Consciousness and that of Afrikaner nationalism: both originated in "the human urge to be oneself and to live in accordance with one's essential nature, as a free intelligence with a particular idiom." Soon, however, Black Consciousness leaders attracted the attention of the Special Branch, and on 12 September 1977 Steve Biko died in detention. Five weeks later all the organizations that had sprung up through the movement were banned.

Black Consciousness had contributed to the Soweto uprising that began on 16 June 1976 in protest against the compulsory use of Afrikaans in African schools. Trouble spread almost throughout the country and hundreds of people were killed. Hundreds more fled South Africa, many of them into ANC camps for guerrilla training. For a number of reasons the ANC, the oldest of the liberation movements, emerged as the strongest force, both internally and externally.

Black Consciousness survives in several groups formed after the 1977 bannings, most notably in the Azanian Peoples' Organization (AZAPO) and an umbrella body of different organizations, the National Forum. It has, however, been overshadowed by the

United Democratic Front (UDF), a similar umbrella organization, which takes as its starting point the Freedom Charter drawn
up by the ANC and its Congress allies, which has a non-racial socialist state as its aim.

While black extra-parliamentary activity was in a ferment
from Sharpeville onwards, the government began to implement
its "homelands" policy—that part of apartheid which, its supporters say, gives it moral legitimacy. Transkei became the first self-
governing homeland in 1963, to be followed by the other nine to
which Africans are meant to owe allegiance. Transkei, Ciskei,
Bophuthatswana and Venda are now all "independent," while
KwaZulu, Lebowa, Gazankulu, QwaQwa, KaNgwane and
KwaNdebele are self-governing.

The homelands policy is less than universally popular. Transkei, Ciskei and Venda are governed under virtual states of emergency. Some African leaders such as KwaZulu's Chief Gatsha
Buthelezi have entered homeland governments under protest.
Millions of Africans in the 'white' areas of South Africa have never seen the "homelands" to which they are deemed to belong and
where, in theory, they should exercise their political rights. The
declared aim of the policy was that eventually there should be no
more African South Africans: when all the homelands were
"independent" every African would be a citizen of one or another, merely coming to 'white' South Africa to sell labour. At the
beginning of 1985, however, a possible shift in course was indicated when Mr. Botha hinted that the question of citizenship was being reconsidered. Later that year, opening the Cape Congress of
the National Party, he said that the government was committed
to "the principle of a geographically united South Africa, a common citizenship and universal franchise." The President's Council would also be restructured to include Africans—the first time
that he had spelled out what he meant when, at the beginning of
the year, he had hinted at a consultative voice in central government for Africans. Mr. Botha, also for the first time, said that he
would include "non-traditional" leaders in consultations. A
month later, a deputy minister said that these could include such
opponents of apartheid as Bishop Desmond Tutu and the Rev.
Allan Boesak. These changes in policy, however, did not mean
that the homelands—"independent" and self-governing—would
be abolished.

If the homelands policy has not proved universally popular,
the new parliaments for Coloureds and Indians have not been
widely welcomed either. (In August 1984 elections for these
chambers were held: fewer than 18 out of every 100 potential
Coloured voters and 16 out of every 100 potential Indian voters
went to the polls) In the Coloured heartland of the Cape Peninsu-
la, the turnout of potential voters was about 5 per cent. This boycott of the polls—encouraged by a wide range of black
organizations—resulted, for example, in the former leader of the
Labour Party (the main Coloured political party), M.D. Arendse,
taking his seat in the Coloured House of Representatives at a salary of R48,000 (£24,000) a year with 118 votes behind him in his
Table Mountain constituency. Mr. Arendse, however, had a
short-lived parliamentary career: a year after his election he was
unseated by the Supreme Court for bribing pensioners to vote for
him. He was sentenced to a 12-month suspended jail term.

Both the present leader of the Labour Party, the Rev. Alan
Hendrikse, and the leader of the National People's Party in the
Indian House of Delegates, Mr. Amichand Rajbansi, are now
non-departmental Cabinet ministers.

The new parliaments for Coloureds and Indians, with the existing white chamber, are meant to cater for the political needs
of 27 per cent of South Africa's total population: 4.8 million
whites (14.8 per cent), 2.8 million Coloureds (8.7 per cent) and
890,000 Indians (2.7 per cent). Excluded are 24.1 million Africans, about 13 million of whom live in the "independent" and self-
governing homelands.

Power, at this stage, still resides firmly in white hands. The
new constitution has been shaped so that the majority party in the
white House of Assembly effectively rules. In the present circumstances this means the National Party, which in turn means the
Afrikaners, estimated at 2.6 million (57 per cent of the white population or 8.7 per cent of all South Africans).

It is the Afrikaners who have become identified with apartheid—unfairly, many of them say. Some South African historians
point out that much of the framework of apartheid has been in
place for years: migrant labour, for example, began to be introduced on a large scale with the discovery of diamonds and gold
in the late 1800s. But whatever the origins and causes of apartheid may be, it is the legislation passed by the South African Parliament, and particularly since the National Party came to power

in 1948, that has focused so much attention on the country.

SOUTH AFRICA'S
RACIAL CLASSIFICATIONS

South African usage of terms to describe the people who live there is both confused and confusing. As elsewhere, it often reflects the political attitudes and position in society of the user. The apartheid system is based on the classification of the population into four main groups, at present officially called 'white', 'Coloured', 'Indian' and 'black'. However, these terms are not the only ones in everyday use. In addition, some words, whether official or unofficial usage, are unacceptable to many of the people they are supposed to identify. This note mentions some of the names historically or currently used to designate sections of South Africa's population.

For many everyday purposes a simple division into 'black' and 'white' is found to suffice. 'White' is used for all those classified and accepted as being of European descent. 'Black', despite its appropriation as the official term for Africans, is used by the majority of the South African population as a generic term for all those on the receiving end of apartheid, whether officially categorized as 'black', 'Coloured' or 'Indian'.

The largest variety of terms has been applied to those of African descent. Someone holding extreme white supremacist views will often refer to Africans as 'kaffirs'. Official terminology was originally 'native', then 'Bantu' (literally 'people'), and is now 'black'. The word 'African' is officially taboo because it translates into Afrikaans as 'Afrikaner'—just the word used for the white, Afrikaans-speaking South Africans who have been largely responsible for institutionalizing apartheid. Nevertheless, except when quoting official sources, 'African' is the term employed here.

The word 'Coloured' is disliked by many of the people of mixed racial origins who are thus officially designated. There is unfortunately no other term in common usage. In South Africa there is an increasing tendency, particularly in more liberal newspapers, for the word to be used in quotes and with a lower-case 'c', but in other English-speaking countries this carries the risk of confusion with the more general sense in which the word is still sometimes used. I have therefore used the term 'Coloured' as it stands.

'Indian' and 'Asian' are used interchangeably by most South Africans to describe people whose forebears came from the Indian subcontinent. Where separate reference is needed the usage of 'Indian' is followed here.

South Africa is a multi-racial society, but four main groups are now officially recognized: white, African (called 'black' in government terminology), Coloured and Indian. What is South African race classification?
It is a government system categorizing every South African in a racial group defined by law. All identity documents, from birth certificate to driving licence, note the race of the bearer.

Has race classification always existed in South Africa?
The Population Registration Act, Number 30 of 1950, was one of the first major pieces of legislation brought in by the National Party government. Before that, some legislation included racial definitions, but they did not all correspond to one another and the system was not rigid: people could "pass" from one group to another if their appearance made it possible.

Why was race classification introduced by the South African government?
The government wanted a system that would end the "passing" of people. It aimed at rigid classification based on appearance, general acceptance and repute. All people were henceforth to be classified on racial lines and entered into a register of the population.

How did the 1950 Act define race?
The original Act classified people as white, Coloured, or Native (later called Bantu and still later black). Coloureds and Natives could also be subdivided according to their ethnological groups.

How specific were definitions of race? Have they been refined at any time?
In Proclamation 46 of 1959, Coloureds were divided into Cape Coloured, Cape Malay, Griqua, Indian, Chinese, 'other Asiatic' and 'other Coloured'. This was, however, declared void for rea-

sons of vagueness by a judge of the Cape Town Supreme Court in 1967.

The Population Registration Amendment Act, Number 64 of 1967, was then introduced. It said that the State President could, by proclamation, classify Coloureds and Africans into sub-groups. This was done through Proclamation R123 on 26 May 1967, repeating the earlier sub-groups declared invalid by the Supreme Court.

Were the original criteria for determining race absolute?

The original Act said that appearance, general acceptance and repute were the tests. In 1962 an amending Act made it obligatory for appearance and acceptance to be considered together— until then acceptability was the main criterion used.

There were many different ways of determining race. Have these definitions changed in South Africa?

The definition of a white was tightened in the 1962 amending Act and was made retrospective to 1950 in another Act in 1964. The Population Registration Amendment Act, Number 64 of 1967, again tightened the criteria used in classification, especially of whites and Coloureds. Descent was now the determining factor. Tests of "appearance" and "general acceptance" were set down for use in cases where people claimed to be white but could not prove that both their parents had been classified white. A white person, according to the Act, is someone who:

a. In appearance obviously is a white person and who is not generally accepted as a Coloured person; or
b. Is generally accepted as a white person and is not in appearance obviously not a white person.

In trying to define who is or is not a white, "his habits, education and speech and deportment and demeanour shall be taken into account."

How do the courts apply the criteria of "appearance" and "general acceptance" in determining who is white?

There are no hard-and-fast rules. In 1981 a Johannesburg magistrate convicted a woman previously thought white for living in a 'white' area. The magistrate said she was Coloured because she had a "flat nose, wavy hair, a pale skin, and high cheekbones." The conviction was set aside by the Supreme Court judges ruling that while the woman was not obviously white, she was "generally accepted" as such.

What kinds of tests have been used in race classification?

Fingernails have been examined. Combs have been pulled through people's hair: if the comb is halted by tight curls, the person is more likely to be classified Coloured than white. In July 1983 an abandoned baby, named Lize Venter by hospital staff, was found near Pretoria. To classify her by race, as the Population Registration Act demands, a strand of her hair was examined by the Pretoria police laboratory: she was then classified Coloured.

Is there any scientific basis for a test using hair as a means of determining race?

Not according to a member of the International Institute of Trichology, which studies the functions, structures and diseases of the hair. He was reported to have said the test was invalid as there was no hair classification for Coloured people.

Can race classifications be challenged?

To some extent. The 1967 Amendment Act removed the right of third parties to take legal action against a classification, apart from guardians of minor children. Third parties were still allowed, however, to object to the Secretary of the Interior—the Civil Service head of the department making the classification.

Can people who believe they have been wrongly classified appeal to the courts?

There is a limited right. The 1969 Amendment Act lays down that a person may go to court against the decision of the departmental appeal board only if the board has altered his or her existing classification. Further, a person may go to court if the appeal board disagrees with the classification made by a lower official. But if the board confirms the lower official's classification, the person concerned cannot go to court.

Can a person socially accepted as Coloured be legally classified as belonging to another group?

It can happen. The 1969 Act says that a person can be classified African if he or she appears to be African, even if that person has white or Coloured blood and is generally accepted as Coloured.

Can Coloureds change their sub-group?

If a person's father is classified in one Coloured sub-group, that person must be classified in the same sub-group, according to the 1969 Act.

How many legal subdivisions are there of the racial group defined as African?

In terms of various laws, nine African "national units" are recognized: North Sotho, South Sotho, Tswana, Zulu, Swazi, Xhosa (two units), Tsonga and Venda. Government policy assigns every African to one of these groups.

Although people cannot physically change race, can they do so in the eyes of the law?

Thousands of people have been affected in this way by the Population Registration Acts. In 1984, the Minister of Home Affairs told Parliament, 795 South Africans were re-classified. They included 518 former Coloureds who became white, two whites who became Chinese, one white who became Indian, 89 Africans who became Coloured and five Coloureds who became African. In 1983, a total of 690 people changed: two thirds were Coloureds who became white; 71 Africans became Coloured; and 11 whites were classified to other groups. In the year July 1981 to June 1982 a total of 997 "changed race." Among them were one Indian who became white, four Cape Coloured to Chinese, 15 white to Chinese, three 'other Asian' to Cape Coloured, and three African to Griqua.

Do people always know what race they are assigned to?

No. In 1984, for example, a government commission studying the courts found that two pre-school children were held in detention for three years while they awaited a government decision on their race. In the 1960s Sandra Laing, born to white parents in the eastern Transvaal, was asked to leave her white school at the age of 11 because she "looked Coloured." She was re-classified Coloured, but after a long legal battle the decision was reversed. She then lived with an African man and applied to be reclassified African so that the relationship could be legalized.

There have been many reported cases of families being split by race classification. Branches of some families have been classi-

fied white while others have been classified Coloured. Dark-
skinned children of Coloureds trying to pass for white are said
sometimes to have been abandoned or sent to relatives of a
deeper hue. Dark-skinned children of white parents, as the Sandra Laing case shows, have also caused problems.

Have people been re-classified more than once?
Yes. In late 1984, for example, a 'white' father was re-classified
Coloured—the fifth time he had crossed the racial divide. His
'Indian' wife also changed and was classified Coloured. The
change meant that the couple, Vic and Farina Wilkinson, could
live together legally as man and wife. Mr. Wilkinson was originally classified 'mixed', then 'European' (white), then Coloured,
then white, and finally Coloured.

Is there a "pure" white race?
Not according to evidence given to a parliamentary select committee investigating the Immorality and Mixed Marriages Acts in
1984. Dr. E. D. du Toit, senior lecturer in the University of Cape
Town's department of human genetics, said there was a considerable admixture of so-called Southern African genes, mostly Khoi-
san (Hottentot and Bushman) as well as Negro and Asiatic. White
South Africans in general had more than seven per cent mixed
blood.

A major row broke out in 1985 over the claim made by an academic, Dr. Hans Heese, in his book *Groep Sonder Grense* ("Groups
Without Boundaries") that the forebears of many leading Afrikaner families had married or had relationships with Asian slaves.
At least 18 MPs in the whites-only House of Assembly have sur-
names indicating a racially mixed genealogy. In the ensuing row
about the book:

  • The heart transplant surgeon Chris Barnard challenged the
leader of the far-right Conservative Party, Dr. Andries
Treurnicht, to verify his claim to pure white ancestry by submitting to a medical test.

  • Sixteen people said they would sue the *Sunday Times*, which
gave extensive coverage to Dr. Heese's findings, for R320,000
(£160,000) unless the paper undertook not to quote again from
the book. They said that they had been embarrassed and humiliated by the suggestion that they might be descended from people
of colour.

• A member of the extremist Herstigte Nasionale Party and of the Pretoria City Council punched a fellow-councillor in a row over mixed ancestry. Piet Rudolph said the impression was given that he was "not worthy of representing a white electorate—that my ancestors were people who acted disgracefully towards their race and *volk* by sexually mixing with other colours."

An admission that race classification, an important pillar of apartheid, is widely resented came in a report by the Human Sciences Research Council in October 1985. It found that the system was "probably the root cause of ill-feeling between South Africa's different groups" and that there was a "clearly apparent link between population registration and the establishment and maintenance of white supreme authority." The HSRC report proposed that, instead of a system where appearance and origin were the determining factor, the emphasis should be on freedom of association and acceptance.

DIAMONDS AND MIGRANT LABOUR IN SOUTH AFRICA, 1869–1910[2]

Racial discrimination in South Africa is based on the migrant labour system. Unlike other South Africans, Africans are treated as foreigners outside strictly defined areas of residence, the so-called "homelands," and their movement is controlled by the notorious system of pass laws. Typically, men contract to work in the major cities while leaving their families and political rights behind them in the "homelands." Migrant labour has ensured a supply of cheap wage labour to the mining sector and secondary industry, and is a system which has been condemned throughout the world.

Migrant labour is not a system unique to South Africa. Migrant labourers from countries in southern Europe contract to work in France, Germany, Sweden and Britain on a large scale. They are genuine foreigners, and while they suffer from different forms of exploitation and prejudice, in time they are allowed

[2]Article by historian Rob Turrell, a fellow at the Institute of Commonwealth Studies, London. *History Today.* 36:45+. My. '86. Copyright 1986 by History Today Ltd. Reprinted by permission.

to settle with their families in host countries. What is unique about South African migrant labour is the prohibition on internal migrants from settling at their work places. The system is far more pervasive and coercive in South Africa than in Europe. In South Africa it has existed in different forms for over 140 years.

So how did it all begin? In the seventeenth and eighteenth centuries, during the period of Dutch rule, slave labour dominated the wheat and wine farms of the Cape Colony, but there were also pockets of wage labour in the main towns. After the arrival of the British in 1806 and the abolition of slavery in 1834, wage labour spread unevenly through town and countryside. The first major growth of wage labour occurred after 1869, following the discovery of diamonds between the Vaal and Harts rivers, some 700 miles from Cape Town.

Fortune hunters flocked to the "river diggings" and then to the "dry diggings" a short distance away at Kimberley, where one of the four mines turned out to be the most valuable four acres of real estate in the world. The mine, also called Kimberley, was so fabulously rich that by 1872 there were 10,000 men picking, digging, shovelling and sorting its diamondiferous ground. The majority of manual labourers were Africans and for them wage labour, let alone minework, was a new experience.

Wage labour was a novelty because no such relationship existed within independent African chiefdoms. Bonds of kinship determined production and reproduction within economic systems based on subsistence agriculture and the herding of cattle. Chiefs and lineage heads governed access to land, controlled the allocation of labour and ensured the payment of various forms of tribute. Crucially, marriage was controlled by the elders who owned the herds of cattle necessary for bridewealth. So, when Africans went to work in the diamond mines they were not "free" wage labourers, in the sense of labourers "free" from the land and labourers "free" to sell their capacity to work. In any case, their social responsibilities denied them the freedom to dispose of their labour as individuals.

Africans went to work in the Kimberley mines for a variety of reasons. Many went to earn cattle for bridewealth or ploughs to improve their farming for the market. Others went to earn guns on the instructions of chiefs and elders. Take, for example, the Pedi, a Sotho people who lived in the north-eastern Transvaal and dominated the Kimberley labour market in the 1870s. Before the discovery of diamonds the Pedi had been travelling to the Cape Colony for some forty years or more to work as migrant labourers. They earned money because their chiefs understood the importance of acquiring guns to protect themselves against white settlers, who had begun to move into the Transvaal region in the 1830s and 1840s. The Pedi sold their labour to buy guns because they did not have easy access to commodity markets for agricultural produce. In this respect the Pedi differed from other African peoples, who were able to sell produce rather than labour for guns. In the 1870s the need for guns grew as the pressure of white settlers on African land increased. Consequently, the discovery of diamonds was opportune for Pedi; Kimberley was a shorter distance than the eastern Cape, wages were higher and less time was spent in working for a gun and/or bridewealth.

The diamond mines provided the largest and most accessible labour and gun markets for Africans from the interior of southern Africa. Africans went to do a spell of minework, which became culturally institutionalised as a rite of manhood. They left at the command of their chiefs and were subject to headmen in the mining camps. They commonly worked between three and six months in the mines, bought guns or other commodities and then left for home. Some never returned, others made it an annual affair. Yet, in the early days, they remained cultivators and pastoralists who complemented their primary activities with a stint in wage labour.

Such Africans were not ideal mineworkers. They were unaccustomed to the heavy work of digging and loading, but more importantly, most did not stay long enough to learn industrial discipline. Mine-owners tried to control the supply of labour to the mines through recruitment, government sponsored schemes to protect the labour routes to the mines and the informal system of labour touting. They were not as successful as they would have liked.

Mine-owners also explored ways of controlling and holding Africans once they were in Kimberley. From 1872 all Africans (Pedi, Sotho and Tsonga from outside the boundaries of the Cape Colony were in a majority) had their freedom restricted by the pass system. This was a complicated set of changing controls which attempted to inhibit desertion. At its heart was the pass an African received once he had made a contract to labour for an employer. Without such a pass Africans were liable to arrest and imprisonment for up to three months. Despite the rigorous application of the system, it did not guarantee the uninterrupted labour of African mineworkers.

In Kimberley Europeans were dependent on an anonymous African workforce for the first time in southern Africa. Africans made up nearly 90 per cent of the mines' labour complement: this varied from 10,000 men during slumps in production to 30,000 during boom periods (1878–81, 1886–90). Between 50,000 and 100,000 Africans went to Kimberley in any one year. This was a far greater movement of workers than had ever taken place in southern Africa before. While Africans did not settle permanently in Kimberley, they threatened new political and social problems, and aroused deepfelt fears amongst Europeans.

What could European mine-owners do to dominate and discipline such a labour force? What they would have liked to do—to turn them into slaves or indentured labourers on long contract—had to be balanced against what was possible. For the first fifteen years of diamond production all the cards seemed to be in the hands of African workers and their chiefs. Wages were high, the pass system was ineffective, workers were more suited to pastoral or agricultural pursuits and they were subject to recall at a moment's notice if their chiefs required their military service. In this period of South African history there were numerous colonial wars which were bad for mining in the short term. In such a situation the strength of African workers lay in their ability to withdraw their labour at will. The mine-owners' problem was simple: their workers were not dependent on mining for a livelihood.

In the early 1880s a number of changes tipped the balance of power against Africans in the labour market. Firstly, after 1880 the growth of joint-stock mining companies, in place of numerous small diggers, provided the political and economic cohesion to push through radical solutions in the industry. Then, the onset of a deep depression from 1882 to 1885 bankrupted weak mining companies and encouraged the destruction of worker organisations. Next, after 1885, the development of underground mining, which precluded the close supervision of the labour process possible in open-cast mining until then, made new forms of control desirable. Finally, the wholesale conquest of African chiefdoms in southern Africa pushed a considerable number of Africans off the land and into the colonial economy. These conquests of, for example, the Pedi and the Zulu, were quite remarkable. In the space of thirty years or so, between 1870 and 1900, all independent African chiefdoms were subordinated to colonial, imperial or republican rule. These military conquests were in no small measure influenced by the increasing labour demands made by the diamond and gold mining industries on the African societies of southern Africa.

Joint-stock companies, the depression, underground mining and the conquest of African chiefdoms all shaped the decision to introduce closed compounds in 1885. Compounds provided the framework for the total control of African workers. Once inside these military-style barracks, workers lost all access to the outside world for the length of a contract. In 1902 Gardner Williams, General Manager of De Beers, described the largest compound:

Fully four acres are enclosed by the walls of De Beers' Compound, giving ample space for the housing of its three thousand inmates, with an open central ground for exercise and sports. The fences are of corrugated iron, rising ten feet above the ground, and there is an open space of ten feet between the fence and the buildings. . . . Iron cabins fringe the inner sides of the enclosure, divided into rooms 25 feet by 30 feet, which are lighted by electricity. In each room twenty to twenty-five natives are lodged. The beds supplied are ordinary wooden bunks, and the bed clothing is usually composed of blankets which the natives bring with them, or buy at the stores in the compound, where there is a supply of articles to meet the simple needs of the natives. Besides these stores there is a hospital and dispensary. . . . In the centre of the enclosure there is a large concrete swimming bath.

While this description contained some recent improvements, the basic features of the compound had been the same since its inception. The compound system denied Africans the freedom to respond to market forces and to sell their labour for the highest wage. It enabled the mine owners to turn the initial disadvantage of migrant labour into the great political and economic advantages of cheap and controlled labour, a system so advantageous to mining capitalists that it continues to operate throughout the mineral industries in South Africa today.

The mine-owners justified such a system of compounds to a colonial governing class, which believed in free trade (and to metropolitan Parliament, which kept a watching brief on "slavery"), by arguing that they were being extensively robbed by their African workers and that compounds were the only fail-safe way of protecting themselves. Diamonds were often very small and easily stolen. A worker in the claims could unearth a stone with his toes, swallow it and wait for it to appear again in the course of nature.

From there it was a simple matter to sell it, for a fraction of its value, on the illicit diamond market in Kimberley. IDB (illicit diamond buying) kept a vast quantity of money in circulation to the benefit of local traders and merchants. It was the extent of this illicit trade, argued mine-owners, that had so seriously undermined the profitability of the industry and exacerbated the crisis diamond mining faced during the depression.

Yet this was a self-serving justification and one which played on an issue, the defence of private property, with which the governing class in the Cape Colony was most likely to sympathise. For one thing, it was next to impossible to judge how many diamonds were being stolen, and mine-owners took advantage of this by magnifying the extent of theft to explain away their failure to make a profit. For another, reckless promotion and speculation during the formation of joint-stock companies in 1880–81 had so inflated the market value of the diamond industry that it was impossible for many companies to declare dividends at all. Who was the real villain: the diamond thief in the pit or the dishonest promoter in the board room? And who was to say the diamond thief was black rather than white?

Of course, mine-owners wanted to prevent theft, but they wanted compounds for other reasons as well. Most managers and directors had noted the advantages in labour efficiency, discipline and cost that Cecil Rhodes' De Beers Diamond Mining Company derived from the use of convict labour. They wanted to imitate the convict labour system without turning free workers into slaves. In time, though, the compound system turned the distinction between waged and convict labour into a matter of words, rather than the fundamental divide between free and unfree labour.

The development of underground mining was experimental in nature as there were no tried mining techniques for Kimberley's type of diamondiferous ground. Going underground was tunnelling into the unknown in more senses than one. It was vastly expensive and the stakes were high for those companies who mastered the underground caverns. A constant supply of Africans accustomed to minework was essential in such a situation. Workers had to be encouraged to remain longer than three months so as to increase labour efficiency. The coercive features of the compound system played a crucial role in turning migrant labourers into experienced mineworkers, good at drilling, loading and picking. That was its essential function.

Once Africans were isolated from the towns and camps in closed compounds, labour discipline was easier to enforce. Absenteeism declined, piece-work was introduced and liquor and women were forbidden. Mineworkers worked full twelve hour shifts, although they did not necessarily work a full week. Isolation also made it easier to force down wages, as strikes could be put down by compound guards as faction fights. And it is remarkable how the wages of workers were forced down to the maintenance costs of convict workers by the middle 1890s.

In short, the compound was the key institution of labour control in early industrial South Africa. It provided the link between a capitalist enclave in Kimberley and its labour-supplying hinterland. The mine-owners had struggled to control the supply of labour throughout the 1870s and 1880s, but had failed in the face of the greater control of chiefs and elders over the labour-power of their young men. In the 1890s it was the compound system that turned migrant labourers into experienced and cheap mineworkers, while reducing the threat of an organised working class in Kimberley.

TALES OF AFRIKANERS[3]

Some 40 miles from Cape Town, on the fringe of the wine-farming region of the Cape Province, lies Stellenbosch, the second-oldest town in South Africa. Though it is the seat of a major university, Stellenbosch is not a notably liberal place. Its students are well behaved, its white voters have always stood firmly behind the National Party, which has held power since 1948. Liberals have gained no footing here, but then neither has the ultraright.

A few months ago, the highway between Cape Town and Stellenbosch was effectively closed: bands of black and Coloured, or mixed-race, youths hung about on the verges or waited on overpasses to stone cars; burning barricades sometimes blocked the road; on bad days even the airport, which lies along this route, could be reached only under police escort.

[3]Articles by South African novelist J. M. Coetzee. *New York Times Magazine*. 14–22+. Mr. 9, '86. Copyright © 1986 by The New York Times Company. Reprinted by permission.

Today, as I drive out to Stellenbosch, the highway is reputed to be safe. I pass an armored troop carrier parked under a tree. A soldier, crouched on the embankment, stares at something through binoculars. From the vicinity of the Crossroads squatter camp, an illegal shantytown that has been the scene of recent violence, a pillar of yellow smoke rises into the air. The sun blazes down. All is quiet on this southern front, by South African standards.

I am on my way to meet some of the citizens of Stellenbosch, strangers as yet to me, to hear how they feel about what is going on in our country. My mind is open; I am ready to be surprised.

A week ago, in the village of Greyton, I overheard a farmer, a fat, apoplectic-looking man in khakis, everyone's notion of the brutal slavemaster. "P. W. Botha and his promises!" he growled. "If he won't put up, he should shut up!" (The idiom he used in Afrikaans was a good deal cruder than the English version.) If, even in the somnolent remoter valleys, Afrikaners were irritated by the snail's pace of change, the gap between talk and action, how much bolder might they not be nearer the big city?

As I will discover, the people I interview do not conform to the reigning stereotype of the Afrikaner. They do not speak contemptuously of blacks. They are not notably intolerant in their attitudes, heartless in their conduct or indolent in their daily life. They seem not to bear the worst marks of apartheid, a doctrine and a set of social practices that scars the moral being of whites as it degrades and demeans blacks. Whether they can be said to be representative of their three million compatriots—in other words, of 60 percent of South Africa's whites—I do not know. They all identify themselves as Afrikaners, but their allegiances seem to lie as much with the broad South African middle class as with the Afrikaner tribe. In this respect they are typical of the generation born after 1948, a generation that, having grown up under Afrikaner hegemony, can afford to be more self-assured, less belligerently nationalistic than their fathers.

Indeed, I am struck above all by the *calm* of those I interview. They do not talk like people perched on the lip of a volcano. All of them believe the world around them is changing (and should be changing faster), but nowhere do they seem to envisage an eruption of change that might sweep them and their children away. Yet they live in a country seething with black anger, and at war on its borders. Have the ring of steel around the black townships and the clampdown on news coverage fostered in them an unreal sense of security, a culpable ignorance, a foolish calm? Or do they in truth have darker fears, more dire visions of the future, than they are ready to divulge? Are they telling the truth, the whole truth, or have they chosen to engage in acts of self-presentation for an audience of strangers?

I put the question, yet it seems to me falsely put. How often in our lives does the truth of ourselves, the whole and unmixed truth, emerge? Are we not routinely engaged in acts of self-presentation, acts which it would be excessively Puritanical to condemn as insincere? Surely, in getting to know the truth of another person, we neither accept nor reject his self-presentations, but *read* them, as best we can, in whatever context we can summon up. A few hours of conversation will not give us privileged access to "the Afrikaner": It would be naive to expect that. What we have below are excerpts from the texts of four lives, uttered (I believe) with due deliberation, for the record, at particular moments in four life-histories—fragments of the text of a national discourse, to be read and weighed alongside whatever other fragments we can come into possession of.

In one of the pleasanter white suburbs, I meet Kaffie Pretorius, an attractive, matronly woman in her 30's. Brought up in Lambert's Bay, on South Africa's west coast, where her father kept a store, she married an academic, settled in Stellenbosch, paints in her spare time. But she still hankers for the desolate west-coast landscape: when she goes there on vacation, she takes her children on long rambles in the veld to teach them the plant-lore she learned as a child.

We speak in Afrikaans, our common tongue, the language of most of rural South Africa. Like everyone else I speak to, Kaffie Pretorius is depressed about the failing economy, about accelerating inflation and the collapse of the South African currency, which has led in only a few months to a doubling in the prices of imported goods, including gasoline. Yet, to my surprise, she observes that these economic woes may not be such a bad thing: "For the first time, whites are truly affected—for the first time they must think seriously about the future." And then, after a pause: "How did we think we could hold on to all of this?" She waves a hand to embrace her spacious home, the prosperous neighborhood, and beyond it the town of Stellenbosch, surrounded by thousands of acres of farmland. "How did we ever think we could hold on to it?"

I have no reply. I am touched by her words, by their suddenness, by the feeling behind them. Perhaps one can be so naked only with strangers. Yet afterward, I wonder whether I would not have been equally touched, though in a different way, had she lamented: "How can they take all this away from us?" And is it a good idea to indulge, in oneself or anyone else, these fits of voluptuous self-recrimination?

"Things go in phases," she resumes. "We are the generation that will have to make the adjustment. Our children will find it easier. Already, children find it easier to relate to Coloured friends than we ever did."

In what spheres of life, I ask, are whites going to find it hardest to adjust? "First, education. When schools are integrated, standards drop. It's unfortunate, but it's a fact. Look at Zimbabwe. Second, neighbors." Would she personally mind black or Coloured neighbors? "Not at all," she replies. "If a black family could afford to move in next door, I would welcome them."

I am struck, as we talk, by how vague and shifting her fears are, and by how typical she is of most whites in this respect. At one moment, she envisages a future social order much like the present one, though without the racial laws. At other moments, she seems to have a grimmer picture before her eyes: a hand-to-mouth existence as an unwelcome guest in the land of her birth. It is one of the bitterest consequences of the decades-long suppression of black dissent that ordinary whites now not only have no one with whom to imagine negotiating their future, but have not the vaguest idea of what blacks might be prepared to settle for.

"Our women are the worst," Kaffie Pretorius remarks. "It is because domestic help is so easy to get. Utter idleness. They get into their cars in the morning and drive around aimlessly all day. If they are the most conservative, it is because they have the most to lose."

Does she herself have a servant, and how have interpersonal relations been during the present unrest? "Martha is going to have a baby soon, which has led us to talk to each other more openly. It strikes me how hard we find it to think our way into the life our servants lead. I wonder how I would feel, in this awful summer heat, living in a corrugated steel house in Ida's Valley."

After lunch, some teen-age friends of the family stop by. They have just written their school-leaving examinations. For the boys, the choice is whether to enroll in college and postpone military service or to go into the army. I ask whether they have any doubts about serving in Namibia (still called South-West Africa by most white South Africans), or patrolling South Africa's black townships. No, they reply: one must be prepared to make sacrifices for one's country. All the same, they are cynical about South Africa's occupation of Namibia and its professed aims there (to protect the right of the territory to self-determination). As for the strife at home, they agree that blacks should be given more freedom. But then, says one of them, Dawid, whites should have freedom too—freedom to found a state in which they will be their own masters. I ask where this state should be, thinking he will propose some tiny Spartan colony on the Orange River. "The Transvaal, the Orange Free State, and northern Natal," he replies, naming a vast area containing perhaps three quarters of South Africa's economic resources—"our forefathers shed enough blood for those parts of the country to justify our claim to them."

He speaks the language, arrogantly possessive, of the enduring right-wing dream of a national homeland where the Afrikaner will be left to run his affairs without interference, and where blacks will face a clear and simple choice: to stay on as rightless, wage-earning sojourners, or to pack their bags and seek their salvation elsewhere.

Dawid's friends shake their heads and smile. Clearly they don't take him seriously. As for Dawid, his face is inscrutable. Does he believe in what he says, or is he trying to shock me? I know the streak of sly humor behind the Afrikaner's mask of dourness. Is Dawid a joker? "What are your ambitions?" I ask him. "To qualify as a clinical psychologist and then go into a career in politics," he replies.

"I travel widely, I talk to many people," says Michiel le Roux. "I would say that, down to the smallest town in South Africa, there is a perception that things have changed, totally and drastically; 1985 has left a mark on everyone. There is an awareness that the country is in a crisis situation, and this cuts across boundaries of age, class, language.

"No one thinks we need only take a few deep breaths for things to go back to normal, as they did in 1977," he says, referring to the 1976–77 uprisings in Soweto that shook the country for 18 months. "For this reason it has become possible for a strong leader to take South Africa in a direction that would have been unthinkable in 1984. Anything is thinkable in 1986, provided that the leadership is strong enough."

Le Roux, a graduate in law, is, at the age of 36, an executive in a Stellenbosch-based liquor company. We meet in his spacious office overlooking a courtyard in which stands an old wooden wine press, tall as a house, preserved for posterity.

Does the strong leadership he refers to exist? "No, clearly it doesn't. President Botha gave strong leadership—stronger than one expected—up to a certain point. Then he faltered. The issue over which he faltered was residential segregation. The feeling that we are directionless is widespread. People have no feeling of being on the road anywhere, or of knowing where we are on the road to."

If the last year has been a year of crisis, how has the crisis manifested itself in this quiet, civilized town with its oak-lined streets and painstakingly restored 18th-century houses? Race relations are good, or seem to be, Michiel replies. He is conscious of no hostility when he visits Coloured areas; calls for a boycott of white business have met with little success. Yet, he concedes, it is quite possible he is deluded. A Coloured school principal warned him of a "tremendous level of aggression" just beneath the surface. What more can he say? One can report only what one sees.

Where we go from here neither of us is sure. I remember the soldiers I passed on the highway, the smoke over the shantytowns. Which is the true face of South Africa—Crossroads, burning, or Stellenbosch, on the surface so placid? Months ago, I remember, on a quiet Sunday afternoon, I cycled through this town. "Amandla! (Power!)," shouted a voice behind me. I glanced around. A man, not black, but Coloured, waved a fist at me from the sidewalk. "Amandla!" he shouted again, in case I had misunderstood him. Was his the true, hidden face of Stellenbosch?

We talk about American stereotypes of the Afrikaner. Michiel shrugs them off. "Stereotypes are always a generation out of date—that is their nature." Would he regard himself as a representative modern Afrikaner? "It is curious how a society changes," he replies. "It is like a child growing: day by day you see no difference, then all of a sudden the child is grown up. For Afrikaners of my generation, born after 1948, the old issues have never really had relevance. It is a question of self-confidence. The Afrikaner's language is no longer threatened. He rules the land. The things that matter to him today are the same things that matter to an American, an Englishman, a German: his children, his job, his salary, his car, his vacation. He has been absorbed into a cultural pattern that is basically American. If you ask me to put my finger on anything that is *different* from a political point of view about the Afrikaner, I would say it is simply that he tends to be 20 or 30 years behind the times. Take racial discrimination. Before World War II, racial discrimination was a fact of life all over the West. The West came to realize it was wrong. Now it is gradually becoming accepted here that you don't judge a person on the basis of skin color."

If Afrikaners have been swallowed into an American life style, is the same future in store for blacks?

"The black man is oppressed in his own country. That is why, at the moment, it is important for him to assert his own culture—black art, black writing, black theater. But the American cultural current is very strong. Ultimately, black theater doesn't stand a chance against *Dallas*. It is *Dallas* that blacks will prefer to watch.

"It is striking what a hold Western values have taken among blacks, values like freedom of choice, freedom of speech, freedom of assembly. Who knows, perhaps blacks will guard these values all the more jealously because they have been denied them so long. On the other hand, if black liberation comes only after a long military struggle, we may have a military cast of mind imposed over everything—military discipline, military organization, as in so many other African countries. It is a matter of *how* the transition takes place."

My next stop is at the farm of Jan Boland Coetzee. Whether Jan Boland has heard of me I doubt: he is not much of a novel-reading man. But I have seen him scores of times, from the sidelines, in his rugby-playing heyday, and can make a fair guess at his approach to life: hard work, no nonsense. Within minutes we have compared genealogies, as is the custom in our country, and established that, like so many Afrikaners, we are probably distant relations—fourth or fifth or tenth cousins.

For our interview he conducts me into the cavernous cellars of his wine-farm, which are lined with huge oak casks imported from France (the craft of cooping has died out in South Africa, he tells me). In a subterranean hush, we sit down to talk.

How is apartheid faring in the countryside, I ask. "Apartheid has never been a word in my book," he replies, establishing his footing at once; and he proceeds to reminisce about the farm on which he grew up, where his grandfather drove to town to do the shopping for everyone, black and white alike. "It was only later, when I left the farm, that I first experienced apartheid." For a while he muses: "Apartheid has created a gulf between people. We no longer know each other. Also, we whites have simply appropriated things for ourselves, leaving the blacks and Coloureds to do the producing. It is not just. It is not a healthy state of affairs."

He is not, strictly speaking, answering my question, and knows it. I understand the difficulty he is having. Like me, he was born in the twilight of a centuries-old feudal order in which the rights and duties of masters and servants seemed to be a matter of unspoken convention, and in which a mixture of personal intimacy and social distance—a mixture characteristic of societies with a slaveholding past—pervaded all dealings. To whites brought up in this old order, the codification of social relations into the system of racial laws known as apartheid always seemed gross and unnecessary, the brainchild of academic ideologies and upstart politicians. So for Jan Boland Coetzee to shake his head over apartheid, yet look back nostalgically to an age when everyone knew his place, by no means proves him a hypocrite, though I suspect he forgets the iron hand needed to keep the old order running.

Coetzee is known not only as a winemaker, but for his part in the movement among progressive farmers to improve labor relations in the countryside. The age of the average farm laborer in South Africa, he tells me, is 52 years. Two generations of workers have quit white farms to seek their fortunes in the cities. In another generation, there will be no one left to till the soil. Therefore he has striven to create an exemplary environment on his own farm that will draw younger Coloured men back to the land: decent wages, productivity incentives, comfortable housing, health care, recreational opportunities. "During the present unrest we have found many younger Coloured people wanting to come back to the farm simply in order to be part of an ordered little community with civilized standards and a regular routine. For years we farmers were preoccupied with land and capital. Now we have begun to pay attention to people again, and the result is a change in attitudes that cannot be described—it truly has to be experienced."

There is a certain Utopianism in the vision he projects of a rural order based on small, rationally organized laboring communities. Utopian less because his brand of upliftment does not work—it clearly does, here and now, within its self-imposed limits—than because it draws much of its attractiveness from somewhat sentimentalized memories of a feudal past. Farmers like Coetzee reject such vast centralized blueprints for the future as Hendrik Verwoerd's "grand apartheid" in favor of small-scale, independent, pragmatic local solutions. As long as the politicians (and perhaps the police too) will leave us alone, Coetzee seems to be saying, we country folk can find ways to live harmoniously together. In much of the talk rife among more progressive whites today, the same spirit is to be detected: loss of faith in large-scale national policies, impatience with red tape, readiness for ad hoc approaches to local problems. The irony is that this is precisely the moment in history when black South Africans are grouping together in larger and larger political blocs, and black leaders prepared to limit discussion to merely local issues are proving harder and harder to find.

Only the darkest cynic would claim that the effort Jan Boland Coetzee and his wife have put into the social upliftment of their work force has not been sincerely intended. While their workers are well housed, the Coetzees themselves live in a cramped bungalow—renovation of the old farmstead is barely under way. Nevertheless, looking toward the future, one may ask whether marriage will ever be possible between the kind of enlightened paternalism they stand for and the egalitarian black nationalism sweeping across the land. When I ask Jan Boland what he thinks the effect will be on this part of the country, once restrictions on black mobility ("influx control") have been lifted, he is dismissive: "There is no tradition of blacks living in the Western Cape," he says. True; but only because the full force of the law has been brought to bear to keep blacks out. Can a farm remain an island of tranquillity in a country in turmoil? Can the Western Cape, this tiny tip of the continent, declare itself independent of Africa?

Can Jan Boland imagine circumstances that would make him give up his farm and quit South Africa? Vehemently, he shakes his head. "Never. I stay. I have enough faith in my countrymen, black, white and Coloured, to believe we can work out a solution. I can't believe that South Africans are such bad people as the Americans and the rest say." He tells a story of how, while touring France with the national rugby team, the Springboks, he found himself in a bus with some American tourists. "They asked us what language we were speaking, and we told them it was Afrikaans. They had never heard of such a language, they didn't even know there were such people as Afrikaners. Well, now they know! What I mean to say is: rather be proud of your language than your skin color. As for the norms of the so-called civilized world, we will *live* those norms, not just talk about them."

"You must understand that I am a believing Christian," says Lydia Roos. "I can't sit here and despair, I can't say there is no future for us, I can't say it is too late. Because things have begun to change. But we must move faster. Whether the Government understands this, I don't know. . . . "

Lydia Roos is a domestic-science teacher in a high school. We meet in her home in an unpretentious white suburb of Cape Town. The schools have just closed for the summer vacation. It has been a hard year, a year of bad news and official lies, the lies sometimes harder to bear than the bad news. We all ache for relief. But the end is not in sight. "December 16 Martyrs Day" reads an ominous sign daubed on a wall in the town. Under the writing is a picture of a neat little house, like the one in which we sit, with flames licking around it.

"We are going to have to make sacrifices," she says. "Prices are rising all the time. Yet the other day I thought: if high prices mean that farm workers will at last get a good wage, maybe it's a good thing."

A drop in living standards: will that be the extent of white sacrifice? What of social apartheid? Is she prepared to see the neighborhood opened up?

There is no hesitation in her reply: "Absolutely. Nor do I think other people in the block would object. Coloureds, blacks: if they can afford it, let them come and live here."

Her readiness to jettison the Group Areas Act, which enforces segregation of housing, marks Lydia as, in her word, *verlig,* enlightened. Her vision of the future, she says, is of a South Africa in which there will be many tribes, white and black, the Afrikaners one of them, none in a position of dominance, each maintaining its own cultural identity. "We will keep our *boerekos,* our Afrikaner dishes, just as the Indians have kept their curry."

I am dubious. Is the struggle in South Africa not about more than the preservation of national cuisines? What of the realities of power?

"I think we will end up with a federal system," she says, "provinces with local self-government, and a national government over them. The Western Cape should be one province, with Cape Town as its capital. I don't know about the Eastern Cape— that is a matter for the blacks."

Will whites elsewhere in the country, living in the midst of vast black majorities, not see her prescription as a form of smug isolationism that only the Western Cape, with its small black African population, can afford?

She smiles. "Perhaps," she concedes. "I see my brother once a year. He lives in Pretoria. After the first day or two we don't talk politics any more. We disagree too much. But families don't break up over questions of politics. We have ways of living with our differences."

I think of the poet Breyten Breytenbach and his brother, an officer in the security forces, who do not speak to each other, of the many friendships I have seen break up under the stresses of this last year. Is it uncharitable to think that Lydia and her brother do not yet disagree enough?

Have her *verlig* leanings brought her into conflict with other Afrikaners? No, she replies. Personally she is not combative. When the gulf yawns too wide she prefers to keep quiet. But she finds she has lost respect for colleagues at school who are absolutely unsympathetic to black aspirations. "Within myself I doubt their integrity." *Opregtheid,* uprightness, integrity, is a key word for her. It measures the distance between professed Christian faith and day-to-day practice. Her parents have worked all their lives in the "mission" church, the branch of the Dutch Reformed Church that ministers to Coloured people. She is a regular churchgoer, and on Thursday evenings runs needlework classes for black domestic servants. "We must each do our bit," she says.

At school, among the teen-agers she teaches, she encounters little spirit of conciliation: "They talk only of shooting the troublemakers," she says. "It hurts me, that kind of talk. They pick it up from each other, or they hear it at home. The school I teach at draws on a less prosperous neighborhood. In the better parts of town you will probably find a more thinking attitude. But signs of the unrest are all around us; buses with broken windows, sirens all the time, helicopters overhead, blacks singing freedom songs in the streets. No one can escape it. You can't expect children not to be affected.

"I taught in a Coloured school for a while, in Elsie's River. I went back for a visit. When I taught there I had good relations with the children, open relations. Now things have changed. The old openness has gone. Hostility? I wouldn't call it personal hostility, though I couldn't help hearing remarks passed behind my back. But hostility toward the system—yes, definitely.

"I remember, during my time there, there was never any celebration of our national day, no singing of the national anthem. I suppose one can understand that. The anthem has certain Afrikaner connotations—the line about the creaking ox-wagon and so forth. But I love the anthem. To some extent it is our fault that they won't sing it. But still. . . . "

II. VIOLENCE IN THE TOWNSHIPS

EDITOR'S INTRODUCTION

What is life like for blacks in South Africa? Fifty-five percent of blacks are forcibly segregated in areas called "homelands," impoverished regions that are nominally independent nations but that are in fact totally dependent on South Africa. Often workers must commute hundreds of miles every day to industrial parks near the major South African cities. Others live in barracks near work, seeing their families once a year. The other 45 percent of blacks live in the "townships," shantytowns on the peripheries of white cities. The black unemployment rate in some areas reaches 35 percent; overall it is about 28 percent. A large percentage of black households earn less than the minimum subsistence level. Nor does South Africa provide welfare or dole payments to the poor.

Under the South African constitution, blacks are allotted few legal rights and have no political power. The current state of emergency, imposed by Pretoria in mid 1985, gives police the right to detain anyone without charge for up to six months and protects officers from prosecution for brutalizing or even murdering suspected troublemakers. As the Amnesty International briefing reprinted as the first selection shows, violations of human rights are widespread in South Africa. Adam Hochschild's article from *Mother Jones* gives an eyewitness view of the effects of township violence.

In addition, black-against-black violence is becoming a regular feature of township life. Much of this is the ordinary criminal violence common in many poor environments. Since 1983, politically motivated violence has been on the increase as well. Loosely organized (or unorganized) bands of youths, known as the "comrades," the *amabuthu* (warriors), or simply "the children," publicly assassinate suspected black collaborators and informants. The preferred method of execution is the "necklace," a burning tire placed around the victim's neck. Tom Lodge and Mark Swilling discuss the comrades in an article reprinted from *Africa Report*.

The comrades and many other blacks claim allegiance to or
membership in the African National Congress, an outlawed
group that has vowed armed resistance to apartheid. Few Westerners, and fewer Americans, know much about this shadowy organization, which operates with Soviet support in exile from
bases in Zambia and Tanzania. Mark A. Uhlig takes a look inside
the ANC in the last selection, reprinted from *New York Times
Magazine*.

VIOLATIONS OF HUMAN RIGHTS
IN SOUTH AFRICA[1]

Widespread civil unrest in South Africa's black townships and
extensive violations of human rights by the government and its
security forces have increased markedly in recent years.

The unrest focussed on issues such as rent increases, the poor
facilities available to black school students and the constitutional
changes introduced in August and September 1984.

These created parliamentary assemblies for the "Coloured"
(mixed-race) and Indian communities but not for the black majority population. Two umbrella organizations were formed to
lead a boycott of elections to the new assemblies: the United
Democratic Front (UDF) and the National Forum. About 20
leaders of these organizations were arrested shortly before the
August elections and held in preventive detention.

Particularly serious disturbances broke out in early September 1984 in the industrial areas around Johannesburg, apparently sparked off by rent rises and the arrests of black community
leaders opposed to the constitutional changes. There were attacks by township residents on local black town councillors and
black police officers, who were identified popularly as representatives of the authorities. Substantial police contingents, and subsequently army units, were deployed in the area.

[1]Excerpted from a briefing by Amnesty International, a worldwide human rights organization. Amnesty International South Africa Briefing. 1+. Mr. '86. Copyright 1986 by Amnesty International Publications. All rights reserved. Reprinted by permission.

In November 1984 black workers organized a mass "stay away" (strike) which led to further arrests and disturbances in Johannesburg.

In late 1984 and early 1985 a further escalation of violence extended into the Eastern Cape and East Rand, in particular, and parts of Orange Free State province. In the course of the disturbances large numbers of black township residents were shot by police and many were killed.

The most serious single incident of this nature occurred in the Eastern Cape on 21 March 1985, the 25th anniversary of the Sharpeville killings, when police opened fire and killed 20 people in a funeral procession near Uitenhage. This incident was the subject of a judicial commission of inquiry which found that 20 black people, including several children, had been killed and others wounded. The police had been equipped with firearms and lethal ammunition, but no other means of crowd dispersal, on orders from superior officers. The police patrols were exonerated by the inquiry, although at least 15 of the victims had been shot in the back.

Amnesty International was concerned that the killings at Uitenhage, the only ones to be made the subject of a commission of inquiry, and many others resulting from police shootings in recent years, may have been extrajudicial executions. There is evidence that, on occasions, killings by police and army units may have been the result of a deliberate and systematic official policy of using lethal force against black protestors. The persistence of the killings, the failure to provide non-lethal means of crowd dispersal, the granting of a blanket immunity to all law enforcement personnel under the emergency and the failure to inquire into individual killings by such personnel lends support to this concern.

Between early September 1984 and late November 1985 the number of deaths associated with the unrest was reported to be over 800. Most resulted from shootings by the police.

In July 1985 the government imposed a state of emergency, which greatly extended police powers in large areas of South Africa. In the succeeding months thousands were detained without charge or trial.

Detention without Trial

Several thousand people were detained without trial for political reasons after the outbreak of heightened civil unrest in the second half of 1984. They included officials of black trade unions, black and white student activists, leaders of the Coloured and Indian communities opposed to the elections, officials of the UDF and other anti-*apartheid* organizations, journalists and church and community workers. Many were detained solely for their peaceful criticism of *apartheid* policies.

The state of emergency imposed in July 1985 further extended the powers of the security forces. This was particularly disturbing because the existing security laws already resulted in widespread political detention accompanied by human rights abuses. Section 29 of the Internal Security Act permits police to hold detainees indefinitely without charge, in isolation, without access to relatives or legal counsel. Section 28 allows unlimited preventive detention without charge or trial.

THE STATE OF EMERGENCY

From midnight on 20 July 1985 large areas of South Africa were placed under a state of emergency.

The emergency regulations give all law enforcement personnel, whatever their rank, the power to arrest without warrant and detain without charge for 14 days. Further unlimited detention may then be authorized by the Minister of Law and Order.

Detainees are normally held incommunicado, although in some cases permission for relatives to visit has been granted. While in custody, detainees under the emergency are not permitted contact with other categories of prisoner or with anyone other than state officials.

The police are not required to charge them or produce evidence against them in court, nor is there any means of appeal against detention. The authorities need not give reasons for individual detentions nor are detainees' places of imprisonment disclosed. Anyone who discloses the name of any detainee without authorization has committed an offence punishable by up to 10 years' imprisonment.

The government has granted immunity in advance to all law enforcement personnel, government ministers and state officials for acts committed "in good faith" in their use of emergency powers.

All those detained under the emergency are liable to interrogation. Given the immunity provisions and the record of the police of physical and psychological abuse of detainees, they are at grave risk of torture or ill-treatment.

The scale of detentions under the emergency is massive: more than 1,100 people were detained in the first week, and by the end of October 1985 the authorities had acknowledged the detention of over 4,300 people.

Those detained included members of black student organizations, particularly those belonging to the Congress of South African Students (COSAS) which was banned on 28 August, and members of black community organizations throughout the Johannesburg and Eastern Cape areas. Many of these organizations are affiliated to the UDF, the anti-*apartheid* umbrella organization formed in 1983 to which more than 600 political, trade union, community, student and other groups are affiliated.

Even children have been arrested and detained for breaking the emergency regulations. On 22 and 23 August 1985 over 800 school students were reported to have been arrested in Soweto for being outside their classrooms during school hours. Some were primary school children as young as seven.

Several black church ministers were detained during the first week of the emergency, including the Reverend Frederick Huskie, who is in his late sixties, and the Reverend de Villiers Soga. They and the other church ministers detained had been active in trying to calm the situation in the black townships and reduce the level of confrontation between the police and the black community.

Many members of predominantly black trade unions were also detained under the state of emergency. There has been a rapid and substantial growth of black trade union membership in recent years and many unions have become involved in campaigning both for improved conditions for black workers and for political and social reform.

For example, leaders of the Motor Assemblers' and Component Workers' Union of South Africa (MACWUSA) were detained in the first week including Dennis Neer, the union's General Secretary. His wife witnessed police hitting and threatening him when they arrested him at home at about midnight on

21 July. Other people in the house were reportedly attacked with teargas and whips.

A new wave of detentions in the Cape Town area began early in the morning of 25 October 1985. Over 70 people were detained including lawyers, church ministers, trade unionists and community leaders. The detainees were initially held under Section 50 of the Internal Security Act which allows the police to detain anyone they believe to be contributing to public disorder on a magistrate's warrant for 14 days. On 26 October the state of emergency was extended to cover eight districts in the Western Cape. Over 100 organizations were forbidden to hold meetings, and those initially detained under Section 50 were apparently transferred to detention under the emergency regulations.

The detainees included Mildred Lesia, a member of the United Women's Organization and an executive member of the Western Cape branch of the UDF who had already spent some eight weeks in detention from August 1985, and Abdullah Mohamed Omar, an advocate who has frequently defended political cases.

Mohamed Saleem Badat, a UDF member and organizer of *Grassroots* community newspaper had also just spent some eight weeks in detention when he was rearrested. He claimed to have been assaulted during a previous period of detention in 1983 and was suing the police.

Amnesty International has repeatedly expressed concern to the South African government about the terms of the state of emergency and about the detention of large numbers of critics of *apartheid*, many of whom are believed to be prisoners of conscience. In particular, it has stressed its fear that those held may be tortured in detention or "disappear."

DETENTION UNDER THE INTERNAL SECURITY ACT

Thousands of people have been detained without trial in recent years for their non-violent opposition to the *apartheid* policies of the South African Government. Since 1982, the main law providing for detention without trial has been the Internal Security Act.

Section 29 permits police to hold detainees for interrogation indefinitely, in isolation and without access to relatives or lawyers. The police are allowed to withhold all information about these detainees, who are held in police custody rather than in prisons administered by the Prisons Department. Detainees are held in solitary confinement. This provision has been used to detain many people in those areas of South Africa not under the state of emergency.

Many detainees have been tortured or ill-treated while detained incommunicado under Section 29. Amnesty International considers that the conditions of their detention facilitate torture and that all detainees held under this provision are at risk of such abuse.

Those detained under Section 29 since mid-1984 have included a number of UDF leaders in the Western Cape and Natal regions, trade unionists, students, members of women's organizations and opponents of compulsory military service for whites.

Section 29 was used, for example, to detain large numbers of leading black trade unionists in November 1984, after a mass "stay away" in the Johannesburg area on 5 and 6 November. On 8 and 9 November Chris Dlamini, President of the Federation of South African Trade Unions (Fosatu), Thami Mali, Chairman of the Transvaal Regional Stay-Away Committee, and at least six other leading trade unionists were detained by security police in Johannesburg.

Phiroshaw Camay and Jethro Dlalisa, also trade union officials, were detained in security police raids on their homes in the Johannesburg area shortly before dawn on 14 November 1984. Phiroshaw Camay is General Secretary of the Council of Unions of South Africa (CUSA). Jethro Dlalisa is Transvaal Chairman of the Transport and General Workers' Union (TGWU), affiliated to Fosatu. Both CUSA and Fosatu backed the November "stay away."

Also arrested in November 1984 were several officials and members of COSAS, which represented black school and college students. Among them were Brenda Badela, a 20-year-old COSAS organizer in Port Elizabeth, and her father, Mono Badela, a former prisoner of conscience.

Arrested at the same time was Kate Philip, President of the National Union of South African Students (NUSAS), the main organization representing students at English language universities, who had played a prominent role in organizing white opposition to *apartheid*.

1984 and 1985 saw an increase in the use of preventive detention, which had been used only in a few individual cases since 1981. Introduced in its present form under an earlier Internal Security Act in 1976, preventive detention orders were imposed on some 135 people in the second half of 1976 following the disturbances in Soweto and other black townships.

In late 1977, a number of black leaders and journalists were held for several months following the death in detention of black consciousness leader Steve Biko and the banning of many black consciousness organizations.

In 1980 more than 150 students, community leaders and trade unionists were detained during a period of schools boycotts and industrial disputes, particularly in the Western Cape area. The 1981 campaign to boycott celebrations of the 20th anniversary of the South African Republic led to further widespread use of preventive detention.

Section 28 of the Internal Security Act empowers the Minister of Law and Order to order the preventive detention of any person he considers engaged in, or likely to engage in, "activities which endanger or are calculated to endanger the security of the state or the maintenance of law and order."

Preventive detention orders may be renewed for an unlimited period. The Minister is not required to disclose specific reasons for such orders and the courts effectively have no jurisdiction over them.

The Board of Review which oversees Section 28 and Section 29 detention orders meets *in camera* and its recommendations are not binding on the Minister. The Minister's specific reasons for the detention are not made available to the detainee.

Among those placed in preventive detention during 1984 and 1985 were leading members of the UDF and other organizations campaigning for an election boycott. They included four black community leaders from Cradock arrested in March 1984 in connection with local protests over rent and education and held for several months. Two of them, Matthew Goniwe and Fort Calata, were abducted and murdered in June 1985 by unknown assailants.

DENIAL OF BAIL:
SECTION 30

Under Section 30 of the Internal Security Act a state Attorney-General may issue an order denying the court its usual authority to release a charged person on bail if he "considers it necessary in the interests of the security of the state or the maintenance of law and order."

This section was used by the Attorney-General of the Transvaal to deny bail to a group of 22 prisoners including UDF officials, civic association members and students arrested between October 1984 and April 1985.

On 11 June 1985 the 22 appeared in the Pretoria Magistrate's Court and were remanded in custody on charges of high treason, terrorism and murder. The charges reportedly related to their alleged responsibility for the unrest in the "Vaal triangle" in late 1984. Before their appearance in court the 22 defendants had been detained incommunicado and without charge in solitary confinement for periods ranging from six weeks to eight months. Several had previously been detained without trial or imprisoned for political reasons, some of them several times.

Despite the serious nature of the charges against the 22, Amnesty International believes that some of them are prisoners of conscience and that others may be. Several had been adopted as prisoners of conscience by Amnesty International during previous spells in prison.

DETENTION OF STATE WITNESSES:
SECTION 31

Under Section 31 of the Internal Security Act a state Attorney-General may authorize incommunicado detention without charge of potential state witnesses until the end of the trial at which they are expected to testify. If they refuse to testify, they may be sentenced to up to five years' imprisonment for contempt of court. If they refute in court a statement made while in security police detention on the grounds that it was made under duress, they may be charged with perjury.

For example Dr. Mvuyo Tom, a medical doctor, was sentenced to three years' imprisonment in early 1984 for refusing to testify as a state witness.

THE HOMELANDS

Legislation similar to the Internal Security Act exists in the four African "homelands" which have been declared "independent" by South Africa, but are not internationally recognized as sovereign states.

Section 26 of the Ciskei National Security Act, for example, allows the Ciskei security police to detain anyone indefinitely, incommunicado and without charge or trial. Many detainees held under this section are reported to have been tortured and ill-treated.

In July 1983 a boycott of bus services in protest at fare increases was organized by black industrial workers and commuters who live in Mdantsane township near East London. The authorities intervened and attempted to break the boycott, which had gathered wide public support, with force. The Ciskei police reportedly established roadblocks and stopped private cars and taxis in which commuters were travelling to East London. Events came to a head at the end of July and in the first days of August when police took up positions outside railway stations in Mdantsane, attempting to prevent commuters from boarding trains and to force them instead to board buses bound for East London. A state of emergency was declared in Mdantsane on 3 August following which there were police shootings which resulted in perhaps as many as 90 people being killed and many others injured by the police.

Between 60 and 100 people, including trade unionists, lawyers and journalists, were detained under Section 26 of the Ciskei National Security Act in connection with the boycott. One of them was Hintsa Siwisa, a lawyer who had been engaged to represent some of the detained trade unionists. He was detained once more (for at least a third time) under Section 26 in September 1985. No reason was given for his detention—none is required by law. However, at the time of this detention he was acting on behalf of a number of people arrested in Ciskei in previous months.

Section 47 of the Transkei Public Security Act permits indefinite detention without trial for interrogation, and has been associated with allegations of torture of political detainees. In August 1984, after several months of unrest at the University of Transkei in Umtata, 200 students were arrested and held under Section 47 after police surrounded the men's residence. They were held incommunicado and without charge for three weeks in police camps, not prisons.

Prince Madikizela, an attorney in Umtata, was banished in October 1984 to a remote rural area far from Umtata. He could not continue his law practice there, and his wife and children live in Umtata. The banishment order stated that he was being excluded from Umtata because his presence there was "not in the general public interest." On 27 August 1985 Prince Madikizela was detained under Section 47. He became ill and had to be admitted to hospital.

On 27 September he was convicted of contravening his banishment order and sentenced to three months' imprisonment, suspended for five years, and to a fine of 250 South African rands (£66) or 60 days' imprisonment. He was then taken back to hospital in Engcobo.

On 1 October the security police removed him from the hospital without a medical discharge and took him to Umtata Prison. On 7 October an appeal was lodged against his conviction and he was released on bail. On 10 October he is reported to have been redetained by the security police at his home in Umtata.

Dumisa Ntsebeza is a relative of Batandwa Ndondo and is a former political prisoner and an attorney in Umtata who has frequently acted for the defence in political cases and who has been subjected to security police harassment in the past. He was apparently compiling sworn statements from eye witnesses of Batandwa Ndondo's arrest and murder when he was detained on 8 October 1985. His elder brother Lungisile, at whose house Batandwa Ndondo was living in Cala, was also detained, as were eye witness Victor Ngaleka and associates of the Ntsebezas, Godfrey Silinga and Monde Mdimbi.

They were held under Section 47 of the Transkei Public Security Act. By law, the authorities may withhold information about such detainees, as in this case, where they apparently refused to provide any reasons for the detentions or to disclose the places of detention.

Banning and Banishment

The South African authorities use banning and banishment orders to restrict and silence their opponents without having to justify those actions before the courts. Banned people may not
—communicate with one another in any way
—be quoted in public or private
—attend any political or social gathering—that is any meeting of more than two people
—move outside the area to which they are restricted
—enter any educational institution or factory without special permission.
Banished people are restricted to places often hundreds of miles from their homes and their previous workplaces.

Until 1982, there was no means of appeal against banning orders. The Internal Security Act of 1982 provided for a Board of Review, but it cannot be regarded as an independent tribunal as its members (whose identities are not disclosed) are government-appointed, and its recommendations to the Minister of Law and Order are not mandatory.

The number of banned people fell to 11 in July 1983, when banning orders issued under the previous Internal Security Act automatically expired one year after the coming into force of the Internal Security Act of 1982. Ten of these orders were immediately renewed. In 1985 restrictions similar to those contained in banning orders were imposed on several people released from detention without trial under the emergency.

When every year many people are prosecuted and convicted of political offences by the courts, the authorities' decision to impose banning orders on certain individuals indicates that they do not possess even the minimum evidence necessary for prosecution.

Winnie Mandela

Winnie Mandela, internationally known anti-*apartheid* activist and wife of imprisoned ANC leader Nelson Mandela, has been banned or detained for all but one of the years since 1962.

She was first detained in 1958 after demonstrating against the introduction of "passes" for black women. In 1963 she was restricted under a two-year banning order to the black township of Orlando, in Soweto, where she lived. The order was renewed for a further five years in 1965. In 1969 she was detained and later charged, with 21 others, under the Suppression of Communism Act. They were all acquitted but were immediately redetained and held incommunicado for a time. All but three were tried again on fresh charges in May 1970, only to be acquitted once more.

Winnie Mandela was then banned for five years and put under partial house arrest. In 1974 she served a six-month prison sentence for contravening her banning order, which expired in September 1975.

However, she was detained once again in August 1976 at the time of the disturbances in Soweto and other black townships. She was released uncharged at the end of December 1976 and restricted under a five-year banning order.

In April 1977 her banning order was amended to "banish" her to the small and remote town of Brandfort.

In December 1981, she was served with another five-year order restricting her to Brandfort. In July 1983, when all previous banning orders automatically expired, Winnie Mandela was one of the 10 people who had new orders imposed.

She has received many death threats. In June 1982 two men were disturbed while apparently trying to plant a bomb in her car. Three days later, she received a letter threatening her with the same fate as two ANC officials killed by a car bomb in Swaziland earlier that month.

Her home in Brandfort was extensively damaged by a petrol bomb on 12 August 1985, while she was in Johannesburg for medical treatment. A few days earlier, police had chased demonstrating school boycotters into her house, thrown tear gas in and ransacked it. The police alleged that petrol bombs were found in the house. Thirty people were detained.

Following this incident, Winnie Mandela stayed in Johannesburg for her own safety, even though this meant contravening the terms of her banning order. In November 1985 the authorities ordered her to return to Brandfort although her house had been burned down.

In the light of the abductions and murders of black community leaders and human rights lawyers and the persistent, though unproved, allegations that the attacks were carried out by, or with the knowledge of, the police, in late 1985 Amnesty International expressed publicly its fears for Winnie Mandela's safety. It also called on the South African Government to lift her banning order and allow her to exercise her right to free expression.

MATHATHA TSEDU

Mathatha Tsedu, once a journalist and Northern Transvaal President of the Media Workers' Association of South Africa (MWASA) was first banned (for three years) in January 1981—along with other MWASA leaders—shortly after the conclusion of a two-month national strike by black journalists and media workers over pay and conditions.

In June 1982 Mathatha Tsedu was detained under Section 29 of the Internal Security Act. In November 1982 nine people were charged with security offences and it is believed that at around this time Mathatha Tsedu was transferred to detention as a potential state witness in the forthcoming trial. However, he was not called to give evidence and was released after 10 months' detention without trial in April 1983.

He was again served with a three-year banning order in July 1983. He is restricted to the district of Seshego, and under house arrest on weekday evenings and weekends. There are few job opportunities in Seshego, a residential black township servicing the neighbouring white town of Pietersburg. His wife (they have two children) is a teacher in Venda; she is able to visit Seshego only once a fortnight.

Acquitted of Treason

Sixteen UDF leaders—all leading nonviolent opponents of the South African Government—were brought to trial charged with high treason in late 1985. All were adopted as prisoners of conscience by Amnesty International. The charges against 12 of the defendants were dropped on 9 December 1985. The remaining four defendants were all leading members of the South African Allied Workers' Union (SAAWU): Sisa Njikelana, Isaac Ngcobo, Thozamile Gqweta and Sam Kikine.

Other defendants were three senior members of the Natal Indian Congress and several members of the Release Mandela Committee. All but two had been adopted as prisoners of conscience during previous periods in detention or under banning orders.

Seven of the defendants were arrested in February 1985 when police carried out dawn raids on the homes of leading UDF members throughout the country. A further eight had already been detained for several months by then, having been arrested in August 1984.

At first, those detained in August 1984 were held in preventive detention. Seven of them successfully challenged their detention orders in the Natal Supreme Court and were released on 7 September, but new detention orders were then issued against them.

Five of the seven, together with Paul David, a former prisoner of conscience whose detention had also been ordered, then entered the British Consulate in Durban on 13 September and sought sanctuary there. This provoked a diplomatic dispute between the Governments of the United Kingdom and South Africa. On 6 October, George Sewpershad, M. J. Naidoo and Mewa Ramgobin left the consulate voluntarily and were immediately re-detained. The three others—Archie Gumede, a national president of the UDF, Paul David and Billy Nair—were still in the consulate on 10 December when all preventive detention orders were revoked by the Minister of Law and Order. They then left the consulate but Archie Gumede and Paul David were immediately rearrested and charged with treason.

Twenty-two other UDF leaders involved in a similar treason case were due to go on trial in January 1986.

Torture and Ill-treatment

For many years Amnesty International has received reports of widespread and systematic torture in South Africa.

Political detainees held incommunicado by security police are at grave risk. Criminal suspects are also reported to have been tortured.

Torture appears to be used primarily to intimidate detainees, to force them to "confess" and to implicate others in political offences.

Detainees held under Section 29 of the Internal Security Act are held in solitary confinement, often for months, and denied access to lawyers and to their families. Many are reportedly subjected to lengthy periods of continuous interrogation during which they are tortured or assaulted. Detainees have often required hospital treatment apparently as a result of ill-treatment and their conditions of detention. These are so harsh—particularly in respect of solitary confinement—that in Amnesty International's view they constitute ill-treatment of themselves. A number of detainees held under this provision have become psychologically disoriented. Simon Tseko Nkodi, a 25-year-old former student leader, who was arrested under Section 29 of the Internal Security Act on 23 September 1984, was reported to have been taken from security police custody under guard to a psychiatric ward in Johannesburg General Hospital on 25 January 1985. There he reportedly made an unsuccessful suicide attempt. Like all Section 29 detainees, he had been held incommunicado and in solitary confinement.

Billy Nair, 55-year-old Vice President of the Natal branch of the UDF and an executive member of the Natal Indian Congress, was detained under Section 29 on 23 August 1985. On 5 September he was referred to specialists by a district surgeon because he had an injured eye and a suspected perforated eardrum. In a letter smuggled out of detention, he told his wife that he had been beaten about the head by security police officers during interrogation.

Vusi Dlamini, a 15-year-old member of the student organization COSAS, was also detained under Section 29, on 27 August 1985. On 3 September he telephoned his mother and told her that he had been admitted to the private Shifa Hospital in Durban on 1 September. He said that he had been severely assaulted while in detention and was unable to hear in one ear, had a broken jawbone and suspected fractures of the skull and forearms.

The Supreme Court later granted interdicts restraining the police from assaulting both Billy Nair and Vusi Dlamini.

Yunis Shaik, a lawyer aged 27 and Secretary of the Garment Workers Union, was detained on 4 July 1985 in the Durban area, released uncharged on 19 July, but redetained on 3 August. After his release on 19 July he informed a lawyer that he had been tortured under interrogation. He claimed that he had been stripped naked and a canvas bag placed over his head. A police officer had then curled a finger around in his rectum while pressure was applied to his kidneys, causing extreme pain.

Detainees held under the emergency regulations are also reported to have been tortured and ill-treated. Mbulelo Goniwe, a leading member of the Cradock Residents' Association, was detained on 25 July 1985. He was reported to have required medical treatment at the Livingstone Hospital in Port Elizabeth for a perforated eardrum. This injury is often associated with a hard blow to the head and several detainees in Port Elizabeth are alleged to have suffered perforated eardrums as a result of being beaten while under interrogation.

Johnny Mashiane, a 15-year-old schoolboy, was detained on 23 July and held incommunicado until 5 August. On his release he displayed serious mental disturbance and was admitted to the Johannesburg Hospital. His family said he had been in good health when he was detained.

Emergency regulations grant immunity in advance to all law enforcement officials for any actions committed "in good faith" in the exercise of their emergency powers. This was reportedly interpreted by police, prison and senior medical officials in the Port Elizabeth area as providing complete immunity against any legal prosecution of the police by detainees.

On 25 September 1985 Dr. Wendy Orr, a district surgeon responsible for medically examining detainees and prisoners in the Port Elizabeth area, submitted evidence to the Supreme Court of widespread and regular torture and ill-treatment of detainees. Her evidence was supported by sworn statements from over 40 people, including detainees.

The court issued an order restraining police from assaulting all detainees held under the emergency regulations in the Port Elizabeth and Uitenhage magisterial districts. It ruled that the police had no immunity from prosecution if they assaulted or threatened to assault detainees.

Dr. Orr had examined hundreds of detainees and alleged that approximately half of them appeared to have been assaulted. Their complaints appeared to be consistent with their injuries— severe weals, bruising and swelling on their backs, arms, legs, hands, and faces.

She reportedly said that: "The overwhelming evidence presented to me . . . convinced me that detainees were being systematically assaulted and abused after their arrest and before being admitted to prison, and also during their incarceration when they were being interrogated. . . . "

Amnesty International has received persistent allegations of ill-treatment of detainees by the Port Elizabeth police over the years.

Among the people allegedly ill-treated and tortured in the area since the imposition of the state of emergency have been a number of leading black trade unionists. Vusumzi George, an executive member of the Motor Assemblers' and Component Workers' Union of South Africa (MACWUSA), was detained at about 2:30a.m. on 22 July 1985. He alleges that he, his pregnant wife and his brother were beaten with whips at that time. On 29 July he was taken from St. Alban's prison to Louis Le Grange Square police station. In a sworn statement following his release, uncharged, from detention, he gave the following account of his treatment:

S . . . and N . . . had a plastic bag which contained the items which had been confiscated during the search at my house. While questioning me about these items they made me sit on the floor with my hands handcuffed behind my back and forced my legs open by beating the insides of my thighs with *sjamboks*. They then attempted repeatedly to kick me in my private parts. They then beat me with a *sjambok* on my back and chest and smashed my toes and head with a short wooden stick . . .

. . . another security policeman came in and ordered me to stand as if I was embracing a metal filing cabinet. He then began punching me in the kidneys from behind and hammering me on my shoulders with two-fisted blows. He repeated this type of assault a number of times and then beat my ears with open hands. He then threw me on the floor and while kicking me asked me questions. Two other policemen then entered the room and assisted with the general assault which lasted about half an hour.

T . . . and the two policemen who had recently entered the room then took me to the next door room and beat me with their fists . . . until I started screaming. Two or three white policemen then came into the room and one of the three brought in a wet towel which was placed tightly around my face and head. While the towel was suffocating me they beat me. They then removed the towel from my face and throttled me. . . .

The prison authorities did not permit him to see a doctor until 1 September.

HOMELANDS

Torture is also reported in the four "homelands" which have been declared "independent" by the South African Government but not recognized internationally.

The Very Reverend Dean Tshenuweni Simon Farisani, effective head of the Evangelical Lutheran Church in Venda, was arrested by security police in November 1981. He had given spiritual support to the family of Isaac Muofhe, a lay Lutheran preacher who died in security police custody two days after his arrest in November 1981. Dean Farisani is reported to have been tortured so badly in detention that he had two heart attacks and had to go to hospital both before and after his release in June 1982.

Dean Farisani gave the following account of his treatment:

A week after his arrest his interrogators told him that they intended to kill him. They said he should write to his wife and to his church superior saying that he had escaped from prison and fled to Mozambique. He was told that he would be killed immediately if he wrote the letter, but that if he refused (as he did) he would be slowly tortured to death.

In early January 1982 he was beaten about his head and body with sticks and fists and his head was repeatedly banged against a wall by interrogating officials. Handfuls of his hair and beard were pulled out and several times he was lifted up bodily and thrown into the air, falling back down onto the concrete cell floor. He lost consciousness several times.

The following day he was stripped and had a canvas bag put over his head. Water was then poured over the bag and he was given electric shocks on the earlobes and back of the head. Electrodes were attached to his toes and genitals and he was given more shocks.

He needed months of medical attention for the two heart attacks he suffered shortly after this.

TORTURE ALLEGATIONS IN COURT

Numerous allegations of torture have been made in court, both by defendants and by detainees who have appeared as witnesses for the prosecution in political trials.

In the majority of these cases the courts appeared to accept police denials of torture at face value and to give insufficient consideration to the problems detainees faced, as a result of their incommunicado detention in solitary confinement, in proving that they had been tortured perhaps many months before.

Auret van Heerden was detained between 24 September 1981 and 9 July 1982. For most of that time he was held in incommunicado detention for security police interrogation. He made a sworn statement after his release that he had been tortured during interrogation: a wet canvas bag was placed over his head, preventing him from breathing, while electricity was applied to his arms, feet, neck and back. A wet towel was repeatedly tightened around his neck and he was beaten about the head. His feet were beaten with a *sjambok* and he was dragged around the room by his hair.

When the authorities would take no action over his allegation of torture, Auret van Heerden brought a civil claim for damages against 10 security police officers. The judge dismissed the claim in September 1984, ruling that Auret van Heerden had not submitted his complaint within the six-month time limit prescribed by law. The fact that he was in incommunicado detention for nine months, and therefore unable to do so, was disregarded.

On the day that the state of emergency was imposed—21 July 1985—Auret van Heerden was once more arrested and held in incommunicado detention without trial until November.

A similar case was that of Linda Mario Mogale, a Soweto student leader whose seven-year prison sentence imposed two years before was revoked by the Appeal Court in June 1981.

The Appeal Court accepted that he had been convicted largely on the basis of a confession which he agreed to make only after he had been subjected to electric shocks and had had some of his teeth pulled out by a pair of pliers by his security police interrogator.

He had then been held for seven months so that there should be less evidence of torture and because a six-month limit existed beyond which victims of torture could not initiate legal actions for damages or redress.

Following the Appeal Court judgment, it was reported that the authorities would take no action against the security police officer who had tortured Linda Mario Mogale because the latter had not laid a complaint against him within the specified time.

LACK OF SAFEGUARDS

Accusations that detainees in South Africa are subjected to torture are met with government denials and references to safeguards. In November 1982 the government issued new guidelines for security police treatment of detainees held for interrogation under Section 29 of the Internal Security Act stipulating that they must not be tortured or ill-treated. Among other things, police are prohibited from taking firearms into rooms where such detainees are held. There is a statutory requirement that all detainees must be seen every two weeks by a doctor and a magistrate. However, these guidelines constitute little more than a restatement of earlier guidelines which had proved ineffective.

The overwhelming evidence of affidavits, inquests into deaths in custody, allegations in open court, medical evidence and eye-witness statements proves beyond a doubt that the terms and conditions of security detention in South Africa provide the context for torture and abuse of uncharged detainees and that existing safeguards against such abuse are wholly inadequate.

Deaths in Detention

Deaths in police custody, allegedly as a result of torture or ill-treatment, have concerned Amnesty International for many years. Between January 1981 and November 1985, at least 12 political detainees are reported to have died in police custody.

In the late 1970s several detainees in the Port Elizabeth area died in police custody, including black consciousness leader Steve Biko who died in 1977. The leader of the police interrogation squad in the Biko case had become the local security police chief by mid-1985. However in October 1985, the chief medical officer in the case, Dr. Benjamin Tucker, was struck off the medical roll for "disgraceful conduct" by the South African Medical and Dental Council.

NEIL AGGETT

Neil Aggett, a white official of a black trade union, was found hanged in his security police cell in February 1982. Auret van Heerden, another security detainee, testified to having seen Neil Aggett briefly several times in the days before his death and to having observed a progressive deterioration in his physical and mental condition.

Neil Aggett had twice complained of torture, alleging that he had been assaulted and subjected to electric shocks and sleep deprivation. The inquest magistrate accepted police denials of torture and ruled that Neil Aggett's death had not been induced by ill-treatment in detention.

Sipho Mutsi

Sipho Mutsi, an 18-year-old organizer for the Congress of South African Students (COSAS), was one of around 20 black students arrested on 2 May 1985. The arrests followed a boycott at a school in the black township of Kutlwanong near Odendaalsrus over the lack of sports facilities. Three days later, on 5 May 1985, Sipho Mutsi died in the custody of the police.

According to a police spokesman Sipho Mutsi suffered convulsions and fell to the floor while being questioned. A post-mortem was carried out on 9 May. The cause of death is reported to have been a brain haemorrhage and the doctors who carried out the post-mortem are reported also to have found whip marks and injuries on Sipho Mutsi's head, chest, back and shoulders.

One of those detained with Sipho Mutsi claims to have witnessed him being assaulted in the police station as he lay on the floor with his hands handcuffed behind his back:

We went into the CID offices. In the office I saw Sipho lying down with his hands handcuffed behind his back. He was wet on the front and water was on the floor. . . . A white stout policeman asked Sipho what he wanted in the Republic. Sipho answered "nothing." The policeman then kicked him in the face. He (Sipho) had been revived with water poured on his face and had been ordered to sit up. He was also given water to drink. But after he was kicked he lay still. There was a cut on Sipho's chin when I saw him. There were also *sjambok* marks on his chest. . . . [A black police officer] said to me while I was in the room "if you and Sipho are killed everything will be quiet in the township."

On 17 May 1985 the Attorney-General of the Orange Free State announced that no one would be prosecuted in connection with Sipho Mutsi's death but that an inquest would be held. It was scheduled for 6 December 1985.

Andries Raditsela

Trade unionist Andries Raditsela died on 6 May 1985—two days after he was detained by the security forces. He apparently died of head injuries, allegedly after an assault by the police.

Andries Raditsela was a senior shop steward of the Chemical Workers' Industrial Union and a member of the executive council of the Federation of South African Trade Unions (Fosatu). He worked at the Dunlop Industrial Products factory in Benoni, east of Johannesburg and was married with a child.

He is reported to have been arrested on the morning of 4 May 1985 in Tsakane, a black township south of Benoni. Uniformed police questioned him about a car which had been hired for him by Fosatu. According to witnesses he was then assaulted and taken away by security forces who were patrolling the streets in a "hippo" (an armoured troop-carrier).

Andries Raditsela was taken to the local administration offices in Tsakane. When his parents saw him a few hours later he was lying outside on the porch, his face swollen and barely able to speak. Later in the afternoon they were informed by the police that he was critically ill and had been taken to a local hospital, from where he was transferred to Baragwanath hospital in Soweto. The next day his parents were unable to trace him at the hospital and he was only finally seen by friends shortly before he died on the afternoon of 6 May. On 8 May it was announced that there would be a police inquiry into his death. By the end of November this inquiry had yet to be held.

In August and September 1985 three young men from Ginsberg, a small township in the Eastern Cape, were reported to have died within hours of being arrested. The youngest, George Thembalake, was only 15 years old. All three were members of a youth league affiliated to the UDF. The last of the three to be arrested—Mbuyisela Mbotya, arrested on 20 September 1985—died the next morning. A post-mortem reportedly showed he had died of head injuries. Lawyers acting for his family state that according to the police he became ill after being arrested and was taken by the police to a hospital in the neighbouring town of East London. His family allege that he was "dumped" outside the hospital by police, who would have driven off but were spotted by nurses.

<small>DEATHS IN DETENTION IN THE HOMELANDS</small>

On 24 September 1985 Batandwa Ndondo, formerly an executive member of the Students Representative Council at the University of Transkei (UNITRA) in Umtata, was reportedly seen being arrested at his home in Cala, about 100 kilometres west of Umtata, by four men and a woman, all plain-clothed. Witnesses later reportedly saw him escape from a van, bleeding and shouting for help, and then being shot several times by one of the men. His assailants took him to Cala Hospital—where they apparently identified themselves as police officers—where he died shortly after.

Two members of the Venda security police were found by an inquest to have brutally assaulted and caused the death in November 1981 of Isaac Muofhe, a Lutheran lay preacher. The two were tried for murder in February 1983 but were acquitted. The officers claimed that multiple injuries sustained by Isaac Muofhe were inflicted when he tried to escape from their custody. The trial judge refused to admit as evidence the officers' testimony before the inquest, which incriminated them and differed from the testimony which they gave at their trial. They were discharged and were apparently still serving in the Venda police in late 1985.

More than 300 criminal suspects also died in police custody between the beginning of 1980 and the end of 1982. It is not known how many of these deaths resulted from torture and ill-treatment but a number of cases did lead to the prosecution of police officers allegedly responsible for assaulting or killing ordinary criminal suspects apparently while attempting to extract confessions from them.

There has been only one case in recent years of the death of a political detainee which has led to the conviction of a police officer. The security police officer who shot political detainee Paris Malatji in the forehead at point-blank range in July 1983 received a 10-year sentence.

Abduction and Murder of Government Opponents

On the evening of 1 August 1985 Victoria Mxenge, a prominent human rights lawyer, was shot dead outside her home in Umlazi township near Durban. Her assailants were reportedly four hooded men. Victoria Mxenge's murder was the latest incident in what has emerged as a pattern of attacks on known critics and opponents of the South African Government.
• In May three community leaders from Port Elizabeth "disappeared"; their relatives believe that they have been killed. Sipho Hashe, Qaqawuli Godolozi and Champion Galela were executive members of the Port Elizabeth Black Civic Organization (PEBCO), affiliated to the UDF. They were travelling between KwaZakhele township and Port Elizabeth airport when they "disappeared."

In a subsequent court case brought by Sipho Hashe's family, his daughter claimed that the police had made threats against him in her presence while she was in detention without trial for 11 months.

The family also claimed that his house in KwaZakhele was attacked the day after his "disappearance" by people claiming to be members of the security police and that his wife was arrested when she went to lay a charge about this attack and was herself charged with public violence. It was also alleged that the security police subsequently indicated that Sipho Hashe had been detained, and threatened his son. The police officially denied that they had detained Sipho Hashe. The authorities have so far failed to clarify the fate of the three community leaders.

• On 28 June 1985 four community leaders in the Eastern Cape with a history of harassment by the security police were abducted and murdered. The four were former prisoners of conscience Matthew Goniwe and Fort Calata, teachers from Cradock; Sparrow Mkhonto, a community leader in Cradock, and Sicelo Mhlawuli, a teacher from Oudtshoorn.

Matthew Goniwe was a founder of the Cradock Residents' Association (CRADORA) at a time of unrest over rents and education in the black township. Attempts by the authorities in early 1984 to transfer him to a school in another area had been followed by community protests and a ban by the authorities on meetings of local community organizations.

Matthew Goniwe, Fort Calata and two other community and youth leaders were detained in April 1984 and held in "preventive" detention without trial for six months. A boycott of seven schools in the township, which started in February 1984, lasted until April 1985 but was unsuccessful in obtaining the reinstatement of Matthew Goniwe and Fort Calata to their teaching posts. Security police allegedly threatened Fort Calata and his wife that they would never work again.

Matthew Goniwe, Fort Calata, Sparrow Mkhonto and Sicelo Mhlawuli were returning home from a UDF meeting in Port Elizabeth when they were abducted and murdered. They had reportedly told others at the meeting, who feared for their safety, that they would not stop on their way home unless made to do so by the police.

• Victoria Mxenge, a Durban-based attorney and well-known supporter of the UDF, had been involved in the defence of many people tried on political charges. At the time of her death she was acting on behalf of the 16 UDF leaders due to stand trial for treason in the Pietermaritzburg Supreme Court.

Victoria Mxenge's husband, Griffiths Mxenge, was also the victim of an apparently politically motivated killing. A former political prisoner who spent several years in Robben Island maximum security prison, he was abducted and died from multiple stab wounds in late 1981. He too had been a prominent human rights lawyer and political opponent of the government. No one was ever arrested for his murder. The Mxenge's left three children.

The authorities announced police inquiries into the murder of the Cradock community leaders and Victoria Mxenge, but no arrests in connection with these killings had been made by the end of November 1985.

Amnesty International has called on the South African Government to establish an independent inquiry into attacks on supporters of opposition organizations to investigate whether any of the attacks have been committed by agents of the government, with or without the government's knowledge.

Death Penalty

Over 100 people are hanged in South Africa every year. Most executions are for murder, but the death penalty may also be imposed for other serious crimes, such as rape, and for treason and certain political offences under the Internal Security Act.

In 1984 there were at least 131 executions in South Africa. A total of 115 people were hanged in Pretoria Prison. Of these, all but three—two whites and one Asian—were Africans or members of the so-called "Coloured" minority. At least 16 people were executed in the "homelands." There were 10 hangings in the Transkei and at least three in both Ciskei and in Venda. All these victims are believed to have been Africans.

As the figures for 1984 indicate, a disproportionate number of Africans and "Coloureds" are executed when compared with the population ratio between these groups and the white and Asian minorities. This has been a persistent pattern over many years and has given rise to the charges that the judicial system in South Africa is racially biased.

In June 1983, three alleged ANC members were executed for treason. They were the first South Africans to be executed for treason since 1914. During their trial in July 1982 the three claimed that they had been forced to make confession statements while in security police custody.

One of them, Marcus Thabo Motaung, had allegedly been denied adequate medical treatment for two days after his arrest after sustaining a gunshot wound in the hip at the hands of the police. In a "trial within a trial" the judge ruled that Marcus Motaung had not made his confession statement under duress and that it was therefore admissible as evidence in the main trial.

Malisela Benjamin Moloise, a 30-year-old poet and supporter of the African National Congress (ANC), was hanged in Pretoria Prison on 18 October 1985 in spite of appeals by Amnesty International, the United Nations Security Council and many governments. He became the fifth person to be executed in South Africa for a politically motivated offence since 1979.

Benjamin Moloise was sentenced to death by the Pretoria Supreme Court in June 1983 after he was convicted of killing a black security police officer in November 1982. He denied the charge and contested a confession he had made to security police during interrogation, alleging that it had been extracted under duress. However, the statement was accepted as evidence of his guilt by the court.

He applied unsuccessfully for permission to challenge the verdict before the Appeal Court, and submitted a petition for clemency to State President P. W. Botha. This too was rejected.

Amnesty International made a renewed appeal for clemency to State President Botha on the eve of Benjamin Moloise's execution.

Recommendations

Violations of human rights on a substantial scale have characterized the situation in South Africa for many years. Recently, there has been a further, marked escalation of political imprisonment and detention without trial, torture and political killings. The judicial death penalty continues to be used at a high rate.

There is an urgent need for action to end these violations. Amnesty International is calling on the South African Government to take the following measures for the protection of basic human rights:

1. To release immediately all prisoners of conscience—those imprisoned for their political or religious beliefs, colour, sex, ethnic origin, language or religion, who have neither used nor advocated violence. In South Africa, these include people sentenced

to prison terms, detained without trial, imprisoned as conscientious objectors, banned or banished and imprisoned under the so-called pass laws, which are discriminatory on racial grounds and lead each year to the imprisonment of many thousands of black people.

2. To abolish immediately the pass laws and all legislation which leads to imprisonment on the basis of race.

3. To release all political detainees without delay unless they are to be brought to trial fairly and promptly for criminal offences.

4. To guarantee that all trials of political prisoners are conducted according to internationally recognized standards of fair trial, and to review the cases of previously sentenced political prisoners with a view to their release or retrial if their trials did not conform to these standards.

5. To curb police powers of arbitrary arrest and detention without trial and withdraw the provisions which allow people to be held for indefinite periods of incommunicado detention.

6. To act immediately to stop torture and ill-treatment of detainees and other prisoners by withdrawing the immunity from prosecution given in advance to police and security forces and by implementing the measures contained in Amnesty International's 12-point program against torture.

7. To establish urgently an independent judicial commission of inquiry into torture and ill-treatment and to investigate deaths in custody of political detainees.

8. To extend clemency in all cases to people under sentence of death and to abolish the death penalty.

9. To establish an independent judicial inquiry into allegations that recent attacks on, "disappearances" and killings of government critics have been carried out by agents of the government, acting in an official capacity or on their own account.

10. To investigate thoroughly all cases of killings of civilians by police to establish whether they constituted extrajudicial executions, and if so, to ensure that they do not recur and to bring those responsible to justice.

GREEN IS DETAINED.
YELLOW IS MISSING. RED IS CONFIRMED DEAD.[2]

From the distance, Johannesburg's Alexandra Township looks as if wisps of fog had collected above it, islands of mist in a sun-scorched day. Coming closer, you see that it is not fog but dust, for the streets here, unlike those in the white suburbs that surround Alexandra, are almost all unpaved. And this morning tens of thousands of pairs of feet are kicking the dust aloft as they walk over the hills in long streams that converge on one spot like a pilgrimage. Seventeen Alexandra youths, from age 12 up, are to be buried today. They are among some two dozen victims of a recent battle with police here, the latest skirmish in South Africa's civil war.

I am heading toward the funeral in a convoy of sympathizers, members of South Africa's small but hardy band of white anti-apartheid activists. They assure me we will be safe, but I am still worried: our skin is the same color as that of the police who shot dead those who are to be buried. Won't we, as the nearest white people in sight on this emotion-laden day, be likely targets for community rage? Furthermore, as if to emphasize that South Africa's race war is also one of class, the group I am with is all in cars, a few of them new Volvos and Peugeots, in a township whose black citizens almost all travel by foot and bus. Indeed, as we drive into Alexandra, we pass its ramshackle bus station: cracked and battered open-air platforms with signs listing destinations— ROSEBANK, FERNDALE, HONEYDEW, PARKMORE —in the white leisured world of boutiques, swimming pools, and well-sprinkled lawns to which Alexandra residents commute to work each day, many of them as domestics.

There is a stench from open ditches at the roadside, and the sound of small gasoline generators: in much of the township there are no sewers, and if you want electricity you have to make your own. Goats, chickens, and an occasional cow are on the streets. The tin-roofed houses are small and cramped together. Some people, desperate for space, are living in abandoned buses. Scattered about are reminders of the recent fighting: the smashed windows of a school, a few burned-out cars.

[2]Article by reporter Adam Hochschild. *Mother Jones.* 11:14+. S. '86. Copyright © 1986 by The Foundation for National Progress. All rights reserved. Reprinted by permission.

Astoundingly, as our little caravan of whites jounces slowly over the rutted road, we are cheered. Older people clap from the roadside. Children smile and wave from doorways. Young men give the clenched-fist salute—right arm extended, thumb outside the fist. The same spirit is visible a few moments later, after we walk into the overflowing soccer stadium where the funeral is to take place. Just outside the stadium is a warehouse under construction, a high skeleton of bright yellow steel girders. Several dozen young black men have climbed up and are sitting precariously astride it. In spite of a police order prohibiting such signs, they hold banners: FORWARD TO PEOPLES' POWER! and UNBAN THE ANC! Two white university students approach the structure, carrying their own banner of support. It takes them ten minutes to clamber up the steel framework; at every level, black hands reach down to help them up. Finally, from the topmost girder, two Alexandra youths reach down, take the students' banner, and hold it aloft.

The ceremony begins. Mourners have now filled every seat in the stadium and the entire dirt field where soccer is normally played. The crowd rises and begins to sing, in spontaneous harmony, the majestic, deeply stirring hymn that for 74 years has been the main freedom song of southern Africa: *Nkosi sikelel' iAfrika/ Maliphakamis'we'pondolwayo. . . . / (God bless Africa/ Let our nation rise. . . .*)

The 17 coffins are lined up in a row, mothers and other relatives sitting next to each. Banners in the black, green, and gold colors of the African National Congress cover the coffins. Teenage boys in berets and red armbands stand guard. For four hours under a broiling sun—a number of people pass out from heatstroke—speaker after speaker comes to the rostrum.

One is Albertina Sisulu, 68, whose husband, Walter, is a top ANC leader serving a life sentence, and who herself has been in and out of jail many times. Everyone here knows she may go in soon again, for refusing to testify against her son in a case now in court. She is introduced, to much cheering, as "our mother, Comrade Mrs. Sisulu."

"This country is governed by frightened cockroaches!" she shouts.

The crowd responds with a distinctive cheer: *"OOOOahhh!"* There are more *OOOOahhhs* as she mentions the names of Nelson Mandela and the other ANC leaders.

But in her talk, as in those of several other speakers, there is an undertone of anxiety: funerals like this have often now become occasions where angry crowds have killed blacks believed to be police informers. "Enough now!" Albertina Sisulu warns the young people. "There is no need for you to be fighting like dogs, man!" Addressing the informers, she says, "We will deal with you when we are free."

This funeral has been organized by ministers from the United Democratic Front, a broad coalition that is the major aboveground opposition group. The speakers talk mostly in English, sometimes in one of the African languages. The sponsors are clearly edgy. "Comrades!" the master of ceremonies urges the crowd, "please be *disciplined.*" And disciplined they are. Almost everyone on the soccer field is sitting cross-legged in the dirt. If more than four or five people in the same place get up, a half-dozen marshals in blue T-shirts that say ALEXANDRA MASSACRE rush to the spot to make sure no violence is about to take place.

A group of diplomats from the United States and half a dozen European countries look hot and uncomfortable in their dark suits and bowler hats. American and British reporters wander through the crowd, distinguishable by the electronic beepers that they wear, like doctors, at their belts. Bunches of pamphlets are tossed into the air and scattered by the wind. One is an appeal from the African National Congress to blacks in the army and police: "Brother soldier, policeman! Refuse to shoot your own people; point your guns at the enemies of freedom."

A poet reads to the crowd, in Zulu and English: "I have been to the mountaintop and seen the dreams of Africa to come." Between speakers, or when the sound system breaks down, the crowd bursts into song, feet stamping and fists rising up and down in rhythm. One song is translated for me as beginning, "We'll kill the Afrikaners." But there is polite applause for the Reverend Beyers Naude, a renegade churchman, who speaks to the crowd with the rolling r's and clipped speech of someone whose native language is Afrikaans.

Several groups of children, some of whom look no older than eight or ten, circulate in single file carrying hand-lettered signs. One addresses the minister of law and order: LeGRANGE, HOW ARE YOU GOING TO FEEL IF WE GO TO WHITE SUBURBS AND KILL THEIR CHILDREN AS YOUR POLICE DO IN OUR HOMES! Another sign provocatively asks a leading clergyman: ALLAN BOESAK, PLEASE ASSIST US TO

GET MILITARY TRAINING IN LESOTHO, BOTSWANA, SWAZILAND, AND ZAMBIA.

Again and again speakers and crowd trade chants, like a litany:

"Viva Mandela viva!"

"*VIVA!*"

"Viva Sisulu viva!"

"*VIVA!*"

"Long Live ANC long live!"

"*LONG LIVE!*"

Mike Beea, chair of the Alexandra Civic Association, speaks to the crowd, his voice almost breaking: "Here are our brothers lying in front of me and you! I am standing here with tears rolling to the bottom of my heart. When is this barbarism going to end?"

When is it going to end? It is impossible to see something like the Alexandra funeral without feeling that massive changes *must* be happening in South Africa. Tens of thousands of people clearly united in their desire for justice—how could gatherings like this not be leading, at last, to majority rule?

But such feelings are deceptive. The eerie thing I found in several weeks of traveling through the country earlier this year was just how unaffected was white South Africa, where the power still lies, by the past two years of black protest and bloodshed. A few nights after the funeral some friends take me to a suburban restaurant. The diners are young white professionals; wine bottles and candlesticks and red-and-white-checked cloths are on the tables; a smiling waitress recites her memorized spiel: "Our specials tonight are. . . . " In a photograph of the scene there would not be one visual clue that it is not in Boston or San Francisco. How many of the diners know that a mile away there has been a massacre, a mass outpouring of rage, a row of grieving mothers beside 17 coffins? They know it, but dimly, in a compartment of the mind that can be switched off, where you consign TV images of far-off places always at war, like Lebanon or Northern Ireland.

I meet several psychotherapists and ask them: how does apartheid enter the dreams of your white patients? They all agree: the remarkable thing is that it doesn't. On Friday afternoons the roads are filled with cars with surfboards on their roofs or boats on trailers behind them. One morning I wake in my room at Johannesburg's Holiday Inn and find that a telex for another room has been slipped under my door by mistake: GILTS HAVE DOUBLED IN VALUE SINCE PURCHASE APPROX 5 YEARS AGO. MOST GRATEFUL YOU PROVIDE COMMENT AND ANY DOCUMENTATION REQUIRED WHILE I AM ON SAFARI. EARNINGS SHOWN ARE TAX FREE AND SHOULD BE GROSSED UP TO ESTABLISH MAXIMUM MORTGAGE ENTITLEMENT. Most white South Africans can go about their days grossing up their earnings because they assume that their lives will go on as normal. For the near future, unfortunately, they may be right.

The atmosphere is far different from a safari, however, one sleepy Saturday afternoon in the Johannesburg suburb of Bramley. The bare, linoleum-floored room in the parish offices of Saint Catherine's Anglican church is almost empty. Audrey Coleman, a short, brisk, red-haired woman of middle age, is sitting at a wooden table with a box of four-by-seven-inch file cards in front of her. The box holds about a hundred cards, each with notations on it and a colored index tab.

"Green is detained," explains another worker in the office. "Yellow is missing. Blue is wounded. Red is confirmed dead."

It is now several weeks after the Alexandra massacre. But many people still do not know where their relatives are, and Audrey Coleman and several other white volunteers have set up a clearinghouse here, near the border of Alexandra, to help them find out. One problem is that the police do not release lists of prisoners. Another is that many people who are hurt are afraid to go to hospitals, where the police frequently come in and arrest anybody with a gunshot wound. On a desk is a list of people still missing and unaccounted for since Alexandra's weekend of bloodshed: there are 15 names on the list, only 3 are of people over the age of 21. At the bottom someone has written, "Check St. John's Hospital." In another handwriting is added: "Not there."

I talk with Audrey Coleman while she waits for people from Alexandra in search of their relatives. She describes one case she has been working on: "There's one young fellow of 17 who's been in detention since August of last year. His mother very soon after his detention had a note left on her kitchen table that her son had been very severely assaulted and tortured. She tried to get a visit to him, to no avail. . . . It's a privilege if you get a visit. She finally got one in November, where she had her visit in the presence of four policemen—one behind him, one behind her, and one on either side. Her son said to her he had to wear a hat because the glare was too much for his eyes now, and he was suffering from blinding headaches. The mother actually shut him up, because she was too scared for him to tell her why, because she thought: he's going to go back into that place with these people again and they're going to beat him up for saying anything. He was perfectly normal when he went in."

No Alexandra residents have stopped at the church today. Audrey wonders aloud whether it is time to close this temporary office: perhaps by now people have either located their relatives or given up hope. Crickets chirp outside, and the hot sun shines on red terra-cotta roofs. We talk awhile longer.

There is a timid knocking at the door.

"Come in!" Audrey calls out.

The visitors are two young black women, both wearing light tan dresses that might be maids' uniforms. One, with a frightened face and a voice so soft it is almost inaudible, says she is looking for her brother. He has been missing since the first night of the massacre.

"The name of the person who's missing is?" Audrey starts going through the box of file cards.

"Thomas."

"What's the surname?"

"Hlangulela."

"How old is he?"

"He's . . . 16."

Virginia Hlangulela is 27. There are nine in the family, she says. She says her work is "to make tea, to clean the offices" at a scaffolding-manufacturing company; the friend with her is from work. She says she has been to the mortuary, to the hospital, to two police stations, no one knows anything about her brother. She speaks haltingly, her eyes always downcast.

Audrey shows her one card from the box: "Is this him?"

"No."

"They aren't in alphabetical order," Audrey apologizes, continuing to go through the cards one by one. After a few minutes she pulls out another card, which reads: "Hlangulela, Thomas; reported Morningside P.S. 23/2/86." She shows it to Virginia:

"Is this Thomas?"

Virginia lifts her eyes and gasps, "Yes!"

"He's at the Morningside Police Station," says Audrey.

"That's . . . gooooood!"

"I'm so pleased for you," Audrey says.

"I'm . . . so . . . happy . . . to know . . . where he *is*," Virginia enunciates every word with great feeling.

Audrey takes down more information: telephone numbers, addresses. She promises to call a lawyer and arrange a visit.

"Thank you madam," Virginia says.

"You've been going around looking for him?"

"For two weeks. We've been spending a lot of money to go everywhere," says Virginia. She says that Morningside was one of the police stations she went to; they told her he wasn't there. Instead, they told her sarcastically, she should "go to the comrades" if she wanted to know where her brother was.

None of us say, because we all already know it, that if Thomas Hlangulela is at a police station he has almost certainly been severely beaten. Virginia is supremely happy just to know that he is alive. She rises to leave with a radiant smile.

"I thought my brother was dead."

From the newspapers: SAA FLIGHTS FOR HALLEY'S COMET ARE ALL SOLD OUT. . . . *Personals:* "Selective top quality Jewish only introductions. Miriam 783-5892." . . . URBAN MAN IN A CAGE: "With grunting rhinos and roaring lions for neighbors, Bernard Rich quietly goes about his business of living in a cage in the Johannesburg Zoo. The 27-year-old salesman is being exhibited as Homo Sapiens Urbanus. . . . 'The hardest part will be having to ignore the public,' says Bernard."

A poster in an activist group's office:
LETTER BOMBS
PUBLIC AWARENESS CHART

Balance. Any letter should be treated as suspect if it is unbalanced, has loose contents, or is heavier on one side than the other.

Restrictive Markings. CONFIDENTIAL, PERSONAL or other restrictive markings might indicate a letter bomber trying to ensure that the package is opened only by a targeted individual.

Protruding Wires or Tinfoil. Letter bombs can be loosened or damaged in the post causing fuses to penetrate the envelope.

Excessive Weight. If it seems excessively heavy for its size it should be treated as suspect.

Public events: Captain Steven Banks, chairman of the SA Antique Collectors' Society, will speak on miniature paintings. The Kennel Association will hold its all-breed championship dog show at the Cape Hunt and Polo Grounds. Swami Yatiishvarananda will lecture on meditation and self-realization. Charlie Parker's Fully Licensed Restaurant and Disco presents the Miss SA Wet T-Shirt Contest.

Black housing: In one set of two rooms, near Cape Town, 12 adults and children are sharing four beds. The ceiling is black from the smoke of a kerosene stove. There is no room for closets: clothes, in plastic bags, are hung high up on the walls. The walls are wallpapered with the shiny paper of Sunday newspaper ad supplements: hundreds upon hundreds of color photos of bathtubs, remodeled kitchens, sofas, stereos, lawn furniture.

TV: In some ways, this is the strangest thing of all. South African TV is tightly controlled by the government. News programs show race riots in Britain but seldom the ones here. The favorite entertainment shows are our own: *The Cosby Show* is tops, followed by two others, shown dubbed: *Misdaad in Miami* and *Die Strate van San Francisco.* I watch, fascinated, as black and white cops joke with one another in Afrikaans on Florida beaches and California streets. What is going on here? Why, in this most influential of all media, is a shrewd and powerful government showing all this black-white camaraderie? And to an audience of all colors? Is this evidence of enlightenment in high places? I think not. There is something more subtle going on. People everywhere confuse TV with reality: "Marcus Welby" used to get hundreds of thousands of letters asking for medical advice. I think the subliminal message of all this racial fellowship flickering across South African living rooms is: *Relax. There is no need for change. It has already happened.*

The wave of violence that has swept South Africa since September 1984 has become, in a strange way, normalized. Each day the *Cape Times* runs an annotated "unrest" map. One day the unrest map and the weather map run side by side, cold fronts and low pressure areas on one, shootings and firebombings on the other.

One place where the symbols on the map become real is in the African townships on the windswept Cape Flats miles outside Cape Town. In the squatter camps here, homes are made of corrugated zinc, tarpaulins, plastic sheets, or pieces of the walls of demolished buildings, with painted advertisements still on them. Children carry water buckets on their heads (one faucet per 33 people); women go door-to-door selling sheep's and pigs' heads, the only meat many people can afford. In these townships, ordinary police cars can no longer drive without being hit by stones or Molotov cocktails, and so the police and the army patrol in armored cars. These look unexpectedly like boats on wheels: a V-shaped, steel-plated hull deflects any land mine blast to the sides. Soldiers and policemen ride in a compartment high atop this hull. Buses here all have wire mesh over the driver's window: buses have been stoned and occasionally their drivers killed. (Current South African humor: How do builders overcome a brick shortage? They send a couple of buses through a township.)

In Nyanga Township, I see a giant Casspir armored car following a small white truck.

"That's the post office truck," explains the African woman whose house I am visiting. "Without the Casspir the comrades would burn it."

That, I think, sums up one particularly tragic aspect of South Africa's violence today: almost all its targets have been in the ghettos themselves. Often, like the mail truck, they are the government services—inadequate though they are—that township residents receive. A Swiss engineer I meet, working on an electrical substation in Soweto, tells me his fellow construction workers wear guns to work because people stone them. All this is senseless but foreordained, because of the way apartheid has bottled up frustrated blacks in isolated townships far from city centers.

The current period of revolt has been the bloodiest in South Africa since the great Zulu rebellions against the British in the early years of the century. Over 2,000 people have died in political killings in the last two years, and there is no end in sight. The violence has had several layers, all grim.

The police and army have been responsible for most of the deaths. Even in some of the so-called black-on-black violence, such as the killing of more than 50 people and the burning of 70,000 people's homes in the Crossroads squatter camp in May and June, police have backed up black vigilantes with volleys of gunfire and tear gas. And beyond news like this that dominates the headlines, much state violence here is routine. Corporal punishment is legal in South Africa, for example, with 40,000 people a year sentenced to whipping. ("Whipping is not more humiliating than imprisonment and will teach a short, sharp lesson," says J. A. D'Oliveira, deputy attorney general of the Transvaal.)

A second type of violence has been the increase in ordinary crime. In South Africa's black townships, as in poor and overcrowded communities everywhere, criminals have always done a booming business: Soweto had over 1,200 nonpolitical murders last year. In such places in recent months, ordinary police work has come to a complete stop. Thieves have had a field day.

To cope with this, in some of the smaller areas like Alexandra or the well-organized townships around Port Elizabeth, a remarkably widespread network of neighborhood block committees has been patrolling the streets, and "people's courts" have been adjudicating disputes. "These street committees are virtually running the townships," says Jon Qwelane, a respected black reporter who has written about them. "They are doing everything except collecting the rent." In Mamelodi Township, outside Pretoria, there is even an appeals court system. But in other areas, like most of sprawling Soweto, whose huge size makes it hard to organize, this has not happened. Sometimes young men come door-to-door or stop cars to collect assessments of money "for the struggle," but no one knows where it goes. And, to encourage them to attack black radicals, police have apparently been arming some traditional criminals: a longtime Soweto gang called Kabasa has recently acquired automatic weapons and tear gas. For ordinary people, even the daily commute to and from work has become a journey of fear.

Finally there is a third type of violence. The most militant political force in the townships now are the amorphous groups of youths, anywhere from 8 to 25 in age, universally known as "the comrades." These are the people whom the cops are out to kill—and who are waging a tough war of their own in return. Terror begets terror. Some of the comrades' tactics have been vicious. During the 1985 consumer boycotts, gangs of comrades searched people returning from downtown and forced them to drink cooking oil or detergent they had bought there. For blacks who are policemen or municipal councillors, or who are thought to be informers, the punishment is being "necklaced," or "Kentuckied" (after Kentucky Fried Chicken): a rubber tire is placed around someone's neck, doused in gasoline, and lit on fire. More than 150 people have been killed by necklacing in the last two years.

Some leaders, like Bishop Desmond Tutu and the Reverend Allan Boesak, have risked their own lives in shielding potential necklace victims from angry crowds. Most activists from established resistance groups like the United Democratic Front or the Azanian Peoples' Organization, some of them prison veterans, strongly condemn these killings. Some, though not all, will say so publicly. But they have been able to do little: as soon as a black leader is seen as being influential, he or she is likely to be arrested. Well over 12,000 people were detained without trial last year and this year; among them were just the sort of respected elders who could have forced the comrades to adopt different tactics. The authorities obviously know this.

Burning people to death is hellish enough; doing so without trial is still worse. The practice has, however, accomplished its intended purpose. When I first visited South Africa some 25 years ago, if you went to a political meeting, someone would pull you aside and say, "Watch what you say to N . . . over there; we think he's with the Special Branch [the security police]." Informers were reportedly paid by piecework, only for information leading to an arrest. Today, I heard stories of people being offered cars, houses, release from jail, and salaries up to the equivalent of $500 a month to become informers. There are few takers. The police network of infiltrators, once widespread, is drying up.

When the current wave of violence began, nearly half of South Africa's police were black. Many have resigned. In many cities, the black cops who remain can live safely only in special tent villages next to police stations. As some of those who stay in uniform take revenge for homes destroyed and companions burned alive, they become as feared as the white cops. I feel I can read some of that history in the face of a black policeman, looking down from the top of an armored car that suddenly roars along the winding sand path—in search of someone? or just on patrol?—next to a clinic I am visiting in Crossroads. His face is grim, his eyes are narrowed; he is holding a submachine gun. Children shrink away from the vehicle's path.

What happens to the survivors of South Africa's multiple layers of violence? And, for those whose bodies heal, what happens to their minds?

Ruth Eastwood is a soft-spoken woman in her 40s, wearing a blue print dress. She is a psychologist attached to Johannesburg's University of the Witwatersrand. On Saturdays, she volunteers her skills to help recently released political prisoners.

"It's not the kind of therapy you can do by asking someone to lie on a couch and let them afford to feel vulnerable," she explains. "For me it's always a question of how far you can go in breaking down a person's defenses when you know they may have to go back 'inside' and get beaten up again."

After asking the patient's permission, she allows me to listen in on one session. The setting is as different as one could imagine from a psychotherapist's office. We are sitting on metal chairs and an old couch in the headquarters of an activist group; at the other side of the room, someone is typing out a list of prisoners. Visitors wander in and out. On the building's front steps sit several people who are almost certainly plainclothes policemen, eyeing everyone who enters. The patient, a 14-year-old Soweto boy whom I shall call Sipho, arrives with his mother, who wears a kerchief and a brown floral dress. She has two other small children in tow. Throughout the interview she breast-feeds and changes diapers; sometimes the children climb onto Sipho's lap as well.

It is the mother, a schoolteacher with a forthright, intelligent face, who first describes the problem: "Sipho is having illusions at times. Sometimes at night he talks to himself. Since his detention his attitude has changed. He was a free child, free in speaking. Now he goes away sometimes and doesn't tell us. He stays by himself. And doesn't want to talk."

Sipho wears a white T-shirt that says Go-Mart, and blue Adidas. His arms and knuckles are scarred. "The whole body," his mother says quietly, noticing my eyes.

Sipho speaks very low and slowly, looking at the floor, sometimes answering questions only with a nod or a sigh. He looks shell-shocked. It takes an hour for Ruth Eastwood, questioning gently but trying not to sound like an interrogator, to get his story:

Eight months ago, he was part of a student group that organized a school boycott. He was arrested and put in a cell with 17 ordinary criminals. During the night, as he tried to sleep, one of them burned Sipho's lip with a cigarette, saying, "No one sleeps here." He was the youngest in the cell. (Afterward, Ruth and I wonder if he was also attacked sexually.)

"I didn't know where he was for three weeks," his mother says. "My husband's cousin is a policeman and he found out."

Soon after he was released, Sipho was attacked in the street by black vigilantes opposed to the school boycott. A friend who tried to defend him was stabbed in the eye. A few days later, while Sipho was in the hospital recovering from his beating, the vigilantes murdered his friend.

"They killed a friend of mine. They stabbed him," Sipho says as if still not quite believing, "the boy who was trying to protect me."

Then there was one final episode: a few months later he was with a gang of "comrades." They hijacked a truck. The police arrived. The other boys managed to escape, but Sipho did not—they abandoned him in the truck, and he didn't know how to drive. A gun was found in the truck, and so he was charged with armed robbery. At the police station, he was brutally beaten until he gave police the other boys' names.

"They kept beating me up. They hit me with their fists. They said they were going to kill me. They said, 'We'll put you away for seven years.'"

Sipho is now out on bail.

By degrees it becomes clear what enormous emotional burdens he is laboring under: rage at the police and vigilantes, guilt at having survived when the friend who tried to protect him died, anger at the comrades who abandoned him, guilt at having been tortured into giving their names, fear of their retaliation—and of the horrors that may await him if he goes back to prison.

Steadily, Ruth Eastwood draws more and more of Sipho's story out of him. There is a layer of quiet wisdom underneath her warmth; he senses it and partly opens up. She speaks so low that I can barely hear her voice, like his. It is frustrating, until I realize why she is doing this: this is a boy whom white people have been shouting and screaming at.

In the idiomatic South African English that they both speak, Ruth tries to help Sipho put his feelings into words: "Did you feel your comrades left you, there in the truck? You must be quite cross with them, hey?" She tries to make him feel that he is not alone: "Every Saturday here we see people who have come from detention. And the same kinds of things that have happened to you have happened to them. They are depressed and sad."

Sipho's mother adds: "He is not just sad; he is bitter. He hates our relatives who are on the police force."

Ruth adds, to Sipho: "The hardest part must be that you can't go and get angry with the people who hurt you. You can't go out there and be cross with the people who made you cross. You keep it all inside you."

"At night," says Sipho's mother, "he is running in the blankets."

At the end of two hours they prepare to leave. Sipho says he thinks it has helped to talk, and that he will come back alone and talk to Ruth again next week. I feel humbled and awed that this boy of 14, to whom so much has happened, is still able to talk at all. It is as if every possible variant of South Africa's current violence has fallen upon his thin, slightly stooped shoulders. And I feel further moved because of something else. If Sipho embodies the tragedy of South Africa's present, the quiet woman he met today embodies an unusual piece of its past.

When the Boers made their legendary trek into South Africa's interior in the 1830s, one of the two republics they set up was what is today the province of the Orange Free State. One of its prime ministers was Abraham Fischer. His son became chief judge of its supreme court. And *his* son, Bram Fischer, was a highly successful lawyer who became an anathema to his fellow Afrikaners when it was discovered that, underground, he headed the Central Committee of the South African Communist party. He is the model for Lionel Burger in Nadine Gordimer's *Burger's Daughter.* In 1966 Bram Fischer was sentenced to life in prison. Nine years later, fatally ill, he was allowed to come home to die. After his death, the police confiscated his ashes, saying they were state property. Ruth Eastwood, who now sees Sipho out the door and invites the next patient in, is his daughter.

One part of the story that Sipho told Ruth Eastwood sounds an ominous note that has been heard more and more in South Africa during the last year: his beating, and his friend's death, at the hands of vigilantes.

There have been sporadic death squad attacks in South Africa for some years, but around the middle of 1985 they sharply increased—suggesting that a nod had been given at a high level of the police. It is only logical, after all: a resistance activist murdered by "unknown assailants," particularly by unknown *black* assailants, is far less embarrassing to a government negotiating for European bank loans than if the same activist dies at the hands of the police, like Steve Biko. By the time I visited South Africa this past February and March, there were small items on newspaper back pages almost daily: MEN SHOT IN RANDOM ATTACK ON WEST RAND; BURNT BODY FOUND; GRENADE FLUNG AT RENTS ACTIVIST.

The vigilantes are both white and black. Among the most feared are those known as "balaclava men" because of the hoods they wear. Particularly active in the Transvaal, they operate at night, cruising through black townships in cars with headlights off, shooting at anything that moves. The police deny any connection. But sometimes the vigilantes don't bother about subterfuge, and the balaclava men are seen driving police vehicles or wearing pieces of police uniforms.

A number of places where the balaclava men have been most active, such as the industrial town of Krugersdorp, where they have murdered one black and injured more than 50, are also strongholds of a Ku Klux Klan–type group called the Afrikaner Weerstandsbeweging (AWB), or Afrikaner Resistance Movement. The AWB is led by an appropriately named farmer and former policeman, Eugene Terre Blanche. Terre Blanche, with an eye on Reagan-era terminology, calls himself a "freedom fighter." He is the voice of South Africa's white backlash: the fury of the poorer Afrikaners who fear they have the most to lose if any concessions are made to blacks. In the last few months, his movement has become a major political force.

A mesmerizing orator, Terre Blanche has attacked President P. W. Botha for his modest reforms, and accused him of laying South Africa's foundations on "curry and samoosas" and "Bantu beer." The AWB has spawned a Nazi-like proliferation of black- or khaki-uniformed militias, known variously as "brandwagte" (sentries), "storm falcons," or "blitzcommandos." By day AWB members attend large rallies; by night no one knows what they may be doing in masks and balaclavas, although there are some clues: one AWB member has been convicted of beating a black man to death with a bamboo pole, and in 1983 police seized an AWB cache of arms, ammunition, and explosives buried on Terre Blanche's brother's farm. Although any African National Congress member found with a stash of machine guns would likely end up on the gallows, Terre Blanche, who has many friends in the police, was given a suspended sentence.

Eugene Terre Blanche is a burly man with a well-trimmed dark beard flecked with gray. His muscular, erect bearing conveys the feeling of a tightly wound spring. His handshake is like a steel trap. He speaks excellent English, in a firm, emphatic, bass voice. During the hour I spend with him at his headquarters in Pretoria, which is filled with stacks of leaflets in Afrikaans, his eyes never leave my face.

What about these militia units of his? I ask. Are they vigilantes?

Oh no, he says, only people training for self-defense. "We must defend ourselves. I am sure there will be a revolution in the next eight or ten months. I know the black man. I've grown up with them. I speak to them. I work with them on the farm. I know them."

AWB literature refers to the corruptions of the "British-Jewish" parliamentary system; Terre Blanche has also said Jews should be stripped of the right to vote. But, faced with a Jewish interviewer, Terre Blanche immediately goes out of his way to say how much he admires Israel: "The Jewish people asked for 2,000 years for their country. For the land which was theirs. And in the end they have it. It's a wonderful example of a struggling people—a nation who wants to be themselves." This, he says, is all he wants for the Afrikaners.

The real art of being a demagogue lies in giving a conquering people a way to feel they are victimized. Terre Blanche does this by harking back to the 19th century, when the Afrikaners were bullied by the British—and when wresting land away from blacks was bold "pioneering." Terre Blanche arrives at rallies on horseback; his women followers wear the bonnets and broad skirts of covered wagon days.

"I think the Afrikaners, especially the poor people, have the right to have their own country," says Terre Blanche. "Their own *land.* And with that I do not mean we want the whole of South Africa. We only want the land which rightfully belongs to *us.* Which our forefathers paid for in installments of blood. By that I mean the whole of the Transvaal, the Orange Free State, and the northern part of Natal. That was rightfully the country of the Boer people. It belonged to us. And the world said so. The English came. They took it away.

"I am not a racist," insists Terre Blanche, sitting in an office bedecked with red, black, and white AWB flags, which look like a Nazi swastika with one leg missing. "I don't see a Coloured person as my enemy. I don't see any person as my enemy, even if he is in technicolor. I just want my Boerland."

On a map, "Boerland" amounts to about 40 percent of South Africa (although part of the remainder is desert). The rest, Terre Blanche says, can be for blacks and English-speaking whites.

Let them figure out what to do with it, he says. "Let them do their sharing there. But they cannot share power in my country."

And the big cities?

"I think they can have Johannesburg," Terre Blanche says, even though it would seem to fall within "Boerland." His dream is of restoring the old rural white South Africa, of the mythical days before urbanization, uppity blacks, and meddling foreigners. He throws up his hands in disgust. "Maybe it will be news for you, but I think they can have Johannesburg and Soweto. I think Americans can have Johannesburg if they are interested."

Despite the rise of neo-Nazi groups like the AWB, there is one way in which South Africa is curiously unlike a fascist state. Americans automatically assume that because a government is totalitarian, its central offense must be against free speech. Yet South Africa's ironfisted police state allows surprisingly open dissent. Universities have Marxist professors and discussion groups; publications from the Eastern bloc or the African National Congress are banned, but books and magazines offering the same ideas under someone else's imprimatur are often available. Although press restrictions imposed in June are far more severe than anything earlier, South Africa—unlike many countries of the world—remains a place where you can get a pretty good idea of what goes on by carefully reading the newspapers. Among them is a wide spectrum of opinions, and even of facts. If you wanted to know, for instance, how many people attended that funeral rally in Alexandra, you can take your pick among various estimates ranging from 20,000–25,000 (the *Citizen*—right-wing white paper), 40,000 (*Business Day*—conservative white), 60,000 (the *Star*—centrist, both white and black readers), or 80,000 (the *Sowetan*—black readers).

Perhaps because the audiences are largely white—most blacks can't afford tickets—the theaters seem freest of all. I saw a one-man theatrical revue that skewered one official target after another. The actor played a South African woman singer return-

ing "from her triumphal tour of Uruguay and Taiwan" (two of
South Africa's diminishing number of friends); he played a German TV producer directing a race riot (President Botha has
charged that the presence of foreign TV crews encourages blacks
to demonstrate); he played a woman in a TV commercial: "My
husband is a prison warden, and Omo is the *only* detergent that
will take the blood out of his uniform"; and he played a salesman
of riot-control gear, offering "vicious Alsatians in three sizes: me-
dium large, large, and bloody large," and "rubber bullets pro-
grammed for full frontal entry no matter where you fire them
from, so they can't say we shot the buggers in the back." When
the show was over, an Afrikaans-accented voice came on the loud-
speaker: "You've got five minutes to disperse in an orderly
fashion."

Why is this being allowed to go on, even during a state of
emergency? Is it a safety valve? Is it to create an illusion, like
showing *Miami Vice* on TV? Mostly I think it is the calculating,
public relations–conscious tolerance of a government that thinks:
*Let the liberals have their precious free speech if they want it; words alone
will never bring us down.*

What will bring it down? I wish I could report that time is running out for white rule in South Africa, and that the long battle
for justice there will at last be victorious. But in the next 10 to
15 years I see no such good news. In this year of the collapse of
dictators, no one should have the illusion that the South African
regime will go the way of Marcos and Baby Doc. Whites have run
the show in South Africa for 300 years; the Afrikaners will not
trade that for Swiss bank accounts or condominiums in Hawaii.
They will fight. They have the best army in Africa. And unlike
the Marcoses of the world, South Africa does not depend on
U. S. military aid: it makes most of its own weaponry—including
guided missiles and counterinsurgency helicopters. Most experts
are convinced it has the atom bomb. And the awesome military
power of the state has yet to be unleashed: the army has never
mobilized its large reserve force, for example. And once the day
finally comes when a combination of pressures forces the government to negotiate, people like Eugene Terre Blanche and the
hundreds of thousands who think like him, all of them armed,
may fight on.

A few years ago, after an earlier trip to South Africa, I wrote in these pages that the country seemed a metaphor to me, a metaphor for how the First World profited off the Third, with both worlds compressed into one country. In this sense, I said, we all live in South Africa. The country now seems to me also a metaphor for something larger. In a world laden with atomic weapons, we live daily with the semiconscious sense that our peace cannot last forever. We are dancing on top of a powder keg. We can deny it, we can temporarily forget it, but in our heart of hearts we know someday it will go off. It is only a matter of time. The longer the time, the more powder, and the more powerful the explosion. It is possible to construct imaginary plans about how the two superpowers might mutually disarm, just at it is possible to draw up blueprints about how power could swiftly be transferred to South Africa's majority without the country's becoming a thousand-mile-wide Beirut. But neither event will happen according to the scenarios we would hope for. Human greed and folly is too great. In this sense, too, we all live in South Africa.

"Looking into South Africa," writes the Afrikaner poet Breyten Breytenbach, "is like looking into the mirror at midnight when one has pulled a face and a train blew its whistle and one's image stayed there, fixed for all eternity. A horrible face, but one's own."

At the Alexandra funeral, the final speeches end. The coffins are hoisted onto dozens of shoulders and carried out of the stadium. As our convoy of cars leaves the funeral, we are stopped at a roadblock. A dozen blue-uniformed police are there in boots and riot gear. Some carry shotguns; bandoliers of buckshot crisscross their chests, giving them the look of guerrilla fighters in Boer War photos. For the first time I see the dreaded *sjambok,* a heavy whip of elephant or hippo hide, containing bits of metal. This one, on a long stock for dealing with crowds, stands higher than a policeman's head. The police open the car trunk and glove compartment and the women's purses, searching for cameras and tape recorders. They find nothing, say little, and wave us on.

The crowd accompanies the coffins, all 17 in a row, down a hill and across a streambed toward the cemetery, a mile in all, through Alexandra's streets. Singing, keening, they pass tiny patches of bare dirt, on almost every block, where people have made miniparks: often in spaces no more than 15 feet square, ar-

ranging rocks or half-buried tires in a semicircle, erecting a small
bench, painting everything green or white, and labeling it with
a small sign: LOVERS' PARK, WILLOW TREE PARK, or, where there is
a wheel embedded in the ground, WAGON WHEEL PARK. Those
with names like MANDELA PARK or STEVE BIKO PARK have all been
crushed by police bulldozers. The crowd is chanting, the pall-
bearers are now running under their burdens, in step, in a slow,
shuffling jog-trot. Around them the dust rises in clouds.

THE YEAR OF THE AMABUTHU[3]

They call themselves the young lions, the comrades, the guerrillas, the soldiers, the Amabuthu—the Xhosa word for the warriors who resisted the settler invasion during the frontier wars of
the 19th century. Their photographs appear almost daily in the
press: ragged children clutching wooden models of AK-47s; kids
playing "chicken" around a tear gas cannister in one of the dusty
battle zones of the townships; the halting orators, their voices as
yet unbroken, signaling their readiness for death. They are
known universally as "the youth," the legion of black teenagers
who for the last two years have provided the shock troops of a na-
tion-wide popular insurrection.

This has been a children's war. The youngest casualty is two-
month-old Trocia Ndlovu, asphyxiated by tear gas when police
attacked her home in Mamelodi, outside Pretoria, last December.
Three months earlier in Soweto, police officers were claiming
that ten-year-olds were joining the front lines in the street battles.
That month they arrested 746 "scholars"—the entire enrollment
of Hlengime high school—and held them in Diepkloof Prison. Of
the 12 political detainees who died in police cells in 1985, three
were age 16 or under and another four were not yet 21 years old.

Statistics do not yet reveal precisely how many of the 879 people killed in the 1985 unrest were children, but it seems likely that
they number over half. Of the thousands detained under emergency regulations since July last year, 26 percent were under 18

³Article by Tom Lodge and Mark Swilling, lecturers in political studies at the University of Witswatersrand,
South Africa. *Africa Report.* 31:4. Mr.–Ap. '86. Copyright 1986 by African-American Institute. Reprinted by permission.

and 61 percent were under 25 years of age. A 10-year-old-boy, Fanie Godoka, was held for two months and children as young as seven have been arrested by the security forces. Some children claim to have been tortured by beatings, humiliations, and even electric shocks. The United Nations proclaimed 1985 as International Youth Year; in South Africa, soldiers and policemen celebrated it with a vengeance.

What has brought the children onto the streets? Demography is one reason. Half of South Africa's black population is under 21. The 6 million black children at school (or boycotting it) represent 24 percent of the population. Economics has also played a major role. Urban unemployment has reached 75 percent in small country towns, but even in the main industrial centers there are few jobs for the ever-expanding flow of school leavers. Black unemployment in most regional centers seldom dips below 20 percent and is especially acute in the Eastern Cape where the recession has hit hardest. The latest unemployment figure for the Port Elizabeth region is 56 percent.

It is perhaps no surprise then, that Port Elizabeth, with 140 people killed in political violence in 1985, leads the township death toll. But not all young combatants have been drawn from the despairing casualties of South Africa's stalled industrial economy. In Cape Town, some of the fiercest fighting was in the Coloured suburbs of Athlone and Mitchell's Plain, where the middle class children of skilled artisans and clerical workers displayed the same ferocious street wisdom as their brothers and sisters in arms in the Eastern Cape shanty settlements.

For in the last 10 years, black South Africa has experienced a cultural revolution, a metamorphosis in values and conventions of the profoundest type. It is perhaps most evident in people's behavior at funerals, for on these occasions, the customary deference of the young to the old has been overturned. Time was when funerals commemorated the lives and achievements of the departed with solemn and timeworn ritual—speeches from peers, black suits, floral tributes, a hearse for those who could afford it, and almost universally, an elaborate religious litany.

Now things are different. Funerals are a time for looking forward, not back. The young predominate among the speechmakers, the time allocated to family grief and religious consolation is severely rationed, and the coffin is no longer borne away in a creaking Cadillac, but carried instead on the shoulders of young mourners wearing the bright tee-shirts of youth congresses, civic associations, and the African National Congress.

Since the Soweto uprising, when a classroom rebellion broke the intimidated silence of the older generation, young people have experienced an unprecedented moral ascendency within the black communities of South Africa. "*Singa magwala,*" wrote Aggrey Klaaste in *Weekend World* in October 1976. "We are not cowards." Today the shame and awe among the parent generation has lessened. It has been replaced with pride—and a bitter anger for the men in uniform who shoot their children outside their homes. On the first day of the fighting in Cape Town's Athlone during November last year, the parents were shouting at their children to get off the streets. By the second day, they were hauling out old tires and passing petrol to the student combatants.

None of the problems which underlay the Soweto uprising have since been alleviated by any actions of the authorities. Despite additional expenditure, classroom conditions remain appalling: overcrowding, unqualified teachers, venal and insensitive administrators, sexual harassment, material shortages, and at the end of it all, only the slenderest prospect of non-manual employment.

In the wake of the events of 1976, schools throughout the nation were rapidly politicized, and during the 1980s, increasingly well-organized. When the United Democratic Front (UDF) was launched in August 1983, its constituency was largely youthful, with a major proportion of its affiliates being school or church-based youth organizations, especially the swiftly expanding Congress of South African Students (COSAS).

But the revolt today does not draw its participants exclusively from the ranks of school children. The Amabuthu of the Eastern Cape—mainly boys between 12 and 16 years old—have had at best only a few years of primary schooling. They are unemployed, virtually illiterate, the offspring of broken or scattered families, living in packs 100- or 200-strong in what they call "bases" on the fringes of the poorer squatter camps.

They have little knowledge of the intricacies of formal political organizations. Instead, they have fashioned their own military structure. Emerging independently from other township associations, the Amabuthu declare their allegiance to the African National Congress. For them, the ANC and its imprisoned leader,

Nelson Mandela, are the liberators; but otherwise, their ideology is limited to a few basic slogans. They may not have a program, but they do have guns and grenades, some of which were captured initially from the South African Defense Force. However, if the arms caches discovered in Mdantsane in January are anything to go by, other weapons have been obtained more recently from the ANC as well.

Similar groups have emerged elsewhere in the country, for in every town the deprivations and restrictions of apartheid have produced bands of feral children. Some of the uglier excesses of last year—the "necklace" burnings of alleged collaborators and informers, for example—were attributable to Amabuthu and their kind, products of a brutal and pitiless social environment, who behave accordingly.

The school movement is more articulate. The young leaders from COSAS and other student organizations can quote the Freedom Charter verbatim and often demonstrate a sophisticated understanding of its clauses. Their advocacy of socialism may be informed by a concept of class struggle, as well as by an awareness of the outside world. Their iconography will include not only Nelson Mandela, Walter Sisulu, and Govan Mbeki, but also Julius Nyerere, Samora Machel, Karl Marx, and even Vladimir Lenin. Unlike the Amabuthu, they will be consciously non-racist; for them the enemy is "the bourgeoisie," not just "the Boer," and the student leaders will often have had a degree of contact with white "progressive" groups and individuals.

The other section of the organized youth movement is provided by the youth congresses, which began to be established after COSAS resolved in May 1982 to organize the youth excluded from schools by the age limit restrictions and barred from the job market by the recession. Twenty youth congresses were formed in less than a year, the most prominent being the Cape Youth Congress, the Port Elizabeth Youth Congress, and the Soweto Youth Congress. Since then, they have proliferated, the network today embracing even the smallest towns.

Their leadership tends to come from the ranks of former COSAS activists, with a sprinkling of veterans from 1976 who have either resurfaced or come out of jail. Young retrenched workers, sometimes with trade union experience, have provided another source of leadership. In the Eastern Cape, the youth congresses, together with women's organizations, provided the orga-

nizational backbone of the dramatically successful consumer
boycotts.

Obviously, the youth revolt of South Africa's black townships
is not a homogeneous movement, containing within it different
social groupings and at least latent ideological variations. The
question then arises to what extent "the youth" are susceptible to
centralized leadership and what likelihood there is of young people forming a movement which could outflank and challenge the
authority of the older political organizations.

Despite their loyalty to the ANC, the Amabuthu, obviously,
are groups who might find it difficult to accept direction from the
older generation of worker and middle class politicians who prevail in local affiliates of the UDF. Certainly during the consumer
boycotts in 1985, there were indications that the teenagers manning the roadblocks which controlled the flow of commuters into
the townships after work acted as a law unto themselves, forcing
women to drink cooking oil, shaving the heads of people with permanent waves, and destroying goods. In the Eastern Cape, community leaders have tried to disassociate themselves from the
necklace burnings and there have been allegations that some of
these savage executions were prompted by *agents provocateurs*
working on the emotions of the wilder kids.

Then, at the beginning of this year, there was a sizeable minority who opposed the return to school called for by the relatively conservative Soweto Parents' Crisis Committee (SPCC), despite
the endorsement of the latter's appeal by the ANC. By no means
were all school children willing to reverse the terms of their 1985
battle cry. "Liberation now, education later." On the other hand,
though, the majority of schools are functioning again, and the
Amabuthu and similar groups in the Transvaal have to an extent
been absorbed into the process of organizational reconstruction
which has proceeded in reaction to the restrictions of the emergency.

In the Eastern Cape and more recently in Soweto, the civic
associations have established street committees. Where these
have taken hold, the Amabuthu have been enlisted as militias,
each under the authority of a marshal who is usually a civic activist. Among other functions, they are used in controlling petty
crime. Last year, the ANC began calling for the formation of
youthful crime prevention units as one of the initial stages toward
the establishment of an alternative popular government in the
townships.

The elements of a new type of social order are beginning to be apparent, one whose spirit is essentially egalitarian rather than hierarchical. As the Reverend Molefe Tsele of the SPCC has pointed out, 1985 brought home a lesson to community leaders: "The youth are a joint and equal partner in all processes of community life. They emerged as a group not to be talked about, but to be talked to."

Today the loyalties of the youth are pure and simple: The youngsters are the frontline cadres in an army of freedom, led by Oliver Tambo in Lusaka and Nelson Mandela in Pollsmoor prison. How the youth will respond if the fighting ever stops and the talking ever begins may not be such a simple question to answer.

South Africa's black teenagers have the least to gain from any concessions to white security and privilege. But unless the country's agonizing conflicts are to endure indefinitely, negotiation of one form or another must occur. The more the revolutionaries have to depend on the reckless heroism of this lost generation of children, the less they will be able to offer their opponents at the negotiation table. For the comrades, the guerrillas, and the Amabuthu are sacrificing themselves for a different world, not the same one in different colors.

INSIDE THE AFRICAN NATIONAL CONGRESS[4]

Each night, when the black workers of Soweto return home to their barren, segregated township, and the haze left by their coal-burning stoves glows overhead in the African sunset, thousands listen on shortwave radios to the fierce, clandestine voice of revolution. Beamed throughout South Africa from distant black nations in English and in South Africa's indigenous languages—Zulu, Xhosa, Tswana, Tsonga, Sotho and Venda—the broadcasts fill the night air with the sound of machine-gun fire and martial cadences, and call upon listeners to rise up in violence against the white Government.

[4]Article by Mark A. Uhlig, an editor of the *New York Times Magazine*. *New York Times Magazine*. 20+. O. 12, '86. Copyright 1986 by The New York Times Company. Reprinted by permission.

"Compatriots! The entire black townships of our country are being engulfed by the flames of revolution. But the battlefield has been confined to the areas where we, the oppressed black people, live. The whites of this country now have to be rudely awakened from the dreamland that they have closed themselves into."

"This is Radio Freedom," the announcer proclaims, "the voice of the African National Congress and Umkhonto we Sizwe, the People's Army."

To an outsider, the program's strident antigovernment tone seems typical of left-wing insurgencies from El Salvador to the Philippines. But to its audience in South Africa, the program carries special authority, asserting the presence of South Africa's oldest and most influential rebel movement, the African National Congress, whose record of opposition to official racism extends back some 75 years, to days when Lenin was still an obscure agitator and Mao a schoolboy.

The African National Congress is, to many black South Africans, both the oldest memory and the brightest hope of black resistance to white rule. Banned in 1960 after generations of nonviolent activism, the group launched a campaign of armed resistance to apartheid, first from clandestine headquarters within South Africa, and then from exile in Zambia and Tanzania. With support from the Soviet Union and a growing number of Western nations, the group began to re-establish its presence inside South Africa in the late 1970's. And as violent protest against the white Government has increased in the last two years, the A.N.C. has become a principal—perhaps a decisive—element in South Africa's deepening political drama.

"The A.N.C. is the only group that has shown itself to be actively fighting the Government, and it is respected for that," says a prominent black newspaper editor in Soweto. "The people are talking A.N.C., the Government is talking A.N.C., everybody is talking A.N.C."

Although conviction for "furthering the aims" of the A.N.C. is punishable by imprisonment and even death, antigovernment protesters regularly carry A.N.C. banners and sing A.N.C. songs. The group's black, gold and green colors are displayed prominently at major opposition rallies and funerals. And the A.N.C. leader Nelson Mandela, jailed since 1962, has become a political celebrity of almost mythic scale.

Most experts agree that the organization cannot claim credit for bringing about the current crisis, but it has benefited strongly from the deep anti-government sentiments in the black townships. And many whites as well as blacks in South Africa agree that no lasting settlement of the country's future can be reached without A.N.C. participation.

That consideration appears to have contributed to a recent reversal in American policy toward the African National Congress: Secretary of State George P. Shultz is planning a visit to Africa, where he is expected to meet with Oliver Tambo, president of the A.N.C. The prospect of such a visit figured prominently in the Administration's attempts to dissuade Congress from applying stiff economic sanctions against the white regime.

The United States has long shunned any formal contacts with the A.N.C., citing its longstanding ties to the banned South African Communist Party. But as the extent of the A.N.C.'s following in South Africa—and of the opposition to apartheid in the United States—has become apparent, Administration officials have begun to qualify their criticism of the organization's leaders and to urge direct negotiations between the rebel group and the Pretoria Government.

To the white South African Government, which pictures the A.N.C. as part of a Communist-inspired "total onslaught" against white rule, any such compromise is anathema. "The A.N.C. is part of the international terrorist network," says Louis Nel, South Africa's Deputy Minister of Information.

Yet many American experts who have studied the organization disagree, and argue that the Administration's delay in understanding the A.N.C.'s importance has already done serious damage to American relations with a group that promises to play a key role in any future black South African regime.

"It's not hard to see the opportunism here," notes Thomas G. Karis, professor emeritus at the City University of New York and a leading expert on black politics in South Africa. "After so many years of indifference to the black struggle, it will take more than talk to convince A.N.C. leaders that we are reversing course."

Ironically, the Administration's shift comes just as the heightening confrontation within South Africa has begun to provoke serious changes in A.N.C. doctrine and tactics, making the organization, if anything, less acceptable to the United States than it was before. Having long attempted to avoid civilian casualties, for example, the A.N.C. this summer announced that it could no longer guarantee the security of such "soft targets." And despite its longstanding commitment to a "nonracial" South Africa, the group has now warned that it will "bring the battle to the white areas."

The A.N.C. is governed by an interracial National Executive Committee of 30 men and women. In extensive interviews with members of that group and rank-and-file members at A.N.C. headquarters in the Zambian capital of Lusaka, as well as in London and New York, I found that tactical issues such as whether to target civilians and whites, far more than broad ideological concerns, now dominate discussions among the leadership. "Our concern is inside South Africa," asserts Oliver Tambo. "And our strategy is necessarily a reflection of the situation inside the country."

Yet that, precisely, is what worries many Western observers. "The question is whether the situation is not already out of control," says Malcolm Fraser, the former Australian Prime Minister who served as co-chairman of a high-level British Commonwealth mission to South Africa this spring. "The anger and resentment among South African blacks is already so high that I worry the West has forfeited any real influence with them."

Seven hundred miles north of Soweto, in the former British protectorate of Northern Rhodesia, now Zambia, the nightly Radio Freedom broadcast is prepared in a small studio outside Lusaka. The studio is located in the back room of a tiny stucco house with a simple corrugated-asbestos roof that reveals the blue Zambian sky through every crack.

Tonight's announcer, Takalani Mphaphuli, skillfully manipulates the dials of an American-made sound-mixer as he blends tribal war chants with the sounds of mortar-shell explosions. His program is chosen from a shelf of tapes with titles that include: "Nzo—Year of the Spear" and "Mandela—Prepared to Die."

Born in Soweto just 24 years ago, Mphaphuli left home in 1980 and, like thousands of other young South African blacks before and after, journeyed overland to A.N.C. headquarters in Lusaka. Sprawled on the dry brown grasslands of central Africa, the city offers few comforts. A.N.C. members assigned there share cramped communal houses owned by the organization, and receive weekly food rations.

"Exile is the worst thing you could wish on your worst enemy," says Tom Sebina, a veteran of the A.N.C.

Life in Zambia is, to be sure, far removed from what most older A.N.C. leaders remember as their glory days in the 1950's. By that time, the organization had a 40-year history as a legal organization espousing nonviolent resistance to apartheid. It acquired a mass following after its populist manifesto, the Freedom Charter, was formulated at a multiracial Congress of the People in 1955. Calling for one-man, one-vote, the Freedom Charter, which remains the organization's principal platform, declares that "South Africa belongs to all who live in it, black and white."

Under the leadership of Mandela and Tambo, who were then partners in a Johannesburg law firm, and distinguished figures such as Chief Albert Luthuli, who won the 1960 Nobel Peace Prize for his African National Congress work, the organization sponsored strikes, stay-aways, bus boycotts and many other forms of peaceful disobedience.

All this changed in March 1960, when policemen in Sharpeville, a black town 40 miles from Johannesburg, opened fire on a gathering of the Pan Africanist Congress, an A.N.C. offshoot, killing 69 unarmed demonstrators as they ran for safety.

"It is hard to overstate the impact that Sharpeville made on us," recalls Tambo, a soft-spoken man of 69, with heavy black-rimmed glasses and precise British diction. "We were unarmed, we were peaceful, and they shot us down in the street. We knew then that we had no choice but to fight."

In subsequent weeks, both the Pan Africanist and African National Congresses were banned and went underground. More than a year later, A.N.C. leaders in hiding announced the formation of an armed wing, Umkhonto we Sizwe (Spear of the Nation), which began a campaign of small-scale sabotage against targets like Government buildings, which it considered symbolic of apartheid.

Within a year and a half, the group's leaders were captured at their underground headquarters near Johannesburg. Mandela and seven other key leaders were convicted of sabotage and sentenced to life imprisonment. Tambo, who had been sent abroad to start an exile headquarters, attempted to cultivate diplomatic contacts in the United States and Western Europe, where he received a lukewarm reception. Later, he traveled to the Soviet Union, where he was offered funds, educational subsidies and military equipment, establishing links that remain a source of important support and controversy.

As the A.N.C.'s influence inside South Africa waned, the country's black townships began to come alive in the early 1970's under the influence of the Black Consciousness Movement, which centered on a defiant assertion of black rights. Epitomized by the slogan "Black man, you're on your own," the movement defined "black" to include all three of South Africa's "nonwhite" racial categories—Africans, Indians and mixed-race "coloreds." And, in direct contrast with the A.N.C., it pointedly rejected collaboration with whites in their struggle.

Under the leadership of dynamic young intellectuals like Steve Biko, the movement's popularity burgeoned. And, in 1976-77, it culminated in the Soweto uprisings. During 18 months of violent demonstrations, some 700 blacks were killed by the police. Biko died in 1977 from beatings received in police custody, and the rest of the Black Consciousness Movement was devastated as virtually its entire leadership was arrested or forced into exile. Thousands of young blacks then turned to the A.N.C., leaving South Africa to join its military arm and revitalizing its exile community. Those recruits now form the most radical wing of the A.N.C., and are largely responsible, for example, for the unusually harsh rhetoric of Radio Freedom.

Since the late 1970's, A.N.C. guerrillas have been responsible for hundreds of attacks inside South Africa, according to South African police officials. In keeping with the group's early policies against risking civilian casualties, most of the attacks have been directed against electrical pylons, police stations and Government facilities, including a series of sophisticated bombings inside high-security state industrial complexes.

But in May 1983, the country was stunned by the explosion of a car bomb in downtown Pretoria. The blast, which killed 19 people, including eight blacks, was the first A.N.C. action to cause extensive civilian casualties. A.N.C. leaders gave notice that it was no accident. "We have avoided civilian casualties because we don't think that individual people are to blame for apartheid," Oliver Tambo told me in Lusaka one month before the attack. "But it's an armed struggle—it's bound to develop into quite a war, and the civilian population will be affected."

You must view our violence in the context of the regime's violence, which is far, far greater," Joe Slovo tells me. "Compared to what the regime has done, we are notable not for our ferocity but for our restraint."

It is a subject that Slovo, a Lithuanian-born white and former Johannesburg lawyer, knows intimately. A longtime left-wing activist and now chairman of the South African Communist Party, Slovo was a founding member of the A.N.C.'s military arm and helped carry out the group's first sabotage campaign in the early 1960's. Now, as chief of staff of Umkhonto we Sizwe, the 60-year-old South African plays a key role in choosing A.N.C. targets and shaping the group's military strategy.

In 1982, his wife was killed in Mozambique by a parcel-bomb assumed to have been sent to her by South African agents. As a result, Slovo, who has given only a handful of interviews in more than 25 years of exile, avoids publicity and keeps his day-to-day whereabouts secret.

For the Pretoria regime, Slovo's involvement in the African National Congress has been a propaganda bonanza. South African officials assert he is a colonel in the K.G.B. And his role in A.N.C. policy making is frequently cited as proof that the A.N.C. is a front for Soviet adventurism, not black nationalism.

As he relaxes over afternoon tea in a Lusaka hotel room, Slovo's appearance belies his reputation as a hardened revolutionary. Resembling an avuncular professor, slightly rounding, with an energetic laugh, glasses and gray hair, he dismisses charges that his party follows outside orders and stresses that Communism in South Africa is unique.

"There isn't such a fundamental divide between what people call nationalists and Communists in the South African scene," he says, "because you don't have to be a Marxist—you just have to be a plain pure black nationalist—to believe that liberation can't just consist of a rearrangement of the voting processes. The whites control 99 percent of the means of production, and if you're going to talk purely in terms of national liberation, you can't leave that undisturbed."

The Freedom Charter, the A.N.C.'s platform, calls for the nationalization of certain industries, as well as of the country's "mineral wealth." But many experts note this is hardly a program for revolutionary change. Some 60 percent of the nation's fixed capital is already controlled by public authorities, and, through state-run monopolies, the white Government controls an enormous share of the nation's industry. Directly or indirectly, analysts say, the Government employs an estimated 50 percent of all employable Afrikaners, the country's predominant white ethnic group, and roughly one-third of all whites.

More troubling to many Western experts are the A.N.C.'s positions regarding broader international questions. A.N.C. leaders, they note, expressed support for the Soviet invasions of Czechoslovakia and Afghanistan, and, condemning Israel's ties to South Africa, have announced their "solidarity" with the Palestine Liberation Organization.

Ties between the A.N.C. and the South African Communist Party, a dogmatically pro-Soviet organization that was banned in 1950, have long been close, and they have been reinforced by Soviet-bloc military aid to the A.N.C., which now accounts for roughly half of the organization's overall support.

"The A.N.C. went throughout the world asking for weapons," said Francis Meli, editor of the organization's official journal, *Sechaba*, and a member of the group's National Executive Committee. "The Socialist countries gave us weapons, training facilities, and all the other things. In America and Britain, we have found ourselves knocking against a closed door—a door that is locked and barred."

In addition, an estimated 400 A.N.C. students receive scholarships each year to study at universities in the Soviet bloc, an experience that has had a visible effect on the ideological leanings of younger A.N.C. leaders. And A.N.C. recruits are also influenced by the instruction they receive from Soviet and East German advisers at A.N.C. military camps in Angola.

Because many of the older key African National Congress figures, including Mandela and Tambo, are noncommunists, some observers now speculate about the possibility of a future Communist-nationalist split within the organization. Pretoria's desire to promote such a split was reportedly behind its decision to separate Mandela and other perceived nationalist leaders from known A.N.C. Communists with whom they formerly shared a prison cellblock on Robben Island, off Cape Town. It is also said to have played a role in the Government's consideration of a plan to release Mandela in the hope that his return to A.N.C. policy making might heighten tensions between the two camps.

The number of Communist Party members in the 30-person National Executive Committee is a matter of much speculation among outside analysts. Figures between 10 and 15 are often cited, although these counts are highly debatable, and most experts agree that the practical importance of this Communist influence is almost impossible to gauge. For their part, Slovo says, party members will not reveal their identities for the sake of such "McCarthyite" counts. To do so, he says, would play into the hands of the A.N.C.'s enemies, and make party members more vulnerable to assassination or attack.

"It's not in our interest to single ourselves out," says Slovo, who has himself been the target of several South African attacks. I walk him to his car, a new Japanese four-door sedan, and, as I open the door, a sharp whistle suddenly pierces the air, emanating from his pocket. "A remote control alarm," he explains, removing the shrieking device from his jacket and shutting it off. "Nothing to worry about."

Paradoxically, after nearly 75 years of struggle, the watershed battle in the A.N.C.'s fight for influence in South Africa was not won by proletarian class consciousness or even military force. Rather, it was won in the carpeted corridors of Afrikaner power, by white politicians anxious to split opposition to the regime. In 1984, they adopted a new Constitution that included a "dispensation" granting parliamentary representation to Indians and mixed-race "coloreds," while denying it to Africans.

The constitutional changes seemed to prove what many blacks had long suspected: that the Government's plans for reform were calculated to prevent, rather than promote, black political participation. And the resulting wave of violent protest has, like the Soweto riots a decade earlier, dramatically fueled the A.N.C.'s popularity.

The last two years have brought the exiled movement important new allies inside South Africa, most notably the United Democratic Front, a federation of some 680 anti-apartheid groups, and the Congress of South African Trade Unions, a new black labor federation with more than 500,000 members. Both organizations are nominally independent, and neither advocates armed struggle, but their political orientation strongly mirrors that of the A.N.C.

The combination of these groups now presents the white Government with a kind of unified opposition it has never before confronted. Though elements of the rival Black Consciousness Movement still exist, they are weak and divided. And the A.N.C. and its allies have largely pushed aside rival black groups, such as *Inkatha*, the Zulu-based political machine of Chief Gatsha Buthelezi.

In late 1985, a group of prominent South African businessmen traveled to Lusaka to meet A.N.C. officials, and, since then, dozens of other informal delegations, including white churchmen, students and political leaders, have made similar journeys. The pilgrimage to Lusaka has also become an obligatory part of the itineraries of foreign diplomats seeking to exert influence on South Africa.

This new popularity has also won the African National Congress a growing set of international contacts and benefactors. The movement now maintains offices in 28 cities, from Moscow to Melbourne. In addition to its ties to the Soviet bloc, the A.N.C. has especially close relations with the Scandinavian nations, which provide it with some $20 million annually. It receives funds and material aid from the Governments of Austria, Italy, several third-world nations, and several million in refugee aid from the United Nations and its related agencies. Other sources of aid include Oxfam, the World Council of Churches, various Catholic aid agencies and Scandinavian charities.

Lusaka is a bush-country capital. In the streets, dusty Land-Rovers pick up supplies, Government trucks rumble by and small foreign-made taxis teem with passengers. So there was little chance that, even with its diplomatic flags furled, the comparatively huge Buick of the American Ambassador to Zambia, Paul J. Hare, would go unnoticed as it slipped through the rusted front gates of A.N.C. headquarters.

The unpublicized meeting, in late July, was the first major step in what has become a series of contacts between the United States Government and the A.N.C. In September, Assistant Secretary of State Chester A. Crocker met for two hours with Oliver Tambo in London in what many observers believe was preparation for a direct meeting between Tambo and Secretary of State Shultz.

The debate within the United States over contacts with the A.N.C. seems likely to intensify as the confrontation inside South Africa grows. "We cannot afford to negotiate with the A.N.C.," says Senator Jeremiah Denton, an Alabama Republican who has sponsored hearings on Soviet and Cuban involvement in southern Africa. "Our evidence shows that it is linked to the Soviet bloc and international terrorist groups."

At this point, a fundamental issue is whether the American approach is even welcomed by the A.N.C. rank and file. Many older A.N.C. members express admiration for the American legal traditions and for the civil-rights movement of the 1960's. But their views are tempered by deep hostility toward what they perceive as Washington's adamant support of the Pretoria regime. Many black activists inside South Africa will no longer meet with American diplomats, and their attitude is mirrored by younger A.N.C. rank-and-file members who express open contempt for Reagan Administration policy in the region.

It also remains to be seen how and whether the A.N.C. will be able to capitalize on its new-found popularity. Many outsiders, such as the members of the Commonwealth mission, this year have advocated direct negotiations between the A.N.C. and the South African Government. Yet, at this point, there is no indication that either the white regime or the A.N.C. leadership is interested in such a meeting. A.N.C. officials point out that even the appearance of compromise could jeopardize support for their group among radical township blacks. "It would be a very dangerous thing for us to undertake," said one National Executive Committee member. "We would stand to lose everything we have worked for."

Tambo is more blunt. "Our target is not negotiations," he says, "it is the end of the apartheid system. There can be no compromise about that." He and A.N.C. leaders insist, moreover, that negotiations cannot even be considered until the white Government releases all political prisoners, including Nelson Mandela.

In the absence of a negotiated solution, the A.N.C. is left with the problems of posing a credible military challenge to the South African regime, something that is still far from its grasp. South Africa's military forces are overwhelming. Exercising its unchallenged superiority in the region, the South African Government has repeatedly attacked suspected A.N.C. bases in nearby states, and has organized civilian defense networks to prevent infiltration of A.N.C. guerrillas through sparsely populated border areas. Perhaps more important, it has used harsh economic and military pressure to extract agreements from the neighboring states of Swaziland, Mozambique and Lesotho, forcing those nations to close their borders to the A.N.C.

The A.N.C.'s response to this stalemate has been to move away from controlled guerrilla operations and to announce a policy of "People's War," calling on its supporters inside the country to rise up and "make South Africa ungovernable" through local violence with arms and explosives supplied by the A.N.C.

In order to maintain their organization's leadership among angry township residents who demand stronger action, A.N.C. commanders have been forced to raise the stakes of the armed conflict, even at the risk of igniting an uncontrollable race war. In 1985, for the first time, Radio Freedom began to urge its listeners to attack white areas. "The point is not to kill whites," said one high A.N.C. official, "but they must be made to understand the situation, to understand that it involves them, too."

Still, they acknowledge that the implications of this strategy are certain to be profound—both for the course of the A.N.C.'s struggle and for Western support.

"In South Africa there is an old African saying," points out the A.N.C. editor Francis Meli. "What is a white liberal? It is someone who sees an African, half naked, being chased by a vicious hound. And the liberal wants to help that poor man. But then the African finds a knife and he stabs the dog with it. And the liberal says, 'What cruelty these Africans are capable of!'

"Many people abroad are supporting us today because we are victims, we are dying, we are being killed. People pity us. But sooner or later, we won't be the only victims—there are going to be quite a number of victims from the white side. And I'm not sure how the Western world will react."

III. A PEACEFUL FUTURE?

EDITOR'S INTRODUCTION

Counteracting the violence, there are strong pressures for a peaceful resolution of South Africa's racial problems. White support for apartheid is by no means universal; even many Afrikaners, including business leaders and academics, oppose it. Perhaps chief among the forces for peace are South Africa's Anglican and black Reformed churches. Two of South Africa's best known personalities—Bishop Desmond Tutu, the 1984 Nobel Peace Prize winner, and the Reverend Allan Boesak, president of the World Alliance of Reformed Churches—are pressing for a peaceful end to apartheid. Often their stinging rhetoric is directed at the United States, which they see as, paradoxically, the chief supporter of Pretoria's policies and the most potent international force capable of influencing apartheid's end. In the interviews with Tutu and Boesak that lead off this section, one can hear both condemnation and entreaty of the West, pleas for peace coupled with a tinge of despair.

Other internal forces are pushing South Africa toward peaceful reform. The country's own economic predicament is an important factor. In addition to a plunging economy, in part due to international sanctions and disinvestment, South Africa also has a severe shortage of skilled labor and high unemployment among unskilled laborers, mostly black. Timothy Belknap, an African-born journalist for the *Detroit Free Press*, claims in his article on the South African labor force that the country's pressing need for educated labor will force whites to train blacks—and that such a strengthening of the black middle class is the best hedge against a bloody revolution.

AN INTERVIEW WITH BISHOP DESMOND TUTU[1]

"Have you heard the latest story they're telling about me?" joked Desmond Mpilo Tutu, the fifty-four-year-old Anglican bishop of Johannesburg, South Africa. He continued: "There's a new Kentucky Fried Tutu. You know what it's got? Two left wings and a parson's nose!" The winner of last year's Nobel Peace Prize sloughs off the criticism with a string of scornful "hmmphhs."

"What do they think they accomplish when they attack me personally?" Tutu asks, his smile turning into a look of puzzlement. "Do they think that by tarnishing my character they are changing the facts of the evil system that I am denouncing?"

That system is apartheid, the institutionalized system of racism that deprives 25 million blacks of the right to vote and subjugates them to the will of 5 million whites. "They" are the white regime behind one of the world's best-oiled police and military machines.

Apartheid became official policy in 1948, when the newly elected Afrikaner-dominated National Party codified 300 years of racial discrimination. Every South African was classified by race after a state-conducted inspection. Racial intermarriage was banned. Colored (mixed race) and Indian communities were stripped of political rights; blacks were stripped of their citizenship entirely. Nonwhites were prohibited from living in certain so-called white areas. Blacks had to apply for temporary permits to work in white areas and could expect as little as one-sixth of what white workers earned.

The government eventually designated ten areas—barren wastelands, really—as so-called homelands for blacks, and since 1948, nearly 4 million people have been forcibly removed from their homes and resettled. Most of those who have been permitted to remain in the white areas must live in squalid, segregated townships.

It is in one of these pressure cookers of humiliation and violence—Soweto—that Bishop Tutu lives today with an estimated

[1]Interview with Bishop Desmond Tutu by journalists Marc Cooper and Greg Goldin from *Rolling Stone*, N. 21, '85. By Straight Arrow Publishers, Inc. Copyright 1985. All rights reserved. Reprinted by permission.

1.5 million other blacks. Just a fifteen-minute drive away from the city center, Soweto might as well be 10,000 miles away. Families live crammed into uninsulated shacks and bungalows, most with tin roofs. Unpaved streets meander for miles through the ghetto, never leading to a center, just on to another row of ramshackle houses. At dusk, a noxious cloud shrouds the township as tens of thousands of coal fires are lit, over which the daily fare of mealy-meal will be cooked.

For the last year, Soweto and dozens of other similar ghettos throughout the nation have been occupied by the white-led army, known as the South African Defense Force (SADF). The troops have been deployed to suppress the most serious revolt in the country's history. Ghetto youths armed with stones and gas bombs, militant black unions, boycotts of white-owned businesses and international condemnation of apartheid have shaken the regime to its foundations. Minor reforms have been enacted, others have been promised. But the basic system remains in place, as does resistance to it.

The SADF troops and security police have arrested more than 10,000 people over the last year, more than 3000 of them detained without trial or charges. Hundreds have been killed in the streets. Others have died while in police custody. Forty-seven of the eighty top leaders of the antiapartheid umbrella group, the United Democratic Front (UDF), have been killed, jailed or indicted in the past year. One of its founders (and a close associate of Tutu), the Reverend Allan Boesak, who also serves as president of the World Alliance of Reformed Churches, has been charged with four counts of subversion. And last July, in a pivotal move, the government of State President P. W. Botha declared a state of emergency in areas that have been the most rebellious.

From exile in nearby Zambia, the outlawed opposition group, the African National Congress (ANC), announced that its commandos operating inside South Africa will step up the war.

Amid this turmoil, Bishop Desmond Tutu has emerged as a leader whose self-assigned mission is to see that the liberation of black people, which he believes is inevitable, comes about peacefully.

His antiapartheid work, dating back to 1978, when he was leader of the South African Council of Churches, drew the attention of the Nobel committee; they awarded him the peace prize last year, thrusting him into international prominence. What gives Tutu such strength and influence is his uncanny ability to look his Afrikaner opponents squarely in the eyes and laugh at the absurdity of their vision. Instead of indulging in a bit of sanctimony, for instance, in condemning the laws that, in effect, force black workers to live in single-sex hostels far from their homes and families, Tutu extends his arms, palms up, and says, with a bitter laugh, "Can you imagine that? This is the only country in the world where it is illegal to sleep with your own wife!"

Last month, Bishop Tutu made time for several interview sessions. His appointment calendar was juggled, rewritten and revised as events exploded around him: six more blacks killed by police in the townships one weekend; Allan Boesak formally charged with subversion; the South African army once again invading Angola; delegations of international lawyers and then British clergy on whirlwind visits to the town.

When we would arrive for our interviews with the bishop, he would come down from his second-floor office and personally escort us upstairs, complaining each time that he had seen us too often, wryly suggesting that we had bought off his personal secretary. His twelve-by-twelve quarters, lit with fluorescent tubes, is dominated by a huge polished desk stacked high with papers, telegrams and lacquered plaques—his latest harvest of honorary awards. Behind him hangs a silk-screen of Christ in subdued colors. To his side, a shelf of books, mostly religious. One volume stands out, its bright red letters reading CALVIN—the patron inspiration of Tutu's Afrikaner adversaries.

Tutu is always smartly dressed: His well-cut suit, imported loafers and designer cuff links are never in conflict with his prominent silver cross and bright-purple rabat. Nor does this touch of flamboyance undermine his essential modesty. The diocesan offices of the Anglican Church on the edge of downtown Johannesburg are next to a rubbish dump, home to an occasional sleeping derelict. The adjoining church, where Tutu prays twice a day, has plastic chairs, no pews, an unpolished wooden floor, a row of makeshift offices in one aisle along the nave. A pile of discarded furniture guards the chapel entrance.

Before becoming the bishop of Johannesburg, Desmond Tutu was the bishop of Lesotho. From 1978 to 1985, he was general secretary of the South African Council of Churches. Educated in his younger years in the segregated Bantu system of South Africa, he attained his master's in theology at King's College in London.

We were amazed by the manifest lack of security precautions taken by the bishop. His family has not been immune to reprisals; his son, Trevor, spent fourteen days in jail in August, detained under the state of emergency. Tutu may have office windows of reflecting one-way glass, and darkened windows on his Toyota, but apart from a lock on his office, he has no other protection. He relies on international vigilance and, as he says, on his faith in God, whose job it is to "jolly well look after me."

How has the system of apartheid personally affected you, Bishop Tutu?

Relative to the kind of life that many blacks lead, I have had a good time. I didn't have a particularly deprived childhood, nor was it particularly well endowed. My mother was a domestic worker; my father, the headmaster of a primary school.

We didn't think it was particularly odd that we were separated from white people. We thought that was the way that God had probably ordered things. I think my first experiences of awakening came when I used to ride my bicycle to town and had to run the gantlet of white boys taunting me racially. But even that was nothing thought to be out of the ordinary. It happened to every black boy. And I supposed that if we had caught a white boy in a similar situation, we might also biff him one!

The other thing I remember very well is seeing black boys scavenging in the rubbish bins of the school where the white children were being given meals by the government. The whites didn't like the food, so they threw it away, preferring to eat the things their mothers gave them. The black children were not getting *any* food at school! That program was introduced much later and didn't last very long because Prime Minister Verwoerd, when he came to power, canceled it, saying because we can't feed all, we mustn't feed some. Isn't that marvelous!

A little later, I began finding things eating away at me. When I went walking with my father, we would get stopped for passes. What that does to you and your feeling as a human being is horrible. Or going to a shop with my father and hearing him addressed as "boy." [*Anguished*] I knew there wasn't a great deal I could do, but it just left me churned. I felt . . . I felt . . . I felt . . . [*takes off his glasses and passes his hand over his eyes*] poor man. What he must have been feeling. What he must have been going through, being humiliated in the presence of his son. Apartheid has always been the same systematic racial discrimination: it takes away your human dignity and rubs it in the dust and tramples it underfoot.

Even now you continue to be the target of government harassment. We have heard that the security forces try to humiliate you the same way those white boys did when you were a youngster.

Oh, yes. You are talking about the roadblocks. I was stopped at a roadblock and my car was searched, and the police wanted to body-search my wife and daughters, and this eventually happened at a police station, where they were stripped. A whippersnapper of a policeman asked me for some identification. Ha! [*Laughs heartily*] I am the bishop of Johannesburg. I am a Nobel laureate. Any policeman who says he does not know me does not deserve to be in the police force. If they treat me like that, what do they do to so-called ordinary people? What do whites know about tear gas, about police dogs, about armored vehicles rumbling through the streets of their suburbs, about rubber bullets that kill three-year-olds? What do they know about having the army deployed against a defenseless civilian population? What are they doing to our children, what are they doing to our beautiful land, what ghastly legacy are they building up for posterity? No country can afford to bleed as much as ours is, where black lives are dirt cheap.

You describe a situation in which whites have imprisoned themselves in their own physical and psychic ghettos, oblivious to what goes on in the black areas. Who then is the black man in the white man's mind?

I think it's easier to say what *most* whites think, because there are some splendid people among them. It's horrible to have to keep saying, "Some of my best friends are whites." [*He bursts into a belly laugh.*] By and large, white people think that we are humans, but not quite as human as they. That, I think, is the sum of it. They would say, "We *do* think you are humans." But if they really believe that, why do they think we get married and then would want to be separated from our wives for eleven months of the year? Why do they think when we come back home from work we don't like to be welcomed by our children? [Under South Africa's Influx Control Law, most blacks are permitted to work in white areas only as "guest workers." They must live in "single-sex hostels" and leave their families in homelands.] And why do they think that in the land of our birth we should have absolutely no participation whatsoever in the most important decisions affecting our lives—that they should legislate about us, that they should determine what is best for us? That's something you would only do for a moron or for little children. And if they think we are children—even when at fifty-four years of age we can be bishops and Nobel laureates, when we can meet up with all kinds of people all around the world—then they can tell themselves that an eighteen-year-old white child has more wisdom and more capacity to make decisions that I do. It must mean they believe that a black person, no matter how high he may go, no matter how educated he may be, is still less than an eighteen-year-old white child, because an eighteen-year-old white can vote and I can't.

And how does the black man see the white?

Many see the white man as something to fear—as one who is out there to squeeze the maximum out of you, and then when you have finished providing your labor, when he has squeezed all of that out of you, he then discards you. And that is what the whites have done. They get men to come and work, and as long as they are able-bodied and can provide labor, they are wanted. When they are no longer able to provide that labor, they are seen only as commodities, things. Things that were once useful and now are not so. One government minister said long ago, talking about these blacks who could no longer work, they were "superfluous appendages." Our mothers and fathers, "superfluous appendages."

Do you think that blacks hate the white minority?

I expect that there are many who do. They must, you know. What do they think happens to you? You work for the white person in a salubrious suburb of Johannesburg, in a huge house that probably has only got two people in it. You have had to leave your home when it was still dark because transport is so inadequate. You go back home to your ghetto, you haven't seen your children, and by the time you get home they've probably fallen asleep. You are in your home, which is perhaps no larger than just the den of the home from which you have just come. What does that say to you? What do they think is happening to you as a human being? However, I think there is still the recurring miracle of blacks still talking to whites. There is an extraordinary fund of good will, still, despite all of what has happened here.

Who can legitimately claim to represent the blacks of South Africa?

The surveys show that Nelson Mandela [leader of the out-lawed African National Congress] is consistently head and shoulders above everybody else. The man they put in a cold jug over twenty years ago, whose picture you are not allowed to publish in this country, whom you are not allowed to quote. Yet people who were not even born when he was sentenced see him as their hero, their leader. Ninety percent, every time. In comparison, let's take who might be considered the best of the lot who operate within the system that the people have rejected: Chief Gatsha Buthelezi [leader of the KwaZulu homeland]. He got barely six percent. Now, these surveys may not be very accurate, but what I am saying is that consistently Nelson is always right at the top and all the others come panting along a poor second, third or fourth.

What would happen if Nelson Mandela were released today? What would change here?

Ohhh! It would be electric. For one thing Bishop Tutu would get on with his work of being bishop, man. [*Laughs*] I said to Winnie [Mandela], for goodness' sake, go and get that husband of yours out and let me carry on my work of being a pastor. I'm having to do his work, which I don't relish at all. Clearly, Mandela must be a remarkable man. He has done nothing—just sat there for twenty-four years—but he continues to be our leader. If he came out . . . well, how did you guys feel about JFK?

We're asking the questions today.

Hmmm. I'm answering them, I'm answering them. But I'm just saying that's more or less where we would be. It would change. It would be a different ball game. And Mandela would be able to say—he's got that kind of authority—he would say: stop that.

Stop the violence?

Yeah, whatever he wanted them to stop. He would be able to get them to do that. I mean, in comparison, we are just puny little things, man.

Are we going to see a black president in this country within a decade?

Yes. It is inevitable and obvious that we will have a truly democratic and majority government. I would not be as rash as to give precise timetables. It could be next year. It could be! You know this is a very strange country.

That's a mouthful. How do you get from white minority rule to black majority rule without an apocalypse?

Basically, there are only two ways. One is bloodshed, violence and chaos, which we are trying desperately to avert. The other is the route of negotiation, people sitting down together, a national convention, a constitutional conference, whatever you call it. That has been the call that the churches have been making now, for donkey's years, it seems, without making too much of an impression on the authorities. Now that the authorities are talking about negotiation, they speak of meeting with *elected* black leaders, knowing very well that the only elected black leaders are those operating within the government. Most of our people have rejected those so-called leaders.

You say negotiation is the preferred route. Is this likely, given an atmosphere of escalating violence?

We already have some of the necessary factors. Business leaders, startled by the run on the rand, have decided it is time to come out more forcefully and unequivocally against apartheid. A delegation of top business leaders went to Zambia to discuss issues with [president] Oliver Tambo and other [exiled] leaders of the African National Congress. Meanwhile, the government, which once said, "Don't push us too far," ends up sending the governor of the reserve bank, cap in hand, around the world saying, "Please extend credit to us." [*Laughing*] And he comes back empty-handed, you see.

Are you saying that economic pressure may lead to a softening of apartheid policies?

If they don't get down to sitting and talking, they are going to be compelled by the business sector, who are seeing their profits slashed because the rand has lost so much of its value. A fifty-percent devaluation! The business community may be realizing that if they do not take action soon they are going to the birds. It is impossible for a minority forever, and ever and ever, to rule over a vast majority as happens at present. Business people are saying, "When the change comes, we don't want to be seen to have been part of the problem. We must indicate that we were part of the solution."

Was the meeting in Zambia with the ANC a hedging of bets by the business community?

Yes, I think so. But maybe not in a kind of cynical way. I think it has been drummed into their heads that no meaningful discussion about the future of this country can take place if you exclude the ANC. I mean, that is just a brutal fact of life.

You point to the meeting with the ANC as one sign of hope for peaceful change. But didn't the ANC itself give up on non-violence when its leader, Mandela, was sent to prison?

No. They said they were forced to take the option of armed struggle because they were banned in 1960. I think many of the ANC leaders said, "If we can no longer operate legally and above-board, we still have to operate. We were set up as an organization to try and ensure that black people had a place in South Africa. It seems then the only way forward is through the armed struggle." I myself still believe—I am naive, of course—and I am not a politician despite *all* appearances to the contrary, but I still believe that if this government says it intends to dismantle apartheid, it is releasing all political prisoners, it is allowing exiles to return home without any risk of persecution, and it wants to talk with those who are the authentic representatives of the black people, then I think the ANC would also be ready to talk.

Recently the ANC announced a stepping up of its guerrilla war. What makes you so sure it would give up its guns?

If you are saying the only thing the ANC wants is to fight to the death, then why did they talk to the business leaders? The ANC is not bloodthirsty, despite what the government says about them. I know many of the ANC leaders personally. I met with them in December in Lusaka. I met with Oliver Tambo in the archbishop of Canterbury's London residence, Lambeth Palace. [*Laughing*] Whites in this country would be shocked out of their skins if they got to know Tambo. I said to the whites once in a public address: You were so surprised when you first got to know Prime Minister Mugabe of Zimbabwe. The whites discovered he was such an urbane, highly educated man. They had always been told if you looked carefully you could see horns on Mugabe's forehead and that he sat very uncomfortably in a chair because his tail was in the way, that he was a Marxist demon. I say to the whites, you were so surprised with Mugabe, so very, very surprised, you will be even more surprised when you meet Oliver Tambo.

But Tambo is leading a declared war against the white majority government.

When you look how the ANC has operated inside this country, it is remarkable how restrained it has been. It hasn't been real terrorism like you get in Beirut and Northern Ireland. The ANC still tends to attack only installations, only property, rather than persons.

If it is true that the ANC is not committed to violence for its own sake, what then can we expect from the government? Is there any willingness on its part to moderate its methods?

Let me make this point categorically. The situation in South Africa is violent. And the primary violence is the violence of apartheid. It is the violence of forced population removals. It is the violence of detention without trial. It is the violence of mysterious deaths in detention. It is the violence that forces children to be stunted through a deliberately inferior educational system. It is the violence of the migratory labor system, which systematically destroys black family life. The catalog is endless. I have declared myself repeatedly as opposed to all forms of violence. But when opponents of this system have challenged it nonviolently, they have gotten it in the neck for their pains.

Last July 20th, a state of emergency was declared in certain areas. What has that meant for the people living there?

This government believes when people get obstreperous, why, just boink them one on the head and you will have sorted them out properly. The state of emergency makes for blacks de jure what has always been de facto. Now they can do some even more bizarre things. My son was detained for fourteen days because he swore at the police. [*Laughing*] He told them what many of us believe about their actions, even though we might not have used equally picturesque language. I ask you, how does swearing at the police constitute a threat to the security of the state? Hundreds of children are arrested, from the age of seven, and many are kept overnight in jail, and there is hardly a squeak, not a semblance of outrage from the white community. An eleven-year-old boy is kept in jail with hardened criminals for fifty-seven days, and not too many are concerned. At a funeral in Bethal, a teenager's teeth were kicked out by the police, and our people are killed as if it were no more than swatting flies—just like swatting flies. There is no more than a whimper of protest from those altruists who are concerned that blacks will suffer most when sanctions are applied. They don't care a bean about our only too real suffering now. I don't know what they will make of the recent surveys indicating that an overwhelming majority of blacks favors sanctions.

The Reagan administration, employing what it calls its policy of constructive engagement, has been reticent to openly condemn the government of South Africa. The administration

argues that its approach of quiet diplomacy has had a greater impact on apartheid than have strict sanctions.

When it was first announced, I said quite firmly that constructive engagement was going to be an unmitigated disaster for our people. I had no idea I was going to be so accurate in my forecasting. Since the Reagan administration took office, our country has seen a new constitution which has excluded the vast majority of us—that is, seventy-three percent of us—from political life. Forced population removal has continued. The pass-law arrests have continued, averaging something like 200,000 arrests per year in this period that is supposed to be of reform. We still have Bantu education, the education that is designed simply for blacks, which has always been a sore point, a very real area of sensitivity. And what about deaths? How many people have died during the period of constructive engagement? Or just since August of last year?

How many have died in the last year?

The figures vary from 600 to over a thousand. So many people have died that it actually isn't newsworthy. *They don't even give the names now.* They just say, "Two people were killed."

But hasn't the white government recently announced they are moving toward reversing the policy of stripping blacks of their citizenship and relegating them to so-called homelands? Might this be a product of constructive engagement?

The government is now rethinking this policy. But this has come only as a result of the unrest and certainly not because of constructive engagement. Constructive engagement itself has had to be changed. Your president has been forced to impose sanctions, which is something he said he would never do.

If constructive engagement is a disaster, then what, ideally, should be U.S. policy toward South Africa?

I would like to see a policy that would end apartheid.

And what would that be?

Oh, I think they know clearly what that would be. It is quite clear that the South African government has known that it can rely on the protection of Mr. Reagan and Mrs. Thatcher and Chancellor Kohl. Look at the *brazenness* with which the South African military forces subvert Mozambique at the very time when they signed an agreement with the government of Mozambique—an agreement that President Reagan claims is a result of constructive engagement. But Reagan's protégé, the South African government, cocks its snoot even at him. Can anyone show me *one positive thing* that is the result of constructive engagement? All we have had is South African military attacks on Lesotho. Attacks on Botswana. On Angola. On Mozambique. It's unbelievable.

You obviously don't believe President Reagan has any sincere interest in doing away with apartheid.

I think that President Reagan's major concern is only for the white South Africans. Why did he not take so long to act against Poland as he did against South Africa? In Nicaragua, Reagan supports the *contras*, who, in the view of the Nicaraguan people, are terrorists. They are not terrorists in the eyes of America—they are freedom fighters. But Reagan is opposed to *our* freedom fighters who are trying very hard to change this system peacefully. For Reagan, our freedom fighters are terrorists.

I want to say to the American people: How about breaking your historical record? You have this extraordinary capacity of supporting the wrong side. Now, could you for once side with those who have right on their side and who are saying they would like to see this country be a genuine democracy where everybody, black and white, will have a stake?

Do you think anyone in the U.S. is listening?

I don't know why, but I seem to have some influence in your country. I guess it's just one of God's jokes.

President Reagan finally imposed sanctions on South Africa, yet you reacted by suggesting he was a racist.

Over the years there has been a fair degree of pressure suggesting that Reagan ought to take far more firm action against South Africa. And all along he has refused. He has made gaffes, like when he said this South African government has been a historical friend of the United States. But he's talking about people who supported the *Nazis* during World War II! Botha was a member of an organization that carried out acts of sabotage against the Allied cause. The people who really fought side by side with the Americans were blacks. Even then, because of the discriminatory policies, our blacks were sent to fight against Rommel's Desert Rats with spears because they were not to be trusted with arms. But our people died, and those are the ones that your president doesn't think about. He thinks about the wrong people because his view of history is horrible. Let's face it, he doesn't know anything about South African history.

How do you know that President Reagan is so ignorant?

Certainly from the statements he makes! Of course, later he backtracked, but remember when he said that racial discrimination of the sort you once had in the South had been eliminated here? Many of us responded by saying, what's the point of eliminating whites-only signs that were put up by these guys in the government here—signs on park benches and toilets. [*Laughing*] I mean, who ever said that our ambition was to share a toilet with white people? That's not the height of our ambition.

But you can't deny that in the last few years some of the more outrageous prohibitions have been lifted.

They think that we are now supposed to be thrilled because we can marry across the color lines. Well, who introduced these laws in the first place? The government did. In its orgy of racism, it was separating everything like mad, left, right and center. Anyone who thinks that we should rejoice because the Immorality Act has been properly amended is like someone who wants you to celebrate because some guy no longer beats his wife. Why should we be thrilled when it was the government itself who established all of these obnoxious laws in the first place?

You had a personal meeting with President Reagan in Washington late last year. Did you have the impression that he understood what you were saying about apartheid?

My wife, who was sitting next to me, said she was looking at him, and you know white people have the disadvantage of their faces showing color more easily than ours do [*laughs*]. She said she saw what shook him, and it seemed like it was the first time he heard any of this. I produced the travel document that I was using at the time—now I have a passport, but then I had this document. [*He stands up, walks to his desk and brings back a blue passport-sized booklet, Travel Document No. J 0270296, issued by the South African government. He opens it to the first page.*] "Undetermined nationality." Can you imagine that? That's what it says here. Undetermined nationality.

Did you show this to President Reagan?

Yes.

Well, what did he say?

I don't think he fully understood. But it shook him. At least that was my wife's impression, according to the look that registered on his face. But it was still early in the morning.

How did you feel when President Reagan's pal, the Reverend Jerry Falwell, came here for a few days this summer and then went back to the United States and called you a phony?

Ahhh, I have far more important things to be concerned about than wanting to respond.

We understand that people can be accused of a crime for merely advocating disinvestment. In this precarious legal context, can you tell us whether you favor economic sanctions and divestiture?

I think that although my official position is that I have not yet called for disinvestment, it's really academic. Disinvestment is happening in any case, without virtually any government having passed legislation to insist on it. It has happened because of where the rand is.

Where does this leave us in terms of foreign corporations? Should they be investing in South Africa or pulling out?

They should invest, but under very strict conditions. Not ones that merely ameliorate apartheid.

Many people in the United States point to the so-called Sullivan Principles—which call upon foreign companies to offer equal opportunities in employment—as a model code of behavior for investors in South Africa.

No, no. I told Dr. Sullivan long ago that these principles are totally unacceptable. We don't want apartheid made comfortable and acceptable. We don't want apartheid reformed. We want to be rid of apartheid.

You see, in the past these foreign corporations used to tell you that they were just visitors in South Africa. But I told them that their presence in South Africa was as much a political and moral issue as it was an economic fact. And they wouldn't buy that. They were more interested in trying to discredit me, really, as the South African government has been doing in its newspapers and television.

Discredit you personally?

Yes. They try to show that I am an awful guy in one way or another, that I have feet of clay. Why don't they just say I'm lying when I say apartheid is unjust, that it is immoral, that it is un-Christian. If that is a lie, then why don't they just say it's a lie and prove it.

The animosity toward you goes beyond the halls of government. On the streets of Johannesburg, we have met many whites who have called you everything from a bloody bastard to a communist. Many blame you directly for the unrest.

I am not the cause of all of this. If anything, some of us, like Allan Boesak and all these chaps they have been trying to vilify, have in fact been standing between them and the revolution! But they don't want to believe that. People like me are risking the danger of rejection by our young who say we are standing in our way. When I said that if some of our people go on burning collaborators, I will leave South Africa with my family, some of these young people said, "Good! Good riddance! Because you keep stopping us from finishing what we have started." So instead of white people—so many of them—being nasty to me and regarding me as some sort of ogre, they should be saying, "Oh, Bishop Tutu, we have a lot to thank you for." I don't really want them to thank me, but I want them to understand that even if they get rid of me, they will not have gotten rid of the problem.

There were brief-lived uprisings here in 1960 and again in 1976. What makes the current unrest deeper reaching and a greater challenge to the system?

Now I think the whole black community is basically at one in its opposition to apartheid. Given the way the authorities have been acting, especially against the young people, they have helped, perhaps unwittingly, to politicize and raise the consciousness of the older, more reluctant parents. Many of these young people do what they do now because of what their friends and colleagues did in 1976. There is a tradition of resistance. Also, the world has changed, it has awakened to apartheid. Most of Africa has become decolonized, and South Africa is surrounded by countries that have become independent. Just look at your country—it's a prime example of the change. If a year ago you had told me that *your* president would be signing a decree for sanctions against South Africa, and that your Congress, or at least the House, would vote so overwhelmingly in favor of sanctions, I would have answered, "Who is your psychiatrist? Don't you want to go visit him?"

What impression did you get on the U.S. college campuses when you traveled through our country in May?

For quite a while, people had been saying that the youth of the United States are not like they were in the Sixties, that most of them are worried only about getting on in the rat race. Then, suddenly, this South African thing came on, and now their fervor is something like during Vietnam. It is strange, because during Vietnam, they were worried about themselves being involved—

they were likely to be drafted. There was a kind of self-interest being served. But on this issue of South Africa, there isn't, and that's what's remarkable. I was at UCLA, Berkeley, Davis. It was an incredible thing! Those students helped us recover our faith in humanity. They should have been busy with their final exams and worrying about grades. But at Davis there were 15,000 of them sitting in the sun, waiting for me to speak. Incredible. Incredible.

Does that sentiment get transmitted back, say, to the youths in Soweto battling apartheid?

They get reports here, but of course not the kind of major coverage that you would get in a free country. Nonetheless, young people are aware of what's going on outside.

Are white South African students any different than earlier generations?

Now you are getting young whites who are saying, "Man, if I go into the army, I may be sent to a black township. I may have to shoot someone who was my friend in the university. If I'm not defending my country against an outside enemy, what is it that I am defending? I'm defending this system."

I find young people to be a great sign of hope. And one needs to look for hope [*pauses*]. I have a lot of time for young people. I think they are tremendous.

The mood of the black youth seems to be militant, if not explosive.

Many of the young people have, in my view, become determined to the point of recklessness. They believe the system will be changed only by violence, and they believe that they will die. And the frightening thing is, they don't care if they die. And we have authorities who do not appreciate and understand this. Or if they do, then they don't care, either. I think that the police and the army say to themselves, "Who cares? What is another black life?"

Your son has been arrested, you have been the target of many government media attacks. Do you fear for your personal safety and for that of your family?

I think you get to the point where you know if you oppose apartheid, you will at one point or another have to face government wrath. And while you will be concerned, there is not a great deal you can do. If they are after you, they're after you. And if they want to assassinate you, they'll assassinate you. If they want to boink you one, they can. If you begin worrying about that, you might as well just stay at home and sleep. Even then you are not safe because they can petrol-bomb your house.

Moreover, if you are doing God's work, it's his job. He will jolly well have to look after you. And no one is indispensable.

Is there any doubt in your mind that South Africa will one day be free?

Ohhh! We don't even discuss that, man! I mean, no, no, no! I say this also to people when I preach. Certainly in the black congregations. I ask them, do you doubt? And they say, quietly, no— rather unenthusiastically. And I say, *what?* Is that how you feel about it? Then they really get warmed up about it. No. I may not be around, but I hope I will be here to experience it.

I am going to be talking at a major private school, and I'm thinking that I want to talk about what it will be like when apartheid goes [*pauses*]. This will be a wonderful country. I will say to them that one of the things that will happen is that you won't have to listen to addresses such as this one anymore [*laughs*].

What are your greatest hopes and fears?

My greatest fear? That on the one side our people will get so impatient that they will say to hell with it. We are probably getting close to that point, to where we will have a bloodbath. On the other side, you'd have the authorities saying let us hold on for dear life, let's hold on as long as we can. So you would have that classic situation of an irresistible force meeting with an unmovable object. That needn't be the case if these guys can still listen and be ready to sit down and talk with the genuine representatives and leaders. We can still get that.

What would it mean for the rest of the continent for South Africa to be free?

Ohhh. I was saying the other day, can you imagine Oliver Tambo sitting in the Union Buildings, the headquarters of government, and he calls on his intercom, "Eh, Nelson, could you please come here? What do you think we should do about this guy Botha?" [*Laughs.*]

We would be the breadbasket for most of Africa. We would be the launching pad to propel not just Southern Africa but most of Africa into the twentieth century. I mean, can you imagine a time when most of our resources are not invested in protecting a system that is totally indefensible? When *all* the people of this country will be trained to their fullest capacity?

One more question.

Hooray! Freedom!

Partial freedom.

Goodbye [*laughs*]!

Okay. Last question. In that future free South Africa, where are we going to find Bishop Tutu? Somewhere in the government?

I will be a pastor. That is what I want. I am quite clear in my own mind. I don't want anyone to think that I have any public political ambition. I'm not as smart as these politicians. I'm really not. It's not that I'm trying to be modest. I just try to be a little bit of a visionary and to leave it to politicians to translate those visions into reality. I want to be around to maintain this critical distance so that I can say to them [the new government], *that* is wrong. Just as I stand around and say something is wrong on the basis of the gospel, I want to be able to be around to say just because *you* are doing the same thing doesn't make it right. If it is evil, it is evil, and I'm going to tell you so.

IS RECONCILIATION POSSIBLE
IN SOUTH AFRICA?
AN INTERVIEW WITH ALLAN BOESAK[2]

The churches planted by Western missionaries around the world have taken firm root in their host cultures and have become increasingly critical of their parent denominations' failures to live up to the demands of the gospel. Nowhere, perhaps, has this been so evident as in the churches of South Africa. And few have voiced the demands of the developing world's people and churches as forcefully as has South African churchman Allan Boesak, a member of the Nederduitse Gereformeerde Sendingkerk, a Reformed communion whose membership is drawn from the mixed-race population which the South African government labels "colored."

[2]Interview by David A. Hoekema, assistant professor of philosophy at St. Olaf College in Minnesota. *The Christian Century.* 101:546+. My. 23, '84. Copyright 1984 by The Christian Century Foundation. All rights reserved. Reprinted by permission.

Boesak's election as president of the World Alliance of Reformed Churches in 1982 and the expulsion of the two major white Reformed churches of South Africa from that body at the same meeting were signals of the growing consensus in Reformed communions worldwide that the apartheid system of legally enforced racial segregation can no longer be tolerated. Boesak's invitation to address a plenary session of the World Council of Churches in Vancouver in July 1983 was a further sign of the international Christian community's support for nonwhite South Africans whose rights and lives are threatened by government policies. Despite pressures imposed by the government and by white missionaries, Boesak's own church in South Africa has condemned apartheid as a heresy.

Allan Boesak serves as chaplain at the "colored" University of Western Cape. His book *The Finger of God* was published by Orbis in1982, and he has helped to organize *Broederkreis*, a group of nonwhite Reformed pastors opposing apartheid. In this interview, Boesak talks about his perceptions of the dangers and the causes of violence in South Africa, and the possibilities for reform.

Hoekema: Let's begin with the frightening but inevitable question: Is war likely in South Africa? And if war comes, what will be its causes? Are there ways to avert widespread violence?

Boesak: The key to peaceful change in South Africa does not really lie in the hands of the black people. It is the white people—who have the right to vote and who hold so much political and economic power—who can bring about the changes in that society which will avert the danger of war. And it is influential outside agencies like the United States government and other external economic and political forces that could apply enough pressure to bring about peaceful change. Our dilemma is that none of these forces seems genuinely interested in applying the kinds of pressure that could bring about peaceful change in Africa. They are most interested in pursuing short-term goals, in ready profits and in immediate political gains. I will not say that it completely takes the possibility for change out of the hands of black people, but it makes it very difficult for us.

Consistently, for many, many years now, we have tried to bring about peaceful transformations in South Africa and to bring peaceful pressure to bear on the South African government. Through the African National Congress, established in 1912, and even before that in the late 19th century, black people have made many efforts to help successive white South African governments see the dangers inherent in the kind of policy they have been pursuing.

All of these efforts have been to no avail. Peaceful demonstrations have all ended in massacres. The government has consistently replied with violence—which means that we have come, in a very real sense, to the end of our possibilities. In South Africa we are not facing a government that can be morally persuaded to bring about necessary changes. We cannot, through our nonviolent ways, bring enough pressure on that government to get it to respond to black people's legitimate demands for the recognition of their human dignity. Therefore, many black South Africans have concluded that the only way to make white people see their determination to be free is to engage in violent conflict.

The South African government, with the support of most white South Africans, long ago decided that there would be no change if they could help it, and that they would employ the considerable military force at their disposal to prevent change. This is the dilemma in which we find ourselves. The longer that the government is allowed to continue on this road, and the longer Western governments, which are supposed to support movements toward peaceful change and democracy, continue, instead, to support the violent and unjust South African regime, the closer we will come to the moment when the whole black community will realize the futility of negotiation. That may trigger a release of the violence that has been building up for so many years now.

Hoekema: So if violence comes, it is likely to come at the hands of the black majority, but from causes that have been created by the white government and its supporters around the world.

Boesak: South Africa is not a peaceful place, to which violence may someday come. Apartheid is intrinsically a violent system. Violence is built into its inequality, its disrespect for black human beings. The undermining of our human dignity, which is part and parcel of the South African legal system, is a kind of systemic violence; and there is also the physical, military violence which the South African government has to employ in order to maintain its power and to intimidate the people. All of these kinds of violence are already there. So what we are talking about is the possible decision of black people at long last to engage in counter-violence.

Hoekema: Yet there are some South Africans—I think especially of C. F. Beyers Naudé and his associates at the now outlawed Christian Institute—who maintain the hope that change can still come through reconciliation, through meeting violence with a more powerful form of reconstruction.

Boesak: We all retain that hope. But I must tell you that Beyers Naudé has just given a lecture at the Free University in Amsterdam, outlining the situation in South Africa. It was a decidedly pessimistic statement. He spelled out as clearly as anybody can that revolutionary violence—the final cataclysmic moment—has become unavoidable. He no longer believes that the government of South Africa is capable of responding in a human way. And I must say that that analysis is shared by most of us. So it is a question of hoping against hope.

One cannot talk about nonviolence if one is unable to do anything about it. In such a situation, nonviolence becomes an oppressive ideology. It aids and abets the oppressor and paralyzes the people in their struggle for justice unless they can translate it into some kind of action. It is just such actions, however, which are prohibited in South Africa. And I do not know whether it is possible for me to say to people, "Let us engage in nonviolent direct action in South Africa," when I know that the government will come out in full force and will shoot to kill—and when I also know that such an incident would stir the conscience of the world for maybe a day or two, but that the money and profits to be made in South Africa would speak louder than the anguish, despair and suffering of our people. We can forget about the West turning on the South African government and saying, "We will not allow you to do that." Hundreds of children, young people and older people were killed in Soweto in 1976. The same thing happened in Cape Town in 1980. The world has not blinked an eye.

Hoekema: But the church, at least, is beginning to blink an eye. Could you have predicted even a few years ago the changes that have occurred, particularly in the Reformed communion—the denunciations of apartheid as heresy, the distancing of the Reformed churches from their sister churches in South Africa? You have said that you believe these shifts have caused some anguish and uncertainty in the ruling Dutch Reformed churches.

Might this be the seed of a more far-reaching change in Western actions and attitudes toward South Africa—the beginning, perhaps, of a worldwide demand that the world community should not accept the South African government as a member until it recognizes the human dignity and the basic rights of all South Africans?

Boesak: I would really hope so. I believe that pressure works. There is one area where we have seen this in the South African situation—the only area where there is visible change—the realm of sports. It is not nearly enough; it does not touch upon the basic fundamentals of South African society; it does not change the political or economic situation fundamentally. Still, matters are far different than they were ten years ago.

Now, how did that change come about? Not because the sports administrators in South Africa all of a sudden went through some heartrending transformation themselves, but because they were being put under pressure by the sports bodies of the world. South Africa cannot participate in the Olympics. It cannot play rugby or soccer or cricket internationally. And that not only hurts, but it makes clear that the country's policies are so unacceptable to the world that unless there is change, South Africa will not become part of that wider world again.

In the churches, too, outside pressure has brought about change. For almost a century and a half the Dutch Reformed church had no qualms about its support of the ruling class in South Africa. During that time it was always able to maintain contact with other Reformed churches around the world, and that kept it from having to face black people in South Africa itself. It is much easier for an oppressor to speak to former oppressors who are also white and who understand—who understand so well, from the distance of Europe or America—the impossibility of real change. It is very different for the oppressor to face the victims of his policies in his own country.

We have succeeded in getting the Reformed churches of the world, one by one, to suspend their discussions with the white South African Reformed churches. So they are facing only us right now. That has brought about a totally different context for the discussion of our situation. If the same could happen in the economic, cultural and political fields, we would begin to see some more meaningful changes.

Hoekema: You have said that the South African reform movements have been encouraged over the years by the civil rights movement and the black consciousness movement in the United States. Do you feel that you are included in the agendas of today's growing European and American peace movements? Is the concern for peace inclusive enough to recognize the situation that you face? Or do you feel that these movements have excluded you?

Boesak: They have not excluded us, but neither have they made us a top priority. There is some justification for the cynical observation of Third World people that the peace movement is a response to the possibility of the nuclear destruction of the First World. Since World War II, we have had dozens of wars in different parts of the world. Many of them have been caused not by the countries in which they have been waged, but by the conflicting interests of the superpowers. There has been far too little concern about that. There has been far too little concern about conventional wars in which millions of people have died—or about the obliteration of meaningful life for the people who are dying of hunger all over the continent of Africa, or whose human rights are denied in Latin and Central America. But now, when Americans and Europeans discover that they might be the victims of the next war, then suddenly they get upset and excited about war.

I do not conclude from this that the peace movement has nothing to do with the Third World. I do think, however, that those in the peace movement will have to work a lot harder to make people understand just how interconnected these concerns are. Unless that happens the peace movement is going to find itself tragically isolated. Peace is a worldwide concern which touches the heart of the gospel, which ought to be part of the life of the church of Jesus Christ universal.

Hoekema: When I visited the Netherlands last year, during the churches' annual Peace Week, I was impressed by Dutch Christians' awareness of the connection between nuclear disarmament and issues of violence and human rights in the Third World—a greater awareness than one finds in many elements of the peace movement in the United States.

Boesak: The Dutch churches have always been more sensitive to these issues than perhaps any other churches in the world. I think other churches are becoming more aware, but it is still an uphill struggle. All the same, in the Third World I always speak up for the European and American peace movements. It would be dangerous if we could not find a common ground.

Hoekema: The United Nations has tried to bring about reform in South Africa, to protect the oppressed, and to protect neighboring lands from South African attack, but its powers are limited. Do you think that stronger UN measures or different forms of international power might indeed change the situation of nonwhites in South Africa?

Boesak: The UN is the only body that has international political power. Its weakness is that it has to depend on the wholehearted cooperation of all of its members. The UN is only as strong as each of the superpowers allows it to be, and that is its essential weakness.

I think that the UN is very important. It is a shame that its authority has been undermined in the past few years—especially the past two years. As long, for instance, as the U.S. government humiliates and treats the United Nations with disdain, the UN will not be an effective instrument anywhere in the world. People must not be upset that the UN is not capable of maintaining the peace in Lebanon. After all, in Namibia—where the organization could have accomplished something—the Western nations have come in with typical Western arrogance, taken the responsibility out of the UN's hands, and mapped out a strategy that does not represent the agenda either of the Namibian people or of the international community.

It is ridiculous that the Western nations have been led by the nose by the South African government. No Western government could really be as naive and as stupid as they all seemed. They must have known what they were getting into—they must have known from the very beginning that there would be no settlement in Namibia. When we undermine the UN's authority in one area, we cannot expect it to solve our problems in another. The same is true for the Soviet Union's actions. If that country ignores the UN's pleas concerning Afghanistan and the right of the Polish people to determine their own destiny, then it cannot be upset with the organization when it is not able to stop South Africa from destabilizing its neighbors.

We have very few international instruments for seeking peace and justice. It is so tragic when we purposefully and willfully undermine the tools that we need for our own safety. On the issues of nuclear destruction or nuclear deterrence, it is once again the two superpowers that will make the decisions, and the rest of the world will have to look on. And that is a very sad state of affairs.

Hoekema: Is an international order an important part of your dream for the world?

Boesak: I have long realized that the one word that best describes our world is "interdependency." It is not possible for a nation to go its own way, even though Mr. Reagan seems to think that it is. That Lone Ranger mentality is not only dangerous, it is simply foolish. In order to maintain that stance you have to undermine all the other agencies that might deny you the feeling of being on top of the world. In an international order that had checks and balances, where nations had to account to one another, Russia could not with impunity march into Afghanistan and do what it does, nor could the United States with impunity march into Nicaragua and do what it does. Weak nations must be given the right to demand that justice be done. We must have a stronger international community, and an international code of conduct in order to accomplish that.

I am too much of a Reformed person to trust to the goodness of human nature. I say with the Catechism that we are corrupt, and by nature prone to hate God and our neighbor. And so we all need the corrective, loving influence, the chastising context, of a Christian community. We cannot simply go out and do whatever we want to do; our acts must be judged and, if necessary, disciplined by the rest of the believing community. In political terms that means that we need an international order of checks and balances.

If only we could create a world order in which weak nations would not always suffer simply because they are weak—and stronger nations would not continue to live in the eternal illusion that their strength gives them the right to do whatever they want! Finally and ultimately, this is God's world. One cannot do with God's world and with his people whatever one wants without finally paying a price.

Hoekema: So we must build an international order, you are suggesting, that will demand an accounting from all the nations of the world not only for their behavior toward other nations but for their internal affairs as well.

Boesak: Is there really such a thing as merely internal affairs? The internal policies of the South African government have become a basic cause for the instability in South Africa, therefore the destabilization of southern Africa, therefore the turmoil on the continent—because South Africa is the superpower of the continent. The internal policies of the Salvadoran government have plunged the whole of Central America into an abyss of war, strife and conflict—with the active participation of the United States.

Eastern Europe probably remains socialist by choice. But does it remain totalitarian by choice? Undemocratic by choice? I don't believe that. I recently spent a week there, and even in circumstances where half a word has to count for ten, you can feel the people's dissatisfaction with the "internal affairs" of their socialist countries. I told the minister of church affairs in Czechoslovakia that I will never give up fighting for the freedom to be a human person and to make my own choices, following my conscience and what I believe are the demands of the gospel. I believe the people of the Eastern bloc countries want that freedom.

Hoekema: Yet surely one of the first requirements for an international order must be the preservation of diversity. Countries which are experimenting with democratic socialism must not be squeezed into a different pattern because of the economic or ideological interests of the superpowers, for example. We must not try to impose a homogeneous pattern on all other nations.

Boesak: I would not plead for that at all. But there is a difference between laying down certain conditions concerning democratic participation, which would be meaningful for the people of every country, and forcing them to follow economic patterns which would be uniform all across the world. Social democracy is what I would work for and vote for in my own country. I do not believe that capitalism responds to the gospel's demands for justice—nor do I believe that the totalitarianism that communism seems to bring with it is any kind of answer. But the people's right to participate in economic, political or social decisions must always be respected.

Hoekema: The increasing contact between Eastern and Western Europe—not on the diplomatic level, which is under severe strain, but on the level of ordinary citizens traveling back and forth and talking about their concerns—seems to me to have been important in the growth of the peace movement. Do you also see this as a sign of hope?

Boesak: Yes, indeed—the one thing that is doing more than anything else to bring Europe together is the peace movement. I think that the peace movement has begun to alter a situation of political paralysis.

Hoekema: Do you find this paralysis particularly in Eastern Europe or is it in other parts of the world as well?

Boesak: All over the world there is the same paralysis. From my South African perspective, there is not much difference between Mr. Reagan and Mr. Chernenko. I wouldn't like either of them to be my president. But there is at least this difference between Chernenko and Reagan: in November it may be possible to get rid of Reagan and thus to take a little step forward. But no one will be able to get rid of Chernenko. And I do not think that anyone in the world—including the pope—ought to have a position from which he cannot be kicked out. That is too much power.

Hoekema: It's a good thing you're Reformed and not Catholic.

Boesak: Yes, I'm afraid that I would be a bad priest in that regard. I think the pope ought to be re-elected every four or five years—if he does well—by the believers in the pew.

Hoekema: Democratic election of the pope would be quite a change in church polity! But the idea seems very much in keeping with the central concept of liberation theologies—that the ordinary believer in his or her concrete situation knows a great deal about the meaning of the gospel.

Boesak: Oh, yes. That is the life of the church. Today I travel all over the world and sit in conferences with people whom as a little boy I would never have dreamed of meeting—I look at myself and what I do now with a constant sense of amazement. And yet the most meaningful things happening to me happen when I am with ordinary people back home. In May I went up to a place about 600 miles from Cape Town, way out in the boondocks, a little place near where I was born. When it was announced that I would preach in the evening, all of the people in that rural city—more than 2,000, half of whom cannot read or write—flocked to the church on a Sunday night. And what a conversation we had with one another! They know so well what they want the church to be and what they expect of me.

I am not saying that dialogue with theologians or other people is worthless. But in terms of commitment, depth and wisdom,

I am more persuaded by those people who speak not out of book learning but out of their life experience, out of the commitment of their faith, than by almost anybody else. They have the right to participate much more fully in the life of the church.

LABORING UNDER APARTHEID[3]

It is nearly 7 a.m. in Johannesburg's main railroad station, and the weekday influx of tens of thousands of black workers from the townships to their city jobs is under way. Third-class cars crammed with workers, some of them singing, lurch by the whites-only platform to unload further down the track. A white railroad policeman standing on the platform flicks a short leather strap across the chest of a worker hanging out of a train door-way—apparently a transgression. Two white women waiting for a suburban train see the incident, but don't really notice it. There's no break in their conversation.

At 8:30 p.m., Lawrence Lindepasi takes his last look of the night at the starry sky of the western Transvaal. Steel doors shut and a huge elevator drops the 33-year-old Xhosa and 90 other men at about 10 yards per second into the depths of the Margaret shaft of the Stilfontein gold mine.

Although Lindepasi is a native of South Africa, he is officially listed as one of the country's 1.5 million migrant workers. When he was 24 years old, the Transkei where he lived was declared an independent country by South Africa and thus became the first of the bantustans, the so-called tribal homelands.

Lindepasi receives free food and lodging at one of the mine's hostels. He sees his family once a year. For every 52 weeks of work, he gets 56 days of vacation, half of them paid. As a team leader, he has done as well as a black can do underground. All better positions are reserved for whites. He earns relatively good wages—about $12 a day—most of which he puts into his tiny farm at Willowvaal in the Transkei where his wife and three children live, and where he hopes to retire as soon as possible.

[3]Article by Timothy Belknap, an editor for the Detroit Free Press. *Africa Report.* 30:57+. My.–Jn. '85. Copyright 1985 by The African-American Institute. Reprinted by permission.

He hopes his children will become sufficiently educated so they will never have to work in the mines. Last year, 19 of Stilfontein's 10,100 mineworkers died underground. The men in Margaret shaft go down as far as 5,400 feet, surrounded by rock that is under tremendous pressure to obliterate their working vacuum, which, to the visitor, seems equal part heat, humidity, and noise.

These glimpses at facets of the South African workday will probably not jar most people's perceptions of an economy fueled by cheap labor and shored up by decades of apartheid. But the economy of South Africa is evolving and the doctrine of apartheid, already somewhat adjusted, faces a severe test not only in the light of international and internal political pressure, but also in terms of a long-term shortage of skilled manpower.

Every Sunday, the Johannesburg newspapers carry a dozen or more pages of personnel ads. Along with good salaries and medical and pension benefits, eye-catching perks are offered: "A 30 percent tax-free gratuity at the end of each two-year renewable contract" . . . "new housing" . . . "subsidized mortgage" . . . "100 percent house purchase loan" . . . "financial assistance for parents who prefer their children to attend boarding school" . . . "generous leave" . . . and "annual bonus and a company car." The latter, for managers, is often a BMW or Mercedes. Even for the young foreigners down a notch or two—"contract workers" from Scotland, Italy, Israel, from wherever the ads reached them—life is comfortable and there is plenty of spending money.

Underlying this boomtown ambiance is a manpower shortage with significance beyond the economic realm, as South Africa begins to tap into its largest potential skilled labor pool: its black workforce.

Only in recent times, between 1979 and 1983, have laws reserving skilled jobs for whites been abolished everywhere except the mines. There the white unions used their political muscle to preserve the 1911 law, section 12 of the Mines and Works Act, that guarantees their jobs.

Black trainees are just starting to filter into the new job market. With their ascent has come a groundswell of criticism from the corporate community in South Africa against one of the cornerstones of apartheid, separate economic development for each race.

In the past few months, business leaders of such prominence as Michael Rosholt, chairman of Barlow Rand, South Africa's second largest company, have urged repeal of the government's urban decentralization policies, particularly the "influx control" system that, in a variety of ways, impedes blacks from living permanently in the urban industrial centers. Firms are insisting that they must have stabilized labor forces, that their black trainees and employees be able to live and work where they want without being subject to arbitrary arrest and relocation.

By 1987, South Africa will need more than 1 million semi-skilled workers and nearly 4 million skilled workers, according to projections by economists. Even in the current recession, practically the entire white workforce of about 2 million is engaged in skilled work, and there has been no significant unemployment among whites since World War II.

"After water, the most scarce thing here is labor—semi-skilled, skilled, and middle-management," says Robert Connan, commercial officer at the U.S. consulate in Johannesburg. "You can see it's a sophisticated country, but part of it remains in the Third World because of the lack of technicians and managers."

Spearheaded by mining, the industrialization of South Africa has been evolving from a farming economy for more than a century. In 1980, the ratio of skilled to unskilled wages in South Africa was 1 to 3. It has now narrowed to 1 to 2.5, closing in on the 1 to 2 average in the industrialized West.

There is no shortage of unskilled labor. South Africa is estimated to have an "economically active" population of 5.7 million blacks and about 1 million other non-whites with respective unemployment rates running at 8.1 percent and 6.8 percent. Unofficial estimates, though, put the black unemployment rate as high as 25 percent, taking into account rural and bantustan residents who were not considered in government surveys.

The surplus of unskilled labor is providing the push to the same dynamics that are being pulled by the shortage of skilled labor. Last October, in a study for the University of the Western Cape, economist Brian Kantor reported that the ratio of blacks to whites has increased during the past two decades in all the main sectors of the South African economy.

"To an ever-increasing extent, white workers have left the factory floor and the mine pit for administrative work of one kind or another," Kantor reported.

The trend, which correlates with those in Western countries, is not surprising given the fact that five generations of white South Africans have been compelled to attend school.

Importing workers to fill the skilled blue-collar vacancies offers no long-term solution to an economy that, with a 1984 inflation rate of 13.25 percent and a severely weakened currency, nonetheless must offer competitive salaries to draw foreigners. Already some skilled fields such as spot welding in the auto industry and production jobs in the chemical and plastic industries are just about exclusively black.

"The migrant system is only suitable for manual labor," says Bobby Godsol, labor consultant for Anglo American Corp., Ltd., one of South Africa's six major mining companies.

"The moment a worker is imbued with a set of skills, which can take as little as three weeks' training, it becomes unproductive to lose him within a year."

The transient nature of the workforce, due in good part to government policy, is compounded by the skilled labor shortage.

"It's not that ships or buildings or bridges are not being built," Godsol says. "What we have is an inflated labor price with turnover rates ranging from 50 to 100 percent because of the short supply of artisans as opposed to a 5 to 10 percent [annual] rate, which is considered ideal."

South Africa has about 50,000 registered artisans, workers who have undergone three to five years of training. About 80 percent are white and the rest are mostly Indians.

"The artisans are constantly being offered a few cents more to work next door," Godsol said. "In the metal industry, the minimum wage is 4.60 rand [about $2.40] an hour. A lot of artisans are earning double that, and that's a measure of the shortage. Almost all operating managers would say they want more artisans, and better ones."

The three-year-old recession has blunted the demand for skilled personnel in some fields, but not in export industries such as mining, nor in the service industries. Electricians are in great demand.

"If you know what you're doing, you've got a job," said Geoffrey Fry, who runs his own suburban Johannesburg business selling and installing appliances.

"I've had several black helpers in the past," Fry said. "As soon as they thought they knew something, they buzzed off."

"My black guys were handicapped, first, because they had difficulty reading English," he said. "They could put a TV together, if it was the same job every day, it was fairly easy. But you couldn't ask them to look at new electrical circuits and do fault-finding." Obviously, effective training is needed, and American companies, which employ one out of every 100 South African workers, pride themselves on being at the forefront of that effort. The American Chamber of Commerce in South Africa (AMCHAM) represents about 300 of the 350 U.S. firms there. Its senior vice president, Don Devine, is chairman of the Norton Co., which sells abrasives, tools, and other industrial materials.

"We, like many other firms, felt an acute shortage of skilled labor in 1980 and 1981," Devine said. Since then, he said, the company, without resorting to contract workers, has stocked up manpower in the most critical areas—sales persons, accountants, computer technicians—with in-house and external training programs. It operates two training centers where a three-year apprentice artisan program involves 33 trainees, 22 of whom are black. The firm gets tax incentives, but not funding, from the South African government for the training.

Right now the program more than meets the needs of the company, Devine says, "But we know full well if the economy picks up in '86 or '87, we could face a shortage."

Meanwhile, government-sponsored training programs for blacks are being expanded. The decades-old standard of 10,000 apprentices training in any given year to qualify as artisans was swollen in 1984 by the addition of 1,000 blacks who for the first time could legally hold many of the artisan positions.

Another 33,000 blacks are enrolled in non-apprentice technical classes. Further down the educational pipeline, about 370,000 blacks are enrolled in schools offering "practical" subjects such as woodworking and 138,900 in schools offering "commercial" courses such as accounting, economics, and typing, according to government figures. (This schooling no doubt has been affected by rampant boycotts and violent disruptions that began last fall and continue.) Last year, the first correspondent college offering technical courses to all races opened.

Clearly there is progress. In 1970, 3,652 blacks attended technical and trade classes, according to government figures. That reflected political rather than economic reality. Twenty-two years earlier, the De Villiers Commission on Technical and Vocational

Education reported "a rapidly increasing demand for trained native labor in practically all categories and grades of work."

Indeed, by the 1960s, the South African economy was booming, with the annual growth rate at 7 percent between 1962 and 1966. But government policy was still based on the Bantu Education Act of 1953, which held that the black's place in society was as an unskilled worker. In 1959 came the formalization of apartheid economic theory holding that separate races must have separate economies, "a commonwealth of economies," as it was stated.

To say the least, that ideology proved to be very idealistic. It envisioned considerable sacrifice on the part of the private sector to shift industries from the white urban centers to the bantustans where blacks were to resettle.

Outspoken critics at the time predicted that "the mountain would not move to Mohammed." Twenty years ago, Helen Suzman, then the only liberal member of Parliament, asked, "Do you want to be rich and mixed or poor and separate?"

There were heavy penalties for urban commercial expansion as well as the incentive of subsidized low-interest loans to decentralize. But, by and large, industry stayed where it was; the mines, for one, obviously having no choice in the matter.

Black workers needed in the urban areas found temporary housing in the African townships, the official bedroom communities that surround all the cities; in bachelor hostels; in unauthorized, but largely tolerated, shanty towns; and in several contrived bantustans that served as second-tier labor dormitories to the industrial areas.

"Reality has a way of overtaking politicians and social engineers," says Godsol of Anglo American. "Wherever black-designated land is near a white city or industrial area, influx control doesn't work at all. You have people farming shacks instead of vegetables. The sooner influx control goes, the better. In a three-year time frame, I predict it will be out."

"The central conundrum is that if blacks are going to be permanently here, they must have permanent political rights. What the government is looking for is a formula where power can be shared without losing control. If you'll look at the modernization of European countries, there is a precedent for expanding the electorate gradually.

"Even this government understands that it cannot have a stable society unless all can influence decisions. There is already a hopeful model with black unions having a say in how factories are run. This is access to power."

Rarely is power eagerly relinquished. In response to a massive strike by black workers last fall, the government, citing chargeless security legislation, detained 13 labor leaders, including those heading the Council of Unions of South Africa (CUSA) and the rival Federation of South African Trade Unions (FOSATU), each of which claims to represent about 150,000 workers. Altogether, black union membership stands at nearly 700,000, three times what it was in 1980.

Suzman, still in Parliament after 32 years, said the government panicked in its response to the strike. And, in her opinion, a timid business community cleared the way for such a reaction. "I was always disgusted how influential business leaders sat back and said nothing," she said. "No one wanted to get in the government's bad books. Now all sorts of people are opening their mouths. There was this sudden awakening to forced removals [of blacks from urban fringes to bantustans] about two years ago and just this past year they opened up on influx control."

Suzman, whose Progressive Federal Party holds enough seats in Parliament—27 of 178—to be the official opposition voice, said that while world opinion has prompted businessmen to openly criticize government policy, there is a local, practical factor, too.

"Their black employees have to go through this tedious performance of getting official approval and then only to be allowed to come into the mines and cities as a migrant worker. Firms like to stabilize labor because they can train it better.

"Then you get the situation like we had with Ford [Ford Motor Co., which has since merged its South African operations with Anglo American] establishing a good negotiating relationship with the workers and then suddenly finding out the head of the negotiating team had been detained."

According to Devine of AMCHAM, businessmen "for a good many years" lobbied with government leaders behind the scenes before their comments surfaced in public. Last winter, 126 AMCHAM members were, in effect, forced to directly lobby. These were firms that earlier had volunteered to sign the Sullivan Principles—specific steps proposed in 1977 by the Rev. Leon Sullivan, a member of the General Motors board of directors, to improve wages and conditions for black employees of U.S. firms in

South Africa. On December 12, the principles were modified so that the signatories are now required to "support the ending of all apartheid laws."

Will Pretoria heed? "That's the $64,000 question," as one of Connan's colleagues at the U.S. consulate put it.

Devine said, "I think the government in my tenure here has been receptive to listening to businessmen. Only in more recent times has it seemed willing to take direct action."

Such recent steps have included Pretoria wavering on decentralization by allowing long-term leases, and even some home purchases, in the townships; by legalizing resident workforces in some industries; and by giving some urban blacks the right of permanent residence.

When he opened Parliament in January, President Pieter W. Botha promised to completely review influx control, declared a moratorium on forced removals, and said freehold rights for blacks would be extended.

But the country's administrators themselves are an obstacle to further reform. A huge bureaucracy has been created to enforce apartheid—actually four huge bureaucracies to deal with each official race category of white, Asian, black, and Coloured (mixed race). Bureaucracies being bureaucracies, there is an instinct for self-perpetuation, and election analyses have indicated that the most conservative bloc of the electorate is the 155,000 white civil servants of the central government. Like the other big conservative bloc, the rural whites, they are mostly Afrikaners.

The incumbent National Party is also under pressure to placate voices even further to the right of its mainstream constituency not only to stay in office, but to avoid an internal "dirty war." Targeting opposition figures, some hardliners are already involved in a low-level campaign of terrorism—thuggery would be a more precise term except that large arms caches have been uncovered.

Also weighing heavily on Pretoria are overseas proposals to initiate or broaden disinvestment laws and other sanctions unless reforms are forthcoming. Already in the U.S., five states, 14 cities, and about 40 colleges and universities have divested securities held in companies doing business in or with South Africa, and 22 states are considering following suit.

Such action is by no means uniformly embraced by black leaders and white liberals in South Africa. Many of them agree with the business community's assertion that to retard the country's economic growth is to retard the economic advance of its blacks.

With prospects of sanctions from the U.S. and the United Kingdom intensifying, the South African press in recent weeks has been citing a 1976 study by the University of Witwatersrand that estimated that a hypothetical 50 percent cut in all foreign investments would cost 52,000 blacks their jobs. A 50 percent trade boycott against South African exports would cost 1.08 million jobs, most of them held by blacks, the study projected. The hypothetical impact a decade later is hard to gauge because there has since been a net outflow of direct foreign investment, and foreign capital has a proportionally smaller role in the South African economy.

Domestic and exile dissidents counter that the anti-sanctions proponents "don't know their own best medicine," that long-term gains come from short-term sacrifices.

If the pro-sanctions argument prevails on Capitol Hill and in Westminster, South Africa will have to take further reform measures to pacify its trading partners or re-chart its current course, which is directed toward free trade and an open economy.

If it chooses to do the latter, it won't be the first time South Africa has adjusted its century-old relationship with the capital markets of the West. The arms embargo imposed on South Africa by the UN Security Council in 1977 gave birth to the success of ARMSCOR, the nationally-owned company that exports its weaponry throughout Africa and to many overseas customers. Although South Africans pay increasingly steep fuel prices, a 15-year-old oil embargo resulted in the country establishing huge coal-to-oil conversion facilities and has recently led to successful explorations.

While South Africa needs foreign capital to dig its mines, it escapes the double bind of most Third World countries that also need outside financing for technology before they can exploit export markets. Mining technology is a homegrown industry in South Africa because the country has geological conditions that exist nowhere else.

As for capital, it is not particularly hard to reroute investments through third countries. "If someone has the capital and sees a good return, he'll find a way," says Robert Craig, who researches mining prospects for investors scouting the Johannesburg stock exchange. (Under last year's version of the proposed

U.S. Export Administration Act, individuals violating an outright ban on new U.S. investments in South Africa would face a $50,000 fine and five years' imprisonment and companies would be fined $1 million. Similar penalties are included in current versions yet to be legislated.) American direct investments in South Africa total $2.3 billion, with another $13 billion in indirect investments such as portfolios and bank loans.

South Africa's biggest trading partners—the United Kingdom, then the U.S. and West Germany—are well aware that sanctions-busting reached a state-of-the-art level in southern Africa during the Rhodesia era. Countries that in other regards have taken a wide range of actions to show their opposition to apartheid have shied away from sanctions, saying they won't work.

The Canadian government, for example, states as part of its policy on South Africa that "comprehensive economic sanctions would not be effective without the commitment and cooperation of South Africa's major trading partners. Even then the size and strength of South Africa's economy and the resources available to it would enable it to withstand economic measures of this kind."

Selective disinvestment by U.S. firms that supply South Africa with such crucial goods as high technology equipment has been suggested by CUSA as well as several American anti-apartheid figures. CUSA's general secretary, Phiroshaw Camay, said, "We would consider calling for total disinvestment but we don't think this would work." His counterpart in FOSATU, Joe Foster, said any call for disinvestment on his part would antagonize FOSATU auto workers: "Our members at Leyland would kill me."

Actually, the issue is so sensitive to the South African government that any public call for disinvestment or other sanctions is illegal, an act of treason. The law has proven to be more of a cobweb than a trip wire. Attribution is often indirect, but all sides of the sanctions debate are presented to South African newspaper readers every time there is a noteworthy development.

Nor does the law seem to have any bearing on the fact that sanctions simply are not a political issue within the white electorate. Even Helen Suzman thinks they are a bad idea.

Furthermore, there is widespread feeling throughout South Africa that the recent escalation of lethal confrontations between police and protesters in the townships will certainly lead to stern overseas reaction, and there is little at this stage Pretoria can do to appease.

Whatever happens on the sanctions issue in the next year or so, South Africa still faces the fact that if it is to tend to its own consumers, let alone export markets, it has no more than a decade to solve its massive manpower shortage. The latest warning came in April from the country's Manpower and Management Foundation: "Unless the skilled labor force increases 3.2 percent each year for the next 15 years, there will be severe unemployment." The Foundation reported that at most, only 25 percent of the needed jobs could be expected to come from the white workforce.

In the words of Anglo American executive Godsol, "There is no doubt this country is going to have to modernize its human capital."

IV. SOUTH AFRICA AND THE UNITED STATES

EDITOR'S INTRODUCTION

South Africa presents a knotty and potentially dangerous foreign relations problem for the United States. In this country, apartheid is the subject of an emotional debate on the national, state, and local levels. Nearly all Americans agree that apartheid should end; the question is what, if anything, the U.S. should do to bring that about.

The Reagan Administration has pursued a policy of "constructive engagement" with the South African government, applying diplomatic pressure for change but avoiding direct confrontation or heavy criticism whenever possible. The philosophy behind constructive engagement is articulated by the president himself in the first selection. Critics of the policy believe that constructive engagement is both ineffective and out of step with the current sentiments of the American people. They call for economic sanctions on South Africa as a way to register American displeasure and force change. Supporters of sanctions seem to be gaining the upper hand. In fact, it was over this issue that President Reagan suffered his worst defeat by Congress, which overturned his veto of a bill to increase sanctions in 1986. U.S. Representative William H. Gray III, writing in *Africa Report*, presents the case for sanctions in the second selection. Sanford J. Ungar, an American political historian, and Peter Vale, a professor at South Africa's Rhodes University, provide a more detailed analysis of just why constructive engagement has not accomplished its basic aim—to encourage the end of apartheid—and offer an alternative policy framework. Their article is reprinted from *Foreign Affairs*.

Still, the United States is unlikely to sever its ties with South Africa. In the fourth selection, from *Current History*, Rhoda Plotkin points out that South Africa is currently the only source for certain strategic materials necessary to U.S. defense, such as the chromium used in jet fighter engines. Plotkin notes that the United States must decrease its strategic dependence on South Africa before any effective challenge to South Africa's policies can be made.

In 1986 several major American corporations, including IBM and General Motors, terminated or sold their operations in South Africa, citing falling earnings and political uncertainty as the main reasons for leaving. Goodyear is one company that does not plan to leave—at least not yet—as the fifth article, from *Fortune,* shows. Another kind of withdrawal is disinvestment, the removal of foreign investment from South Africa or from companies that do business there. In the final selection, from *Foreign Policy,* Gavin Relly, chairman of South Africa's largest corporation, discusses the heavy costs—to whites and blacks alike—of disinvestment, and argues that whites and blacks will be more likely to solve their differences if not abandoned by the rest of the world.

U.S. ECONOMIC RELATIONS WITH SOUTH AFRICA: APARTHEID, SOME SOLUTIONS[1]

For more than a year now, the world's attention has been focused upon South Africa, the deepening political crisis there, the widening cycle of violence. And today I'd like to outline American policy toward that troubled republic and toward the region of which it is a part, a region of vital importance to the West.

The root cause of South Africa's disorder is apartheid, that rigid system of racial segregation wherein black people have been treated as third-class citizens in a nation they helped to build. America's view of apartheid has been, and remains, clear: apartheid is morally wrong and politically unacceptable. The United States cannot maintain cordial relations with a government whose power rests upon the denial of rights to a majority of its people, based on race.

If South Africa wishes to belong to the family of Western nations, an end to apartheid is a precondition. Americans, I believe, are united in this conviction. Second, apartheid must be dismantled. Time is running out for the moderates of all races in South Africa.

[1]Speech by President Reagan delivered on July 22, 1986 from Washington, D.C. Reprinted from *Vital Speeches of the Day,* 52:1+, Ag. 15, '86.

But if we Americans are agreed upon the goal of a free and multiracial South Africa associated with free nations in the West, there is deep disagreement about how to reach it. First a little history. For a quarter-century now, the American Government has been separating itself from the South African Government. In 1962, President Kennedy imposed an embargo on military sales. Last September, I issued an Executive Order further restricting U.S. dealings with the Pretoria government.

For the past 18 months, the marketplace has been sending unmistakable signals of its own. U.S. bank lending to South Africa has been virtually halted. No significant new investment has come in. Some Western businessmen have packed up and gone home. And now we've reached a critical juncture. Many in Congress, and some in Europe, are clamoring for sweeping sanctions against South Africa. The Prime Minister of Great Britain has denounced punitive sanctions as immoral and utterly repugnant. Well, let me tell you why we believe Mrs. Thatcher is right.

The primary victims of an economic boycott of South Africa would be the very people we seek to help. Most of the workers who would lose jobs because of sanctions would be black workers. We do not believe the way to help the people of South Africa is to cripple the economy upon which they and their families depend for survival.

Alan Paton, South Africa's great writer, for years the conscience of his country, has declared himself emphatically: "I am totally opposed to disinvestment," he says. "It is primarily for a moral reason. Those who will pay most grievously for disinvestment will be the black workers of South Africa. I take very seriously the teachings of the Gospels, in particular the parables about giving drink to the thirsty and the food to the hungry. I will not help to cause any such suffering to any black person." Nor will we.

Looking at a map, southern Africa is a single economic unit tied together by rails and roads. Zaire and its southern mining region depends upon South Africa for three-fourths of her food and petroleum. More than half the electric power that drives the capital of Mozambique comes from South Africa. Over one-third of the exports from Zambia and 65 percent of the exports of Zimbabwe leave the continent through South African ports. The mines of South Africa employ 13,000 workers from Swaziland, 19,000 from Botswana, 50,000 from Mozambique and 110,000 from the tiny landlocked country of Lesotho. Shut down these productive mines with sanctions and you have forced black mine workers out of their jobs and forced their families back in their home countries into destitution.

I don't believe the American people want to do something like that. As one African leader remarked recently, southern Africa is like a zebra: if the white parts are injured, the black parts will die, too. Western nations have poured billions in foreign aid and investment loans into southern Africa. Does it make sense to aid these countries with one hand and with the other to smash the industrial engine upon which their future depends?

Wherever blacks seek equal opportunity, higher wages, better working conditions, their strongest allies are the Americans, British, French, German and Dutch businessmen who bring to South Africa ideas of social justice formed in their own countries. If disinvestment is mandated, these progressive Western forces will depart and South African proprietors will inherit at fire-sale prices their farms and factories and plants and mines. And how would this end apartheid?

Our own experience teaches us that racial progress comes swiftest and easiest not during economic depression but in times of prosperity and growth. Our own history teaches us that capitalism is the natural enemy of such feudal institutions as apartheid.

Nevertheless, we share the outrage Americans have come to feel. Night after night, week after week, television has brought us reports of violence by South African Security Forces, bringing injury and death to peaceful demonstrators and innocent bystanders. More recently, we read of violent attacks by blacks against blacks. Then there is the calculated terror by elements of the African National Congress—the mining of roads, the bombings of public places, designed to bring about further repression, the imposition of martial law, and eventually creating the conditions for racial war.

The most common method of terror is the so-called necklace. In this barbaric way of reprisal, a tire is filled with kerosene and gasoline, placed around the neck of an alleged collaborator and ignited. The victim may be a black policeman, a teacher, a soldier, a civil servant—it makes no difference, the atrocity is designed to terrorize blacks into ending all racial cooperation and to polarize South Africa as a prelude to a final climactic struggle for power.

In defending their society and people, the South African Government has a right and responsibility to maintain order in the face of terrorists but by its tactics the Government is only accelerating the descent into bloodletting. Moderates are being trapped between the intimidations of radical youths and counter gangs of vigilantes. And the Government's state of emergency next went beyond the law of necessity. It too went outside the law by sweeping up thousands of students, civic leaders, church leaders and labor leaders, thereby contributing to further radicalization.

Such repressive measures will bring South Africa neither peace nor security.

It's a tragedy that most Americans only see or read about the dead and injured in South Africa, from terrorism, violence and repression, but behind the terrible television pictures lies another truth. South Africa is a complex and diverse society in a state of transition. More and more South Africans have come to recognize that change is essential for survival. The realization has come hard and late but the realization has finally come to Pretoria that apartheid belongs to the past.

In recent years there's been a dramatic change. Black workers have been permitted to unionize, to bargain collectively and build the strongest free trade union movement in all of Africa. The infamous pass laws have been ended, as have many of the laws denying blacks the right to live, work and own property in South Africa's cities. Citizenship wrongly stripped away has been restored to nearly 6 million blacks. Segregation in universities and public facilities is being set aside. Social apartheid laws prohibiting interracial sex and marriage have been struck down.

It is because state President Botha has presided over these reforms that extremists have denounced him as a traitor. We must remember, as the British historian Paul Johnson reminds us, that South Africa is an African country as well as a Western country. And reviewing the history of that continent in the quarter-century since independence, historian Johnson does not see South Africa as a failure. "Only in South Africa," he writes, "have the real incomes of blacks risen very substantially. In mining, black wages have tripled in real terms in the last decade. South Africa is the only African country to produce a large black middle class. Almost certainly," he adds, "there are now more black women professionals in South Africa than in the whole of the rest of Africa put together."

Despite apartheid, tens of thousands of black Africans migrate into South Africa from neighboring countries to escape poverty and take advantage of the opportunities in an economy that produces nearly a third of the income in all of sub-Saharan Africa.

It's tragic and in the current crisis social and economic progress has been arrested. And yet, in contemporary South Africa, before the state of emergency, there was a broad measure of freedom of speech, of the press and of religion there. Indeed, it's hard to think of a single country in the Soviet Bloc, or many in the United Nations, where political critics have the same freedom to be heard as did outspoken critics of the South African Government.

But by Western standards, South Africa still falls short— terribly short—on the scales of economic and social justice. South Africa's actions to dismantle apartheid must not end now. The state of emergency must be lifted. There must be an opening of the political process. That the black people of South Africa should have a voice in their own governance is an idea whose time has come. There can be no turning back.

In the multiracial society that is South Africa, no single race can monopolize the reins of political power. Black churches, black unions and indeed genuine black nationalists have a legitimate role to play in the future of their country. But the South African Government is under no obligation to negotiate the future of the country with any organization that proclaims a goal of creating a Communist state, and uses terrorist tactics and violence to achieve it.

Many Americans understandably ask, given the racial violence, the hatred, why not wash our hands and walk away from that tragic continent and bleeding country. Well, the answer is, we cannot. In southern Africa, our national ideals and strategic interests come together. South Africa matters because we believe that all men are created equal and are endowed by their Creator with unalienable rights. South Africa matters because of who we are. One of eight Americans can trace his ancestry to Africa.

Strategically, this is one of the most vital regions of the world. Around the Cape of Good Hope passes the oil of the Persian Gulf, which is indispensable to the industrial economies of Western Europe. Southern Africa and South Africa are repository of many of the vital minerals—vanadium, manganese, chromium, platinum—for which the West has no other secure source of supply.

The Soviet Union is not unaware of the stakes. A decade ago, using an army of Cuban mercenaries provided by Fidel Castro, Moscow installed a client regime in Angola. Today the Soviet Union is providing the regime with the weapons to attack Unita, a black liberation movement, which seeks for Angolans the same right to be represented in their government that black South Africans seek for themselves.

Apartheid threatens our vital interests in southern Africa because it's drawing neighboring states into the vortex of violence. Repeatedly within the last 18 months South African forces have struck into neighboring states. I repeat our condemnation of such behavior.

Also, the Soviet armed guerrillas of the African National Congress, operating both within South Africa and from some neighboring countries, have embarked upon new acts of terrorism inside South Africa. I also condemn that behavior.

But South Africa cannot shift the blame for these problems onto neighboring states—especially when those neighbors take steps to stop guerrilla actions from being mounted from their own territory. If this rising hostility in southern Africa between Pretoria and the front-line states explodes, the Soviet Union will be the main beneficiary and the critical ocean corridor of South Africa and the strategic minerals of the region would be at risk.

Thus it would be a historic act of folly for the United States and the West, out of anguish and frustration and anger, to write off South Africa. Ultimately, however, the fate of South Africa will be decided there, not here. We Americans stand ready to help, but whether South Africa emerges democratic and free or takes a course leading to a downward spiral of poverty and repression will finally be their choice, not ours.

The key to the future lies with the South African Government. As I urge Western nations to maintain communication and involvement in South Africa, I urge Mr. Botha not to retreat into the locker, not to cut off contact with the West. Americans and South Africans have never been enemies, and we understand the apprehension and fear and concern of all of your people. But an end to apartheid does not necessarily mean an end to the social, economic and physical security of the white people in this country they love and have sacrificed so much to build.

To the black, colored and Asian peoples of South Africa, too long treated as second- and third-class subjects, I can only say: In your hopes for freedom, social justice and self-determination you have a friend and ally in the United States. Maintain your hopes for peace and reconciliation and we will do our part to keep that road open. We understand that behind the rage and resentment in the townships is the memory of real injustices inflicted upon generations of South Africans. Those to whom evil is done, the poet wrote, often do evil in return.

But if the people of South Africa are to have a future in a free country, where the rights of all are respected, the desire for retribution will have to be set aside. Otherwise, the future will be lost in a bloody quarrel over the past. It would be an act of arrogance to insist that uniquely American ideas and institutions, rooted in our own history and traditions, be transplanted to South African soil. Solutions to South Africa's political crisis must come from South Africans themselves. Black and white, colored and Asians, they have their own traditions.

But let me outline what we believe are necessary components of progress toward political peace.

First, a timetable for elimination of apartheid laws should be set.

Second, all political prisoners should be released.

Third, Nelson Mandela should be released to participate in the country's political process.

Fourth, black political movements should be unbanned.

Fifth, both the Government and its opponents should begin a dialogue about constructing a political system that rests on the consent of the governed, where the rights of majorities and minorities and individuals are protected by law. And the dialogue should be initiated by those with power and authority, the South African Government itself.

Sixth, if post-apartheid South Africa is to remain the economic locomotive of southern Africa, its strong and developed economy must not be crippled. And therefore, I urge the Congress and the countries of Western Europe to resist this emotional clamor for punitive sanctions. If Congress imposes sanctions it would destroy America's flexibility, discard our diplomatic leverage and deepen the crisis. To make a difference, Americans who are a force for decency and progress in the world must remain involved.

We must stay and work, not cut and run. It should be our policy to build in South Africa, not to bring down. Too often in the past we Americans, acting out of anger and frustration and impatience, have turned our backs on flawed regimes only to see disaster follow. Those who tell us the moral thing to do is to embargo the South African economy and write off South Africa should tell us exactly what they believe will rise in its place. What foreign power would fill the vacuum if its ties with the West are broken?

To be effective, however, our policy must be coordinated with our key Western allies and with the front-line states in southern Africa. These countries have the greatest concern and potential leverage on the situation in South Africa. I intend to pursue the following steps:

Secretary Shultz has already begun intensive consultations with our Western allies, whose roots and presence in South Africa are greater than our own, on ways to encourage internal negotiations. We want the progress process to begin now, and we want open channels to all the principal parties. The key nations of the West must act in concert, and together we can make the difference.

We fully support the current efforts of the British Government to revive hopes for negotiations. Foreign Secretary Howe's visits with South Africa's leaders this week will be of particular significance.

And second, I urge the leaders of the region to join us in seeking a future South Africa where countries live in peace and cooperation. South Africa is the nation where the Industrial Revolution first came to Africa. Its economy is a mighty engine that could pull southern Africa into a prosperous future. The other nations of southern Africa, from Kinshasa to the Cape, are rich in natural resources and human resources.

Third, I have directed Secretary Shultz and A.I.D. Administration representative McPherson to undertake a study of America's assistance role in southern Africa, to determine what needs to be done and what can be done to expand the trade, private investment and transport prospects of southern Africa's landlocked nations. In the past five years, we have provided almost a billion in assistance to South Africa's neighbors, and this year we hope to provide an additional $45 million to black South Africans. We're determined to remain involved diplomatically and economically with all the states of southern Africa that wish constructive relations with the United States.

This Administration is not only against broad economic sanctions and against apartheid, we are for a new South Africa, a new nation where all that has been built up over generations is not destroyed; a new society where participation in the social, cultural and political life is open to all peoples; a new South Africa that comes home to the family of free nations where she belongs.

To achieve that we need not a Western withdrawal, but deeper involvement by the Western business community as agents of change and progress and growth. The international business community needs not only to be supported in South Africa, but energized. We'll be at work on that task.

If we wish to foster the process of transformation, one of the best vehicles for change is through the involvement of black South Africans in business, job-related activities and labor unions. But the vision of a better life cannot be realized so long as apartheid endures and instability reigns in South Africa. If the peoples of southern Africa are to prosper, leaders and peoples of the region of all races will have to elevate their common interests above their ethnic divisions.

We and our allies cannot dictate to the government of a sovereign nation—nor should we try. But we can offer to help find a solution that is fair to all the people of South Africa. We can volunteer to stand by and help bring about dialogue between leaders of the various factions and groups that make up the population of South Africa. We can counsel and advise, and make it plain to all that we are there as friends of all the people of South Africa.

In that tormented land, a window remains open for peaceful change. For how long, we know not. But we in the West, privileged and prosperous and free, must not be the ones to slam it shut. Now is the time for healing. The people of South Africa of all races deserve a chance to build a better future. And we must not deny or destroy that chance.

STANDING FOR SANCTIONS[2]

Ethnic division is not the only goal of apartheid, South Africa's peculiar institution of neo-slavery built on severe racial segregation. The ultimate motivation for apartheid, like most forms of oppression, is greed.

Consequently, it is a mistake for newly-sensitized Americans to view the struggle of the 27 million–strong black majority in South Africa to overthrow their brutal subjugation at the hands of 4.5 million whites only in moral terms.

Apartheid may have been nurtured by a degenerate theocracy born in the 17th century, but profits sustain it in the 20th century. If racism is not the most profitable industry in South Africa, no doubt it is one of the biggest. More than 40 percent of the white population is employed by the bureaucracy which maintains the complex legal and social infrastructure of apartheid.

It is upon this conceptual basis that I first made my decision to introduce sanctions in the U.S. House of Representatives against South Africa's white minority regime in 1982. As an opponent of apartheid, I decided that America cannot be loyal to its own democratic creed and at the same time provide the economic fuel for apartheid.

Moreover, during our congressional visit to South Africa in January, the majority of that country's anti-apartheid forces pleaded with our delegation not only to strengthen America's economic sanctions but, at the same time, to aim new sanctions more accurately at the pressure points of South Africa's economy.

Those who would argue that sanctions won't bring down apartheid are right; they were never intended to do so. Effective sanctions, like those in my bill, as compared to the mild restrictions President Reagan invoked last year, would simply end American economic support for apartheid. The political issues will be decided by South Africans—either at the negotiating table or through violent upheaval—the choice is theirs.

[2]Article by U.S. Congressman William H. Gray III. *Africa Report.* 31:27+. Mr.–Ap. '86. Copyright 1986 by The African-American Institute. Reprinted by permission.

Several American companies doing business in South Africa recently have begun discussing the possibility of selling a small number of shares to select Africans. They hope to invest in a small black middle class that will be able to negotiate with the angry black masses.

Regrettably, these American industrialists believe they can slow down the growing divestment fever by such sleight-of-hand. It is regrettable because, as one non-violent black activist whom we met so poignantly summarized the issue of sanctions, "How are my people to believe that America wants peaceful change in South Africa, when your government and your capitalist businessmen keep undermining the last means of peaceful change—sanctions?"

Cursed by nearly all humanity and unnerved by the mounting restiveness of the non-white majority that they oppress, white South Africans today are struggling to find a way to give up *most* of apartheid without relinquishing any of their power.

Power-sharing, the idea of whites allowing the majority to have a limited voice in the regulation of local institutions that directly affect their schools, city services, or transportation, is now the Afrikaner's favored defense against international condemnation.

"Now we have a message to sell," intoned the urbane, confident foreign minister, Roelof "Pik" Botha, during our three-hour meeting at government headquarters in Pretoria. "Our big dilemma now is how to implement the principle of power-sharing."

Translated into plain language, today's Afrikaner has reluctantly accepted the idea that original "grand apartheid" is no longer feasible because the minority cannot dominate the non-white majority without the assistance of a selected elite chosen from among compliant blacks. However, while the Afrikaner has accepted the idea of no longer singularly ruling blacks, he has not accepted the notion of blacks ruling Afrikaners.

The dominant constant which emerged from my recent trip to South Africa is that every faction agrees change is coming.

• Militant leaders of the newly formed black trade unions, potentially the most powerful anti-apartheid force in South Africa, emphatically lectured our delegation that they want a commitment to full economic sanctions against the apartheid regime and a deadline for total American disinvestment.

• According to a moderate black leader, black anger can no longer be defused or checked. "We've got to get rid of this [Botha] government, put an interim government in office while all parties sit down to reach a negotiated settlement."

• The "comrades," or young street activists in the black townships who have spearheaded much of the spontaneous rioting and rock-throwing incidents, have vowed to make 1986 a "no-go" year for township schools in honor of the 10th anniversary of the Soweto riots.

• President Botha told us there would only be concrete legislative proposals in the 1986 session of Parliament to implement his promised reforms of the pass laws and property rights.

These markedly conflicting opinions about the who, what, when, and how change will come to South Africa are at the core of the unrest threatening to unleash a holocaust of rage across this land of majestic geographical splendor where human savagery has been licensed by the state for almost a century.

If the Afrikaner—who has ruled by strict racial subjugation and economic exploitation since coming to power in 1948—has his way, change will come painfully slow, eked out bit by bit, emphasizing cosmetic reforms, such as last year's repeal of the ban on mixed marriages.

During the 90-minute conference our congressional delegation held with President P. W. Botha, he repeatedly attempted to mitigate his party's apartheid policies, claiming his government was meeting with "responsible" black leaders that he declined to identify.

President Botha pointed to the three-tiered Parliament—one for whites, one for Coloureds, and one for Asians—set up in 1984 as proof of the Afrikaner's commitment to power-sharing. However, he failed to mention that the Asian and Coloured members of Parliament may not use the lavatory and dining facilities used by white lawmakers unless accompanied by a white MP.

But the absurdity of this notion of power-sharing under such an odious arrangement is most clearly demonstrated by the absence of Africans from all sectors of national government.

Clinging stubbornly to his view of separation of the races, President Botha categorically rejected the concept of a unitary state governed by representatives elected under a system of one-person, one-vote.

"One-man, one-vote is out," snapped Botha. "Blacks don't want it." With that repudiation of the key demand of black leaders, Botha revealed how out of touch he and most of his fellow South Africans are.

In all of our meetings with more than 200 persons, from moderate opposition leaders like Zulu Chief Gatsha Buthelezi to the more militant, all black, 230,000-strong workers of the Congress of South African Trade Unions, the refrain we heard is for government by one-person, one-vote, and the complete dismantling of race-biased institutions and privileges.

"I am committed to bringing about one country with one government and to eradicate ethnicity as a determinant of political structures," Buthelezi told our delegation during a breakfast session.

And only a few minutes later in a separate meeting with one of Buthelezi's harshest critics, the Reverend Allan Boesak, a key leader of the multi-racial anti-apartheid group, the United Democratic Front, told us, "A non-ethnic unitary state is what we are fighting for; we will accept nothing less."

It is this communication gulf that is most threatening to South Africa's immediate future. As long as the Afrikaners continue to delude themselves with the belief that all of the unrest and violence is provoked by outsiders and communist agitators, they will fail to appreciate the urgency of the rage burning within the non-white majority that surrounds them. Such self-delusion is actually a precursor to renewed violence, because notwithstanding the more than 1,000 deaths in 1985, in Pretoria today there is no understanding, no dialogue.

The longer Afrikaners resist meaningful change, the more difficult it becomes for moderate non-violent leaders like Nobel laureate Bishop Desmond Tutu and the Reverend Boesak to hold the attention and respect of the impatient "comrades."

It is this intransigence that mandates tough economic sanctions against South Africa. Like the ostriches indigenous to South Africa, the Afrikaners have their heads deeply imbedded in the sand. If white South Africans cannot accept change, the United States and other Western nations must *at least* stop providing the economic fuel for the political engine of apartheid.

The staggering international profits that apartheid fosters are all too apparent when it is understood that South Africa mines about half the world's gold and that gold sales account for about one-third of the country's export earnings.

More than 80 percent of the world's diamond trade is dominated by one South African firm, De Beers, which is part of the Anglo American Corp. group, the largest company in South Africa.

In platinum mining, South Africa exports nearly 90 percent of the 2.86 million ounces annually consumed worldwide. A key element in the automobile, petrochemical, and electronic industries, slightly more than 1 million ounces of platinum were used by the United States and Japan each in 1984, according to industry experts.

When apartheid's pivotal role in South Africa's economy is exposed, it also reveals the impotence of one of the far right's key arguments against tougher trade sanctions—namely, that a strong vibrant economy will enable South Africa to "grow out" of apartheid.

In the meeting our congressional delegation held with Zach de Beer, one of the officers of the mammoth Anglo American Corporation, he tried to persuade us that sanctions only slowed the economic growth needed to prod the ruling Afrikaners to loosen their grip.

"Stronger sanctions will only produce backlash from among those who are resisting reform," explained de Beer. "While I admit the government should be ready to take more risks to get negotiations started, I believe that sanctions will only stiffen their backs. Our best hope is a strong economy that can provide better opportunities for all ethnic groups."

Time has proven the fallacy of that argument. The South African economy grew by 6 percent annually through the 1960s, a high rate in comparison to other countries at similar levels of development. But apartheid only grew more intense. More recently, growth has continued: 8 percent in the 1980 boom, another 5 percent the next year. The fruits of that spurt, however, were not used to start reforming the migrant labor system, or to improve the appalling conditions in the bantustans, or even to upgrade the urban townships in any significant way.

Surely, the need for sanctions has not been obviated. In fact, recent hardline statements made by the apartheid regime demonstrate the urgency to better aim new sanctions at those industries which will have the most direct impact on the rand—mining and energy, for example.

In our meetings with government officials, we searched desperately for some sign that Botha's regime was contemplating fundamental change in apartheid, and specifically the elimination of the pass laws which require all non-whites to carry racial identification cards which must be presented on demand upon threat of arrest; repeal of the Group Areas Act which limits certain residential areas to specific races; repeal of the laws which permit the wholesale removal of non-white settlements; and permission for workers to reside near their place of employment with their families. We received Orwellian double-talk in response to our inquiries.

The human costs of such intransigence never left my mind as we talked, ate with, and walked among the many South Africans our delegation encountered.

Throughout my trip, I could not escape the fact that when the changes—demanded by so many and resisted by so few—finally come to South Africa, many of those we met will not be alive to share them.

SOUTH AFRICA:
WHY CONSTRUCTIVE ENGAGEMENT FAILED[3]

Ronald Reagan's imposition of limited economic sanctions against the South African regime in September was a tacit admission that his policy of "constructive engagement"—encouraging change in the apartheid system through a quiet dialogue with that country's white minority leaders—had failed. Having been offered many carrots by the United States over a period of four-and-a-half years as incentives to institute meaningful reforms, the South African authorities had simply made a carrot stew and eaten it. Under the combined pressures of the seemingly cataclysmic events in South Africa since September 1984 and the dramatic surge of anti-apartheid protest and political activism in the United States, the Reagan Administration was finally embarrassed into brandishing some small sticks as an element of American policy.

[3]Article by Sanford J. Ungar, former managing editor of *Foreign Policy*, and Peter Vale, a professor at Rhodes University, South Africa. *Foreign Affairs.* 64:234+. Winter 85/86. Copyright 1985 by Sanford J. Ungar and Peter Vale. Reprinted by permission.

The Reagan sanctions, however limited, are an important symbol: a demonstration to the ruling white South African nationalists that even an American president whom they had come to regard as their virtual savior could turn against them. Only a few weeks after inexplicably hailing South Africa for an American-style solution to racial segregation, Mr. Reagan, beating Congress to the punch, signed an executive order banning the export of computers to all official South African agencies that enforce apartheid; prohibiting most transfers of nuclear technology; preventing loans to the South African government unless they would improve social conditions for all races; ending the importation of South African Krugerrand gold coins into the United States; and limiting export assistance to American companies operating in South Africa that do not adhere to fair employment guidelines. By any measure, this was a significant development, and Pretoria's reaction of shock, anger and defiance underlined its impact.

But the sanctions, applied at once with fanfare and apologies, do not represent a fundamental change in American policy toward South Africa. Nor do they portend or promote a meaningful evolution in the South African political and social system. On the contrary, they continue the recent American practice of attempting to reform the South African system by working entirely within it and honoring its rules. "Active constructive engagement" (the new, impromptu name the President seems to have given his policy during a press conference) is still a policy that engages the attention and the interests of only a small, privileged stratum of South Africans. It relies almost entirely on white-led change, as designed and defined by a regime that is becoming more embattled by the day. And it ignores the needs, the politics and the passions of the black majority in South Africa.* The policy will continue to fail.

II

Constructive engagement has not merely caused the United States to lose five valuable years when it might have influenced South Africa to begin negotiating a settlement of its unique and extraordinary racial problems. Many would argue that constructive engagement was a necessary step in the evolution of Ameri-

_____
*The term "blacks" is used here in the South African sense, to include black Africans, so-called Coloureds of mixed race and Asians.

can attitudes toward South Africa, but the cost has been great. American policy has actually exacerbated the situation inside South Africa by encouraging and indulging the white regime's divide-and-rule tactics—leading that regime, its internal and external victims and much of the international community to believe that, whatever the rhetoric emanating from Washington, American prestige is on the side of the Pretoria government.

Indeed, from the time constructive engagement took effect, American trade with and investment in South Africa increased, and the Reagan Administration expanded the scope of U.S. cooperation with the South African government. It lifted previous restrictions on the export of military equipment and equipment with potential military uses; permitted (until President Reagan's recent change of heart) the sale of American computers to the police, military and other agencies of the South African government that administer apartheid; and approved the sale of shock batons to the police. The Administration also allowed the return of South African military attachés to the United States and otherwise expanded diplomatic, military and intelligence relationships between the two countries—including the establishment of several new South African honorary consulates around the United States, the provision of American training for the South African coast guard, and the resumption of official nuclear advisory contacts.

In addition, the Reagan Administration frequently stood alone on South Africa's side in the U.N. Security Council—vetoing resolutions critical of South Africa on occasions when Britain and France abstained, and, in some cases, registering the only abstention when Western allies voted to condemn South African actions.

No specific conditions were imposed on South Africa in exchange for these American favors. On the contrary, they were granted at a time when many of the restrictions on black South Africans were being tightened and tensions inside South Africa were growing. One important consequence was that, while America's official gaze was averted, a whole stratum of black South African leaders who had appeared willing to negotiate over the country's future seem to have been pushed aside by groups that advocate violent solutions. The arguments in favor of American-style, if not American-sponsored, conciliation and negotiation in South Africa may now have lost their force, as the South African drama has taken new and significant turns toward a tragic resolution.

Viewed in the context of the events of the past 15 months, South Africa's problem today is a manifestly new one. Unless steps are taken to prevent further deterioration, that country is liable to drift into uncontrollable violence fueled from the extreme right and extreme left. What is needed from the United States is not a withering debate over disinvestment or a domestic public relations campaign on behalf of constructive engagement, but an entirely new and more imaginative approach to South Africa. A policy must be crafted that not only recognizes and works with the current grim realities there, but also tries to ease the transition to an altogether different, albeit unknown, future in which blacks will take part in the government of their country. There is no longer any question that this change will occur in South Africa; the question is how, according to whose timetable and with what sort of outside involvement.

Only by establishing much more direct communication with the South African majority and by granting it far greater and more practical assistance can the United States hope to influence the course of events there. In effect, a new, parallel set of diplomatic relationships is necessary. And only by taking further steps that risk hurting the pride of South Africa's current rulers can American leaders hope to win enough credibility among South African blacks to be listened to in the debate over the country's future—a debate that will have profound consequences in all of Africa, the United States and much of the rest of the world.

III

From the start, constructive engagement meant quite different things to the four constituencies that would be most affected by it: the Reagan Administration itself, and by extension the American public; the South African government and the white population it represents; the South African black majority; and other countries in southern Africa.

The policy of constructive engagement was spelled out in 1980 by Chester A. Crocker, shortly before he became assistant secretary of state for African affairs. One of its first principles was that the previous U.S. policy of putting overt, public pressure for change on the South African regime had seemed to promise much more to black South Africans than it could deliver. "Americans need to do their homework," wrote Mr. Crocker in a landmark article:

A tone of empathy is required not only for the suffering and injustice caused to blacks in a racist system, but also for the awesome political dilemma in which Afrikaners and other whites find themselves. . . . American powder should be kept dry for genuine opportunities to exert influence. As in other foreign policy agendas for the 1980s, the motto should be: underpromise and overdeliver—for a change.

Ironically, the Crocker approach made its own very ambitious promises, this time to the American public and the international community. Among other things, it offered the prospect of increased American prestige in southern Africa (with the implication that Soviet influence there would correspondingly be neutralized); a solution to the diplomatic and military conflict over Namibia (or South-West Africa), the former German colony that South Africa has continued to rule in defiance of the United Nations; and a withdrawal of Cuban troops and advisers from Angola. The latter—the prospect of an apparent setback for the Cubans—carried particular domestic political appeal in the United States, and it alone seemed to justify the sudden focus of high-level attention on Africa.

Finally, and most fundamentally, constructive engagement promised that if the United States could, as Crocker put it, "steer between the twin dangers of abetting violence in the Republic and aligning ourselves with the cause of white rule," then it could contribute to the achievement of change in South Africa. The Reagan Administration seemed to believe that P. W. Botha, who had become prime minister in 1978 and elevated himself to state president in 1984 under a new constitutional scheme, was significantly different from other, more orthodox postwar South African leaders. Botha's program of limited reforms, Crocker felt, should be encouraged and applauded by the United States, if only to safeguard American interests in South Africa and the region.

In the early days of constructive engagement, Botha appeared to be impervious to, or at least capable of outsmarting, the increasingly assertive South African right wing, composed mostly of disaffected members of the ruling National Party. What is more, the domestic situation in South Africa seemed to be secure. The nationwide upheavals associated with the Soweto riots of 1976 had subsided. Despite localized incidents of black unrest and sporadic attacks inside the country by members of the exiled African National Congress, there was no obvious political force that might be able to dislodge, or even unnerve, the Botha government. When ANC attacks got out of hand, the South African government seemed capable of neutralizing the organization with commando raids into neighboring black-ruled countries.

Reinforcing all this was the widespread impression that the South African business community—led primarily by relatively liberal English-speaking men with extensive ties to the outside world—was not only poised to play a more active role in setting the pace of reform and determining the country's future, but was also being encouraged to do so by the Afrikaner-dominated political establishment. After the uprisings of 1976, business leaders had established new foundations that would attempt to improve the lives of black people in ways that the government itself was not yet prepared to attempt. At a widely publicized meeting in Johannesburg in 1979, Botha had explicitly asked the captains of South African business and industry to help him lead the country along a new political path, and they had, for the most part, responded enthusiastically.

The Reagan Administration seemed to believe that with its domestic situation under control and improving all the time, South Africa, with American backing, could also play the role of a regional power promoting peace. Once Namibia had achieved independence under U.N. supervision (in direct exchange for the withdrawal of the Cubans from Angola, a linkage that Washington introduced into the negotiations), other regional tensions would be reduced and, the State Department hoped, recalcitrant South African whites would see the advantages of peaceful coexistence with neighboring black-ruled states.

IV

The Botha government had different expectations of constructive engagement. Indeed, for Pretoria, Ronald Reagan's victory in 1980 stirred ambitious hopes. It seemed to signal a return to the days when the South African white regime could get away with portraying itself as a protector of the Western way of life, a bastion of freedom, decency and economic development at the tip of a continent afflicted by tyranny, chaos and abject poverty—above all, a bulwark against communism.

For the four previous years, that pose had been weakened, if not entirely rejected, by Washington. Jimmy Carter, with his emphasis on human rights and his public criticisms of apartheid (made, for example, during a visit to Nigeria), had come to be regarded as public enemy number one by many South African whites, who believed that he was trying to humiliate, or perhaps even destroy them. During a press conference at the end of a dramatic confrontation with then Prime Minister John Vorster in Vienna in 1977, Vice President Walter Mondale had appeared to advocate a one-man/one-vote system for South Africa. Two of Carter's other lieutenants who applied pressure on the country, U.N. Ambassadors Andrew Young and Donald McHenry, were black. Some white South Africans held Young and McHenry personally responsible for forcing a supposedly unwitting and, at the time, somewhat disorganized National Party government into a fateful concession—an agreement that Namibia should move toward independence under the terms of U.N. Security Council Resolution 435.

Anti-Americanism became a powerful force in South African white politics during the Carter Administration. In an election held some months after his showdown with Mondale, Vorster was able to add 15 seats to his majority in the white parliament simply by focusing the electorate's attention on alleged U.S. meddling in the country's affairs. Indeed, Carter's promotion of a climate of distrust between Washington and Pretoria, his refusal to acknowledge and endorse South Africa's dominant role in the region, may have contributed to the growing determination of the South African military to demonstrate the country's hegemony by destabilizing the governments and economies of neighboring states.

For the National Party government, Reagan's election raised hopes for more than just a return to a "normal" relationship between the United States and South Africa. There was the prospect of a valuable endorsement of the legitimacy of the white regime and the promotion of South African leadership in the region, perhaps through the "constellation of states" concept that Vorster had introduced and Botha had promoted. When President Reagan himself, in a television interview early in his term, extolled South Africa as "a country that has stood beside us in every war we've ever fought, a country that strategically is essential to the free world in its production of minerals," some South African politicians began to fantasize that their wildest dreams might come true.

Pretoria was encouraged that the Reagan Administration viewed the problems of southern Africa in the context of East-West relations, a perspective that South Africa felt had been naively missing from Carter's policy. South Africa's suspicion of the Soviet Union bordered on paranoia, and the new American government's tough line toward Moscow was greeted in South Africa as "political realism." Indeed, white South Africans hoped they would finally be regarded as an integral part of Western defense requirements.

In a "scope paper" to brief then Secretary of State Alexander Haig for a meeting with South African Foreign Minister Roelof F. "Pik" Botha in 1981 (and later made public by TransAfrica, the black American foreign policy lobbying organization), Crocker gave every indication that the Reagan Administration might be prepared to trust South Africa with just such responsibilities. He wrote:

The political relationship between the United States and South Africa has now arrived at a crossroads of perhaps historic significance; the possibility may exist for a more positive and reciprocal relationship between the two countries based upon shared strategic concerns in southern Africa, our recognition that the government of P. W. Botha represents a unique opportunity for domestic change, and willingness of the Reagan administration to deal realistically with South Africa.

If the South Africans cooperated on the Namibian issue, the Crocker memo went on to argue, the United States could "work to end South Africa's polecat status in the world and seek to restore its place as a legitimate and important regional actor with whom we can cooperate pragmatically." The United States was prepared to begin this process of new, "realistic" dealings with South Africa by taking "concrete steps such as the normalization of our military attaché relationship." In other words, the State Department leadership was so enthusiastic and hopeful about this course that it was willing to make symbolic gestures to Pretoria without any advance indication that reciprocal measures would be forthcoming.

Aware of this attitude, the Botha government expected still more concessions out of constructive engagement—perhaps even some form of American recognition of the South African-designed "independent homelands" of Transkei,

Bophuthatswana, Venda and Ciskei, which had been scorned and shunned by the international community but remained an important part of the grand fabric of apartheid. At one meeting with Crocker in Pretoria, Foreign Minister Pik Botha attempted to promote direct communication between the United States and the homelands by passing along messages from the leaders of two of these pseudostates. The thought was that if America conferred some legitimacy on the homelands, then other Western nations might follow suit and, before long, the established, genuinely independent states of the region, such as Botswana, Lesotho and Swaziland, would be forced out of weakness to deal with the homelands directly and perhaps even to join them in Botha's "constellation."

As far as Namibia was concerned, given the rich enticements that were being offered, South Africa seemed willing to play along with Crocker's patient, if overly optimistic, efforts to secure a settlement. Pretoria was, of course, deeply suspicious of the United Nations and skeptical of any transition to independence in Namibia that would operate in favor of the South-West Africa People's Organization, which had been designated by the United Nations as the sole legitimate representative of the territory's inhabitants. SWAPO, although it included among its membership many old-line nationalists whose views were consistent with those of European social democrats, had long been aided by the Soviet Union and other communist countries and, as an organization, officially followed a Marxist political line. Once the connection of a Namibian settlement with the departure of the Cubans from Angola had been introduced by Washington, however, it was much easier for South Africa to cooperate—or at least to give the impression of cooperating—with the Reagan Administration's efforts, which most South African political analysts thought were doomed to fail anyway.

Whether the Botha government ever could have delivered on a Namibia deal without provoking a severe crisis in the ranks of white South Africans is another question; the South African Defense Force, whose influence over the country's regional policies is profound, was, and apparently remains, hostile to any negotiations to "give away" the territory.

When it came to the issue of internal reform, P. W. Botha found it relatively easy to satisfy the Reagan Administration with his own limited agenda. Botha, as a lifelong party organizer and

long-standing member of the white parliament from southern
Cape province, where the population is evenly divided between
whites and so-called Coloureds, had very little direct experience
with other blacks. Thus, when he promoted a new constitutional
scheme in 1983 establishing separate chambers of parliament for
the so-called Coloureds and Asians, he was still groping to construct an alliance of minority groups that would exclude, and defend itself against, the black South African majority. When the
United States appeared willing to accept the new constitution as
a step in the right direction, Botha and his reformist allies were
encouraged to think that they had American support on this important front.* It was the impression that the United States was
identifying itself with the South African government's latest
scheme for preserving and prolonging apartheid that was critical
to the view of constructive engagement held by most black South
Africans.

V

A major complicating factor for any outsiders who attempt to
deal with the South African issue is that black South Africans
have a view of the world quite different from their white countrymen. But they have no formal diplomatic representation—the
few overseas offices of the ANC and the Pan-Africanist Congress
(PAC) have no meaningful status, except at the United Nations—
and not even any reliable informal ways of making their views
known to the international community. They are as disenfranchised in the outside world as they are at home.

For years, contacts between Americans and black South Africans had grown stronger, in part through greater journalistic attention to South Africa in the United States, and in part through
the growing inclination of American civil-rights and other organizations to become concerned about the South African problem.
An assumption gained currency in South Africa during the presi-
dency of John F. Kennedy that the United States sympathized
with the plight of black South Africans and tended to take their

---

*The State Department has repeatedly sought to deny that it gave any encouragement to P. W. Botha's "new
dispensation" for Asians and "Coloureds," but statements issued by U.S. Ambassador Herman Nickel in South Africa
and by official spokesmen in Washington had that effect. Some of the statements were later withdrawn or amended,
but the impression had already taken hold; many of the white liberals who campaigned for a negative vote in the
whites-only referendum on the new constitution complained that Nickel seemed to be taking the South African government's side.

side during incidents of repression and violence. Among other gestures, Kennedy's State Department for the first time required the American embassy in South Africa to invite blacks to official functions; the President's brother, Robert, was particularly involved with South Africa, and his visit there in 1964 is still remembered as an important gesture of solidarity with those who were fighting apartheid.

The Carter Administration sought to rekindle this spirit in American relations with South Africa, especially during its first two years in office. After the death of "Black Consciousness" leader Steve Biko at the hands of the South African police in 1977, the Carter Administration led the international chorus of outrage, and for a time it seemed as if American protests had helped to end deaths in detention in South Africa. Although Carter's rhetoric on the South African issue subsided as the practitioners of realpolitik gained the upper hand in his Administration, and although he repeatedly disappointed those who were waiting for the United States to vote in the United Nations for international economic sanctions against South Africa, the Carter years are nonetheless regarded by some South African blacks as a time when America was ready to help.

In the heady early days of constructive engagement, however, the Reagan Administration seemed obsessed with a need to demonstrate classic American qualities of evenhandedness. In one speech in August 1981 to the annual convention of the American Legion in Honolulu, Mr. Crocker stressed that "it is not our task to choose between black and white" in South Africa, where the United States sought "to build a more constructive relationship . . . based on shared interests, persuasion, and improved communication." While reiterating that the Reagan Administration disapproved of "apartheid policies that are abhorrent to our own multiracial democracy," Crocker said that "we must avoid action that aggravates the awesome challenges facing South Africans of all races. The Reagan Administration has no intention of destabilizing South Africa in order to curry favor elsewhere."

To some black South African leaders, not to choose sides between the oppressors and the oppressed was tantamount to buttressing the oppressors. Already, in March 1981, Bishop Desmond Tutu, then secretary-general of the South African Council of Churches, had warned that "a United States decision to align itself with the South African government would be an un-

mitigated disaster for both South Africa and the United States."
Tutu cautioned that the appearance of a reconciliation between
Pretoria and the most influential government in the West would
negate years of attempts by black South Africans to achieve a
peaceful realization of their political ambitions.

Four months later, a well-known black South African academic, N. Chabani Manganyi of the University of the Witwatersrand, told a Johannesburg conference that "blacks, both in South
Africa and elsewhere in Africa, interpreted the policy of constructive engagement as an act of choice—or moral choice. They
see the choice as a very simple matter in that it is a choice between
South Africa and its domestic policies and the rest of the world."
Manganyi called upon the Reagan Administration to fulfill its
moral obligation to the people of South Africa and the international community by applying pressure for change; he said that
whereas the Carter Administration had given blacks hope, "it
could well be that President Reagan is preparing us for despair."

So preoccupied was the Reagan Administration with sending
signals to South Africa's white minority, however, that it is not
clear its representatives paid heed to such warnings. Crocker exacerbated the situation by failing to include formal, public meetings with black South Africans on the itineraries of his many trips
to South Africa, which received prominent coverage in the South
African press. One black South African newspaper claimed that
between January 1982 and December 1984, Crocker had met
formally with only 15 South African blacks, and that all of those
meetings took place in the United States. As a result, it became
all the more difficult for him and other representatives of the
American government to encounter blacks and solicit their views
informally; increasing numbers of them (and even of white liberals) refused to attend functions given by U.S. diplomats in South
Africa.

Especially offensive to some black South Africans was the fact
that the United States expressed no opposition to the Pretoria
government's latest divide-and-rule tactic, the new constitution
creating separate chambers of parliament for so-called Coloureds
and Asians—nor to the conduct of a whites-only referendum in
November 1983 for approval of the constitution. In a speech to
the National Conference of Editorial Writers in San Francisco in
June 1983, U.S. Under Secretary of State Lawrence Eagleburger
stated:

I do not see it as our business to enter into this debate or to endorse the constitutional proposals now under consideration. Nor do we offer tactical advice to any of the interested parties. Yet the indisputable fact which we must recognize is that the South African government has taken the first step toward extending political rights beyond the white minority.[*]

In the view of black South Africans, who were almost universally opposed to the new constitution (even the leaders of six of the homelands urged a negative vote in the referendum), the United States could hardly have devised a clearer endorsement of the proposals.

In August 1983 more than 570 organizations, with members from all races, joined in a movement that pledged to work actively against the new constitution. The result was the United Democratic Front (UDF), which eventually orchestrated a massive boycott of the September 1984 elections for "Coloured" and Indian members of parliament. Only 30.9 percent of "Coloureds" and 20.3 percent of Indians who had taken the step of registering actually cast their votes; some of South Africa's new nonwhite parliamentarians went to Cape Town on the basis of the votes of only a few hundred people.[**] Most blacks saw the new institutions as a farce.

The identification of Washington with some of the most detested devices of the white regime may have helped to discredit black South African leaders who were not entirely ill-disposed to the United States, as well as American liberal politicians who were willing to support only moderate tactics in the struggle against apartheid. Thus, the radical Azanian People's Organization (AZAPO), a "Black Consciousness" group, demonstrated against Senator Edward M. Kennedy (D-Mass.) and succeeded in ruining his visit to South Africa early in 1985. Meanwhile, black spokesmen such as Dr. Nthatho Motlana, who had been an early activist in the ANC and, as chairman of the "Committee of Ten," had the support of his community in confronting the authorities during the Soweto riots of 1976, now appeared increasingly irrelevant to the more militant youths in the townships who called each other "comrade."

So far had things moved by the time P. W. Botha declared a stage of emergency in certain parts of the country in July 1985

[*]"Southern Africa: America's Responsibility for Peace and Change," Document 115, *The United States and South Africa: U.S. Public Statements and Related Documents, 1977-85, op. cit.*, pp. 189-196.

[**]Another way of stating the turnout in the elections for the new chambers of parliament is that 18.2 percent of the "Coloureds" eligible to vote did so, and that among Asians the comparable figure was 16.2 percent.

that it was not clear that the country-wide violence could be halted even if the ANC were brought into the dialogue. It seemed obvious that the ANC leaders sitting in other African capitals were as surprised as anyone else by the turn of events inside South Africa, and perhaps equally unable to control what happened. Whereas the ANC banner had often been displayed at political funerals over the years, on at least one occasion, in Cradock, eastern Cape province, it was now accompanied by the Soviet flag.

VI

American officials who spoke on behalf of constructive engagement liked to stress as often as possible that it was intended not merely as a policy toward South Africa, but as an effort to deal with the entire southern African region and its problems—thus Washington's promotion of direct talks between South Africa and Angola and its pleasure over the signing of the Nkomati accord between South Africa and Mozambique.

Most governments in the region, however, saw few benefits from constructive engagement. On the contrary, they saw evidence of a dangerous new South African military ascendancy, as the South African Defense Force seemed newly emboldened to strike across frontiers—into Mozambique, Lesotho, Botswana and, above all, Angola—in pursuit of ANC or SWAPO guerrillas and activists. The South Africans certainly supplied and trained the Mozambique National Resistance (MNR or Renamo), whose destructive war against the hard-pressed government of Samora Machel drove him to sign the Nkomati accord. (The accord called for Mozambique to expel ANC guerrillas in exchange for a suspension of South African aid to the MNR; documents recently discovered in Pretoria revealed that while Mozambique kept its part of the bargain, South Africa did not.) South Africa also kept up the pressure on the Marxist government in Angola by continuing to supply the rebel forces of the National Union for the Total Independence of Angola (UNITA) led by Jonas Savimbi. What is more, there have been few moments during the past ten years when there were not substantial numbers of South African troops inside Angola itself; last spring, South African commandos were captured in the Cabinda enclave (a part of Angola that is separated from the rest by a thin piece of Zaire) as they were preparing to sabotage an American-owned oil-drilling installation.

At the same time, South Africa also found economic means of destabilizing its neighbors and demonstrating its political hegemony over weaker states. The United States tried to put distance between itself and the South Africans on the issue of destabilization, frequently condemning its cross-border incursions and finally, after the raids in Cabinda and Botswana, withdrawing the American ambassador to Pretoria, Herman Nickel, for several months. Yet it seems clear that South Africa felt comfortable taking these steps against its neighbors without fear of serious recriminations from Washington.

Indeed, the U.S. Congress has been pushing the Administration to resume American aid to UNITA; while intended as a means of demonstrating toughness toward Cuba and the Soviet Union, this action would have the primary effect of advancing South Africa's interests in the region. Savimbi is clearly Pretoria's client, and is regarded as such throughout Africa; in fact, there is no way to aid him without going through South Africa.

For a time it appeared that the Reagan Administration would be willing to complement its new closeness with Pretoria with substantial aid programs for nearby black-ruled states. But those programs rarely materialized, and when they did, as in the case of Mozambique, opposition from conservatives on Capitol Hill made them almost impossible to carry out. In the case of Zimbabwe, where the United States had made an international commitment of aid at the time of independence in 1980, the Reagan Administration decided to punish Prime Minister Robert Mugabe for his foreign policy positions—including his sponsorship of a U.N. resolution condemning the U.S. invasion of Grenada in 1983—by cutting back substantially.

VII

After nearly five years, then, constructive engagement has failed on every front and with all of its constituencies.

The American public has seen little to indicate new U.S. diplomatic or strategic strength in southern Africa; on the contrary, the region is in as much turmoil as ever, and the Soviets have suffered few notable setbacks. The Cubans are still in Angola, and Namibia is no closer to independence; indeed, the South Africans recently instituted a new internal regime there, in direct defiance of American wishes.

Within South Africa itself, the United States has given a great deal and seen little progress as a result. The only concrete achievements of constructive engagement, apart from the shattered Angolan–South African truce and the now-discredited Nkomati accord, were a brief period of leniency by the Pretoria government toward black trade unions and the granting of passports to black spokesmen invited to the United States, such as Tutu and Motlana.

But the Reagan Administration can hardly claim that constructive engagement has brought about genuine improvements in the lives of South Africans. On the contrary, the piecemeal reforms that have been enacted in the past five years have been the object of resentment. The introduction of the new tricameral parliamentary system has coincided with the most devastating internal violence the country has experienced since the formation of the unified South African state in1910. Unrest has flared during the past year in every part of the country, and the imposition of the state of emergency has done little to quell it. In addition to the hundreds of known deaths and thousands of detentions that have occurred in recent months, more than one hundred South Africans have mysteriously vanished, many of them suspected victims of clandestine elements within the state security apparatus. The South African economy is in a shambles, and the country has been forced to postpone payment of many of its international debts. In some rural areas, such as the strife-torn eastern Cape, black unemployment is estimated to be as high as 60 percent.

The South African government, having expected so much, is itself disappointed with constructive engagement. It has reverted to old-style denunciations of American pressure as counterproductive, and it is furious over even the limited sanctions— worried that other nations may do the same or more and weaken the South African economy further. Far from strengthening its network of homelands, South Africa now finds itself having to think about dismantling them altogether or using them to create a new "federation." Its economic and military dominance of southern Africa is apparently intact, but it is not clear how long that will last if domestic turmoil continues. South Africa's formidable military machine is now required almost full time to help suppress internal unrest, despite a recently announced increase of 25 percent in recruitments into the police force.

Black South Africans are, if anything, becoming more disillusioned with the United States. Their impression is that although some sanctions have been instituted by executive order and American officials continue to condemn apartheid and demand further reforms, Washington is still collaborating substantially with the apartheid system rather than calculating further measures against the white government. It was particularly telling that when a clinic run by Winnie Mandela, wife of Nelson Mandela, the imprisoned leader of the ANC, was firebombed during the recent violence, she refused an offer of official American assistance to rebuild it.

According to the limited opinion polls that are available, Nelson Mandela remains the most popular black leader in South Africa; having been ignored by the United States all these years, it is difficult to imagine that he would be sympathetic to American concerns in South Africa's crisis. Some analysts believe that Mandela himself may soon be overtaken by the quickening pace of radicalization in South Africa; it may be that those who inherit his mantle will be overtly hostile to the United States. With President Reagan appearing at times to justify the excesses committed by the South African government under the terms of the state of emergency and at other times seeming to exaggerate the degree of reform that has already taken place, the United States is viewed increasingly by black South Africans as part of the problem rather than part of the solution.

Similarly, other southern African states are blaming constructive engagement for much of their own distress. In some cases, overestimating the degree of actual American influence on the South African government, they have developed unrealistic expectations of what the United States can do to improve their situations, and they are bound to be disappointed.

VIII

It is time for a new American policy toward South Africa that will help restore the reputation of the United States as a defender of human rights and racial justice in that country and will serve the broader interests of all South Africans and Americans.

There are, of course, important limitations on the American ability to affect the situation in South Africa. The U.S. military is not about to intervene on any side in any current or future crisis; it is foolish for whites or blacks in South Africa to believe otherwise (as some of them do). Nor can American leaders wave political or economic wands that will transform South Africa overnight. Indeed, American sanctions or moves toward disinvestment from the South African economy are sometimes more important on both sides as symbols than as practical measures; when sanctions are invoked, they should be carefully calibrated and thoughtfully applied. Given the level of suffering that already exists in the country, it is in no one's interest to destroy the South African economy or to induce further chaos in the country. And despite the frequent declarations from many quarters about the willingness of black South Africans to endure sacrifices in exchange for eventual freedom, it is not for the United States to condemn them to more abject poverty and deprivation. Disinvestment efforts within the United States should be directed only against particular firms that are known to have conducted themselves in an antisocial, regressive manner within South Africa. As for the continued presence of American business in South Africa, individual companies, evaluating their risks on the basis of hardnosed, pragmatic criteria, are making their own rational decisions on whether to stay or not.

But there are some official steps that the United States can take in an effort to move South Africa toward meaningful change and full participation by all of its people in the affairs of the country. If Americans still want to try to assure that the South African transition occurs relatively peacefully and with a minimum of vindictiveness on the part of blacks, then there is little time left to act.

The first step, uncomfortable as it may seem to many Americans, is to restore a forthright atmosphere of public and private confrontation to relations between Washington and Pretoria—precisely the sort of independent attitude that Mr. Crocker has eschewed. Internal and external pressure is the only thing that has ever produced meaningful change in South Africa. American officials need to become far more direct and persistent in their condemnations of apartheid. Speeches at the National Press Club in Washington alone cannot do the job. U.S. representatives in South Africa must be willing to denounce and even defy the system whenever possible, making clear their official and personal support for organizations like the UDF and Black Sash, the women's group that represents the victims of arbitrary "pass arrests" and other government actions. Some things may have to be said or done many times before they are believed or credited by disillusioned blacks.

All of this would have the immediate effect of helping develop a healthier, more vigorous multiracial opposition within South Africa, which would be far more difficult for the regime to crush if it clearly enjoyed outside support. If an American decision to confront apartheid more boldly also stiffened the resolve of other Western nations and ultimately led to a growing international vote of no-confidence in the leadership of P. W. Botha, that too would be a desirable turn of events. It is now obvious that as long as he remains in power, the National Party will not be able to form or endorse the alliances with other political factions that are necessary to head off full-scale civil war.

The current South African government, under the short-sighted impression that it has profited from a five-year interlude of conciliation with the United States, would be bitterly resentful of such a reversion to prior strategy by Washington. It would undoubtedly attempt once again to profit politically from American hostility and would proclaim, as it must, that this is the surest way for the United States to lose, rather than gain, influence in South Africa. But the truth is that South Africa has few other places to turn. It is dependent on the United States, in spirit as well as in fact; fellow "pariah states," such as Israel and Taiwan—its other current friends—simply cannot do for South Africa what America can do. And if constructive confrontation hastened the start of negotiations over real power in South Africa, which constructive engagement has failed to do, that would be a step forward.

IX

Once having restored a proper sense of balance and confrontation to U.S.-South African relations, it would be important for the American government and private business interests to devise additional measures that might hurt the pride and prestige of the white South African government without inflicting undue economic damage on black South Africans. Some of the measures should be selectively instituted for predetermined periods, in response to particular events in South Africa, with the American government making it clear that they may be lifted if circumstances improve. Alternatively, if the situation continues to deteriorate, the pressures could be intensified.

The landing rights enjoyed by the state-owned South African Airways in the United States can be reduced or terminated. The availability of almost daily direct service between Johannesburg and New York, with only a stop in the Cape Verde Islands, is a great advantage to South African businessmen and officials, and since Pan American abandoned its service for economic reasons earlier this year, the South African state airline has a monopoly on the route's substantial profits. Far from considering this step, which has frequently been proposed in the past, the Reagan Administration actually expanded South African Airways' landing rights in the United States in 1982, permitting direct service between Johannesburg and Houston (later suspended). The cancellation of direct air service is a sanction the United States has frequently taken to demonstrate disapproval of actions by other governments—including the Soviet Union, Cuba, Poland and Nicaragua. Because of the importance to South Africans of their links to the outside world, this would probably be more likely to have an effect in South Africa than it did in those other countries.

The United States can take steps to reduce South Africa's privileged diplomatic status here. South African military attachés can be expelled, for example, especially in the wake of external raids and other objectionable actions by the South African Defense Force. The visa-application process for South Africans who wish to travel to the United States can be made as complicated and cumbersome as it is already for Americans who seek to visit South Africa. And if Pretoria proceeds with its policy of making it more difficult for American journalists to travel to South Africa, and to have the necessary access when they do get there, then the number of official South African information officers permitted in the United States can be reduced.

The United States has recently sought South African permission to open a new consulate in Port Elizabeth to establish an official American presence in the troubled eastern Cape. The Reagan Administration must take care not to grant unnecessary concessions in exchange; South Africa already has four full-fledged and four honorary consulates in the United States.

The flow of new American technology to South Africa can be further restricted, especially as it relates to the repressive domestic tactics of the South African government and its raids against neighboring countries. President Reagan's restriction on the shipment of computers to South Africa had little immediate effect because most of the material to which it applied was already in South African hands or could easily be obtained from other countries. Rigorous steps can be taken, however, including the use of U.S. Customs Service agents and other law enforcement personnel, to be sure that other American technological advances do not reach the South African police or military, directly or through third countries. It would also be possible to improve American compliance with the international arms embargo against South Africa and to take further steps to prevent nuclear material from reaching the country. It is widely known that some American companies operating in South Africa are involved in strategic industries, and therefore in the regime's domestic and international war effort; this could be prevented with new federal rules governing American corporate behavior in South Africa.

The U.S. government can severely restrict, or even suspend entirely, its intelligence cooperation with the South African government. There is reason to believe that these ties have helped the South Africans far more than the United States, and they carry the implication that the United States is complicit in some of the worst abuses committed by South Africa against neighboring countries. One of the most troubling aspects of this problem is that some operatives of U.S. intelligence agencies and some State Department employees who have served in South Africa are outspokenly sympathetic to the apartheid policies of the white regime and have occasionally used their positions to thwart official American actions and directives.

The United States can seek to internationalize discussion of the South African issue by putting it on the agenda of the annual Western economic summits. This would be a way of coordinating economic pressures on South Africa, and also of trying to persuade recalcitrant nations, such as Japan, which has richly profited from its pragmatic relationship with South Africa (the Japanese have status as "honorary whites"), to go along with the measures.

X

Even more important, perhaps, are positive, lasting steps that the United States can take to demonstrate its sympathy for the black majority in South Africa and to show that it does not believe all change there must be white-led.

The United States must open a dialogue with the African National Congress and other black organizations that have widespread support among black South Africans, just as Secretary of State George Shultz has suggested the white South Africans themselves should do. Not to know what the ANC, the oldest black nationalist organization in South Africa, is thinking and doing is not only bad diplomacy but also foolish politics. If South African businessmen and white opposition politicians have recently held such discussions, certainly American officials will be taking no great risk by doing so. As it is, there is a feeling among some black South Africans that the attitude of the ANC may now be too moderate, in view of the pace of events within South Africa, and thus the United States may have to open relations with much more radical organizations. This contact with black South African leaders should take place at the ambassadorial level, both inside and outside South Africa, as a means of stressing the American rejection of the notion that the white government is the only meaningful political institution in the country.

The United States should send a black ambassador—a man or woman of international stature—to South Africa as soon as possible, to demonstrate important points of principle to South Africans of all racial groups. Above all, this would be an opportunity to emphasize the valuable role that black people play in a multiracial society and a system which South Africans often compare to their own. Some might complain that such an appointment smacks of tokenism, but if the ambassador behaved in an appropriate manner, his presence would be of more than symbolic value. For example, this new ambassador should attend the funerals of blacks killed by the police, political trials, and church services in black communities, as American diplomats in South Africa used to do. He should provide facilities for the meetings of groups that are trying to organize peaceful protests against the apartheid system and, in other respects, make it clear that he is the ambassador of all Americans to all South Africans, not just of white America to white South Africa. He should not take it upon himself to play American politics in South Africa—as the current U.S. ambassador did when he denounced Senator Kennedy while introducing him at a meeting of the American Chamber of Commerce of Johannesburg—but rather should take it as one of his jobs to convey to South Africans the depth of American feeling against apartheid and the so far inadequate steps to dismantle it.

Massive aid programs, funded by the American government, foundations and business, should be instituted to help black South Africans attain better educations in a broad range of fields, from engineering to international relations. The money for such programs should be distributed to all South African educational institutions, regardless of their nature, but special attention should be paid to encouraging the further integration of the mostly white elite universities. The committees that decide how this money is to be spent should have a majority of black South Africans. American-sponsored educational programs already available have barely scratched the surface; what is needed now is an effort to help black South Africans learn how to help run their country, an eventuality that seems not to have occurred to the ruling whites.

The United States should offer publicly to send forensic pathologists and other experts from the Federal Bureau of Investigation into South Africa to help find South Africans who have mysteriously disappeared and to help determine the cause of death of those who have been found. This has proved to be an effective technique in Central American countries such as El Salvador, where the police do not always care to solve crimes. The South African police are accused of acting to frustrate, rather than advance, the solution of some crimes against black people, and such outside help might well be appropriate. If the South Africans at first refuse such aid, the United States should offer it again and again, until its refusal becomes an embarrassment and a liability to the white government.

The United States government, in conjunction with professional groups such as the American Bar Association, should also send legal aid to black South Africans. Although the legal systems differ in certain important respects, the American experience with public defenders and government-funded legal services is an excellent example for the South Africans. American law schools and private foundations, for example, could help train black South Africans as paralegal workers, who in turn could establish elementary legal clinics in remote areas of the country, where the civil and human rights of blacks are the most egregiously and routinely violated; these paralegal workers could in turn report to lawyers, who make sure that the abuses are brought to the attention of the courts and the press. The American legal community could also assist the South Africans in the creation of a lawyers' organization in which blacks play a prominent role. (Such an association of doctors and dentists was recently established in South Africa, but unfortunately it is still not officially recognized by the American Medical Association.)

The United States should not only support the efforts of the black-led labor unions in South Africa, but where possible, should also send expert American union organizers to help them strengthen their institutions. Until and unless other structures are established, South Africa's black unions represent one of the few ways that the disenfranchised majority can become involved in political action, and American labor organizations have relevant experience to offer in this domain.

The American government should carefully monitor the performance of U.S. companies operating in South Africa, with a view toward creating and publicizing a list of those who treat their black workers badly. Indeed, American companies should be pressed by their government into playing a far more progressive role in South Africa— for example, by ignoring the Group Areas Act and establishing mixed housing areas where black and white South Africans can create de facto integrated neighborhoods. U.S. businesses operating in South Africa should also make every effort to visit any of their employees who are detained on political grounds and should establish a fund to be used for their legal defense.

The United States should help black South Africans increase and improve their means of communication with each other and the rest of the South African people. The exchange of South African and American journalists should be promoted, along with technical assistance in establishing black publications at the grass roots and black-oriented radio stations. Americans can help South Africans understand that a free press can often be one of the most important safety valves available to a society where there is political discontent. Severe consequences should be invoked, such as restrictions on South African diplomatic personnel in the United States, if black publications are closed and banned in South Africa, as they often have been in the past.

XI

In sum, courageous efforts must be made to convince black South Africans that Americans identify with their plight and are willing to help. There have been times in U.S.-South African relations—before constructive engagement—when officials from the American embassy were the first to be called by black activists in moments of crisis, and there were even U.S. officials in South Africa who occasionally sheltered political fugitives or helped them escape from the country. This was a role more consistent with American principles than the current one of keeping a distance from anyone charged by the government.

Recent developments indicate that P. W. Botha, far from responding creatively to the American confidence in him, is resorting once again to repression rather than reform. Concerned about minor electoral losses on the right, he is ignoring the rumbling volcano of discontent on the other side, from blacks and whites alike. His recent curbs on domestic and foreign press coverage of unrest in South Africa are a sign that the last vestiges of decency—South Africa's last claims to be part of the Western democratic tradition—may soon be destroyed in the defense of apartheid.

The United States must clearly and unequivocally disassociate itself from such measures. And it must resist the ever-present temptation to use southern Africa as a place to score points in the East-West struggle. Only after America rediscovers its voice—and its principles—in South Africa can it hope to play a truly constructive role in the region once again.

THE UNITED STATES AND SOUTH AFRICA: THE STRATEGIC CONNECTION[4]

Southern Africa is one of the world's most volatile regions, and one of the richest in terms of strategic minerals. The issues are inflammatory; the stakes are high on all sides. The problems for United States policymakers do not yield to simple solutions. Indeed, the challenges a great nation encounters in international politics are nowhere more clearly outlined than in the United States relationship with South Africa.

President Ronald Reagan's policy of constructive engagement is based on the premise that the United States can help bring about democratic change, that American ideals and inter-

[4]Analysis by Rhoda Plotkin, Lecturer in Political Science, City University of New York. *Current History.* 85:201+. My. '86. Copyright 1986 by Current History, Inc. All rights reserved. Reprinted by permission.

ests can prevail, and that we must "engage ourselves in the politics
of the real world for moral and strategic reasons," dealing "with
the difficult moral choices that the real world presents to us." A
debate has surrounded American—South African relations in recent decades. As tension and violence periodically escalate, the
debate on South Africa's strategic significance to the United
States has been rekindled along the following lines. On one side
are those analysts who maintain that the United States is too dependent on Pretoria's resources for its national security needs to
make any dramatic policy changes. Others have concluded that
despite inconvenience, both economic and political, the United
States can distance itself from South Africa without posing a significant threat to American national interests. An analysis of the
United States—South African strategic relationship can provide
a clearer understanding of the political realities, policy choices
and alternative strategies available to the United States in this decade and beyond.

The 1974 oil embargo made clear the extent and the consequences of American dependence on foreign sources of supply
and vulnerability to stoppages of strategic materials. Ironically,
in the lexicon of strategic and critical materials, oil does not rank
as high as manganese, chromium and the platinum group metals,
because the United States is an oil-producing nation with abundant domestic reserves. In contrast, it possesses little or uneco-
nomic resources of nonfuel materials. Yet the impact of the oil
embargo on consumers and business in terms of across-the-board
inflation, supply disruption, and inconvenience was overwhelming. In fact, it can be argued that the OPEC (Organization of Petroleum Exporting Countries) embargo set in motion dramatic
economic and political changes across America. It raised the
prospect of future interruptions, including strategic nonfuel materials, thereby widening the arena of American dependence on
foreign suppliers and its vulnerability to political upheaval in producer countries like South Africa. By the late 1970's, this situation had provoked enough concern in Congress to develop a
nonfuel minerals policy that would reduce American vulnerability.

In the South African context, the term "strategic" can be con-
ceptualized in two ways. First, a material is considered strategic
to the United States because of the vulnerability of its supply to
interruption, and because of the critical nature of its uses in appli-

cations essential to American national defense and the civilian economy. Second, in the East-West equation, "strategic" refers to South Africa's geopolitical significance to the United States in its rivalry with the Soviet Union. Without strategic materials like chromium, manganese and the platinum group metals (PGM's), "we really couldn't make a jet engine." The extent of American dependence is made clearer when one considers the fact that each engine that powers the F-15 fighter requires over 1,600 pounds of chromium, and "almost all of it comes from the Republic of South Africa and . . . the Soviet Union."

The United States annually imports more than $1 billion in chromium, manganese and platinum for the industrial economy and the national defense. Manganese and the platinum metals are almost nonexistent in the United States, and where limited amounts of strategic materials like chromium exist, they are currently uneconomical to mine because of undesirable grade or potentially low yield. On the other hand, the vast South African strategic reserves include 74 percent of the world's reserves of chromite ore. Most of the world's manganese reserves are held by the Soviet Union and South Africa, and these two countries also own the world's platinum. Together, South Africa and the Soviet Union "hold some 95 percent of the world's vanadium reserves, 94 percent of its manganese, 90 percent of its platinum group metals, 84 percent of its chrome . . . and an important proportion of other strategic minerals."*

According to such statistics, there can be little doubt that South Africa is strategic to the United States economy and national security. In terms of American foreign policy, however, the operative questions are the following: Must we continue on the present course or is there a way out of the dilemma? Are there policy options that would free the United States from strategic dependence while protecting our national security? It is precisely the need to reduce strategic reliance and provide greater flexibility in our southern Africa policy that has generated congressional inquiries into alternative strategic minerals policy. Table 1 shows the outlook for the development of selected strategic resources in the United States.

---

*"Strategic Minerals in the 1980's (Paper presented by W. W. Malan, vice president of the South African Chamber of Mines, Rome, November 25, 1980). Chromite ore is the original ore from which chromium is produced after certain impurities have been removed. Manganese is a hardening agent used in steel making. Vanadium is used as an alloy to make high-strength, lightweight steel. Platinum is a noncorroding metal that is used as a catalyst in alloys. These metals are used to produce strategic materials, particularly jet engines, for the defense industry.

Table 1:   Outlook for the Development of
              Known Domestic Deposits of Strategic Resources

	Chromi-um	Cobalt	Manga-nese	Platinum
Alaska	–	–	–	1–2
Montana	3	–	–	1–2
Missouri	–	2–3	–	–
Idaho	–	2–3	–	–
California	2–3	2–3	–	–
Minnesota	–	3	–	3
Overall Domestic	–	–	3	–

– Not applicable.
1 Economic at current prices.
2 Marginally economic to subeconomic; under consideration for exploitation.
3 Subeconomic—not considered for commercial exploitation at current metals prices.
Source: Office of Technology Assessment

In contrast to the United States, few countries have been as inordinately endowed with such a concentration of the world's mineral wealth as the Republic of South Africa. In addition, South Africa's technological expertise and highly developed infrastructure have made it a very attractive trading partner for the United States. South Africa figures prominently as a producer of 11 of 27 of the world's critical minerals. Of these, manganese, chromite ore and the PGM's are of particular concern to United States defense and civilian industries.

Successive American administrations have hesitated to confront the fact that the United States relies on the critical materials of South Africa to satisfy its strategic and industrial needs. Without substantial evidence to challenge the prevailing view that the United States cannot do without South Africa's critical materials or that if it attempts to do so it will find itself at the mercy of the Soviet Union, little policy reevaluation can be expected. Since 1980, however, several congressional reports have focused on strategic minerals policy options. House and Senate studies have focused on alternatives to United States minerals dependence, and have tried to fashion a comprehensive, workable plan in place of the present ad hoc minerals policy. According to the most recent findings prepared by the United States Congress's Office of

Technology Assessment, data that parallel the Senate Foreign Relations Committee findings, a national nonfuel minerals policy could significantly reduce reliance on South Africa and the Soviet Union, while maintaining the integrity of United States strategic interests.

Thus, a key assumption of administration policy has come under congressional scrutiny. Although present minerals dependence is acknowledged, both congressional inquiries question the premise underlying the President's South Africa policy, that is, that we must continue on the current course, relying on existing foreign sources and technologies because they are cost-effective, reliable and abundantly available. This is not to suggest that dramatic changes in United States minerals procurement and supply can occur overnight, but that policy options are feasible and in the long run will be politically cost-effective.

Under present circumstances, the United States needs South Africa's critical minerals and metals. No single approach to the problem will reduce American dependence. Instead, a combination of technical and economic strategies, in conjunction with the political will to implement them, is the starting point for a minerals policy that can, over time, provide political leverage and strategic security.

The administration must set in motion a comprehensive national minerals policy based on the necessity to reduce United States vulnerability to potentially unstable sources of supply and, in cooperation with the private sector, to provide the economic incentives to overcome barriers and inconveniences that may lie in the way of a more favorable position.

Such a policy would not constitute an immediate decisive break in American–South African trade relations, but it would mark a transition in the nature of that relationship. From the United States vantage point, that relationship would be less subject to the vicissitudes of continuing violence and upheaval. The United States must make advance preparations for the possible disruption of supplies. A comprehensive nonfuel minerals policy "formulated in cooperation with our allies should be a national priority. Failure to take prompt action will risk repeating in southern Africa the same mistakes we have made in the Middle East."* The most promising approaches include stockpiling, con-

*United States Senate, Subcommittee on African Affairs of the Committee on Foreign Relations, *Imports of Minerals from South Africa by the United States and the OECD Countries*, September, 1980, p. xii.

servation, research and development of advanced technologies and a search for alternative suppliers. These policy alternatives should be adopted as soon as possible to enable Washington to deal with supply disruptions, should they occur, without jeopardizing vital American interests.

Stockpiling

In the case of the four critical materials that the United States imports from South Africa—chromium, manganese, vanadium and the platinum group metals—stockpiling is an effective way to cushion dislocations caused by supply cutoffs and to provide the defense requirements of a protracted conflict. The United States stockpile is predicated on a three-year conventional war on several fronts. A comprehensive policy would raise the levels of these critical materials to a minimum three-year standard. (This is the recommendation of independent congressional research groups.) Enlarging the stockpile of platinum, for example, to a three-year supply level was suggested as a means to "ease the adjustment to any interruption in South African supplies. . . . Adaptation could be facilitated by a . . . policy of increasing stockpiles prior to any cutoff."

At present, a lower priority has been put on the stockpiling of critical materials. The Reagan administration has had on hand an approximately 2.5-year supply of chromium, an almost 2-year supply of manganese ore and an 8-month supply of ferromanganese. In 1985, it adopted as a policy "one year's peacetime levels of imports for such materials. . . . " The stockpile is being reduced despite the conclusion in 1978 of the United States National Materials Advisory Board that "the United States is strategically more vulnerable to a long-term chromium embargo than to the embargo of any other natural resource including petroleum."

Conservation Technologies

Conservation, in the form of the reduced consumption of strategic materials, recycling, substitution and design changes where applicable, provides another promising alternative. Present import levels can be significantly reduced through a variety of techniques. For example, "chromium consumption could be reduced by 35 percent . . . within 5 years and by 64 percent within 5–10 years,* by developing industrial processes that consume less chromium, and by recycling and substituting advanced materials like ceramics and composites. In addition, the recovery of chromium from steelmaking, industrial, and chemical waste has begun to rise in the past few years," partly because of the federally mandated cleanup of air and water, which has contributed to the knowledge of conservation technology.

The ability of the United States and the Western democracies to adjust to disruptions in the supply of platinum group metals from South Africa depends on reduced consumption and recycling. Under a comprehensive policy, nonessential uses of platinum could be diverted to defense and the industrial sector. Research and development in the automotive and petroleum industries—major civilian users of platinum—have already reduced consumption through alternative technologies for auto emissions control. More could be done. The petroleum industry currently uses platinum in the refining of high-octane gasoline to control auto pollution. The development of "lean-burn engines capable of using low-octane gasoline, and the possible substitution of non-platinum catalysts, could eliminate this use of platinum."** Finally, the demand for newly mined platinum group metals can be reduced because their major applications are catalytic. Since the platinum is not consumed, the potential for recovery from scrap is very great. It is estimated that "about 70 percent of platinum in the United States is used for catalytic purposes and that 70–80 percent of the platinum catalysts now scrapped are salvageable."

Despite these advances, the strategic minerals recycling industry is a new one. It needs updated information and government encouragement to continue developing recycling technology. Coordinated effort undertaken by government agencies and the private sector will be necessary in the areas of minerals exploration and research and development of other conservation technologies that are vital to the success of a strategic minerals policy.

*United States National Academy of Sciences, National Materials Advisory Board, *Contingency Plans for Chromium Utilization* (Washington, D.C., 1978), p. 87.
**Imports of Minerals from South Africa,* p. 16.

Economic Incentives

Like other political and economic entities, private corporations act in their own interests as they perceive them. They cannot be expected to undertake the enormous costs of developing advanced minerals technologies to meet national security needs without economic incentives and administration guarantees of compensation for the risks involved. To this end, the administration can use fiscal policy as a stimulus for minerals research and development. Such stimulation would include tax advantages like depreciation and retrogressive taxes telescoping deductions into shorter time frames. In the area of risk compensation, the government can underwrite the bulk of new investment for conservation technologies and minerals exploration.

Guarantees for certain corporate ventures have been successfully used in the domestic economy and for targeted areas overseas. For example, OPIC, the Overseas Private Investment Corporation, is a federal agency that encourages American business abroad by guaranteeing much of the risk of private investment considered important to United States foreign policy objectives. In addition, the administration can activate the provisions of existing legislation, like Title 3 of the Defense Production Act of 1950, which "authorizes direct Federal subsidies, purchase commitments, loan guarantees and other instruments to assure availability of essential defense materials and industrial processing capabilities."

Incentives could also be used to encourage investment in the infrastructures of targeted third world countries that need to upgrade productivity and make their current operations more efficient.

Alternative Suppliers

Although South Africa and the Soviet Union have a preponderance of the world reserves of strategic materials, the needs of America's defense industry and the economic well-being of its industrialized society can increasingly be satisfied through trade with alternative suppliers. There is no single approach to a comprehensive minerals policy, but the adoption of such a policy, in conjunction with other strategies, would signal a move away from dependence. A strategy of diversification and action to expand the range of foreign suppliers and domestic producers would give the United States greater control over strategic materials while ensuring a stable flow of goods.

Admittedly, minerals produced elsewhere may be less desirable than those processed by the technologically sophisticated industries that the South Africans have developed without peer. All things considered, however, American worry about strategic vulnerability in the South African context is overwrought. Manganese producers include Australia, Brazil, India and Gabon. All these countries are major suppliers to the United States.

In the case of chromium and the ferroalloy-processing industry, there is no long-term alternative to reliance on southern Africa, because Zimbabwe and South Africa possess about 99 percent of the world's known chromium resources (about 35 billion tons of ore). If these supplies were unavailable, "chromium resources in the rest of the world would be exhausted in 21 years at 1975 rates of consumption." However, supply disruptions lasting that long are implausible, and it is unlikely that disruptions from Zimbabwe and Pretoria would occur simultaneously. By promoting increased trade with Zimbabwe and other producers like Turkey, and by assisting domestic producers to be more competitive, the United States can diminish, although it cannot entirely eliminate, its reliance on South Africa.

Despite Soviet and South African domination of the world's reserves of PGM's (the United States, Canada and Columbia combined have only about 1.3 percent of known quantities), there are reasonable prospects for some domestic production of platinum group metals. With advanced technologies, substitution and recycling, United States dependence on imported platinum can be significantly reduced.

The implications are clear. The United States now relies on the strategic materials provided by a narrow range of foreign producers, increasing its vulnerability and, under specific conditions, influencing foreign policy decisions. But the United States is not a helpless giant. On the contrary, the evidence suggests that an administration commitment to a strategic minerals policy would ameliorate the serious problem of import vulnerability.

Barriers to Policy Implementation

Ironically, while emphasizing a strong America and increased defense expenditures, the Reagan administration has not yet carried out all the provisions of the 1980 materials act. Intended to give the executive branch greater control over managing the problem of import vulnerability, the act "requires the Executive Office of the President to assume a more active role in coordinating and formulating materials policy beginning with a . . . materials . . . plan to be submitted to Congress by the President on a one-time basis."

A strong America requires independent national security policies based on specific goals and timetables. How can we account for the apparent discrepancy between administration words and action? Two possible explanations suggest themselves. First, despite years of civil unrest in South Africa, the volatility of the region and the implications of strategic supply disruptions, the administration does not envision a meaningful change in the politics of the status quo in South Africa. Even so, the assumption that revolutionary violence can be contained or that the policy of constructive engagement will produce a more stable environment for peaceful change should not preclude serious consideration of advance preparations to protect United States vital security interests.

Second, a prominent feature of President Reagan's political style and philosophy has been the call to reduce the size and role of the federal government. But in the area of strategic materials research and development, American national interests demand that the government be a critical player. How to reconcile this dilemma? Ideology and rhetoric must make way for the pragmatism of political reality.

In the past, President Reagan has exhibited a pragmatic side, moving from previously held ideological positions to a more flexible response to key advisers and congressional and world leaders. The same pragmatism must apply to the urgent issue of strategic materials, so that the United States can import more of these materials from countries other than South Africa and the Soviet Union.

Trade in critical materials is one aspect of the United States strategic relationship with Pretoria. The other strategic question deals with the geopolitics of the region, that is, South Africa's military significance for the West and the impact on American interests of a Soviet presence in southern Africa.

Pretoria's economic trade with the West belies the extent to which the political and military relationship has eroded in the postwar years. South Africa has no formal military arrangements with the United States or the NATO (North Atlantic Treaty Organization) nations that affect Western security. South Africa is not an equal partner. Even its historically close military relationship with the British no longer exists because, in 1975 (two years before the United Nations mandatory arms embargo), London unilaterally abrogated the 1955 Simonstown Agreement with Pretoria "that formalized long-standing imperial cooperation for South Atlantic naval defense. . . . The republic's few gains in its effort to become a legitimate Western defense partner have proved to be remarkably ephemeral."*

South Africa serves no significant military interest for the United States or its allies, despite the President's world view and his perception of the role the United States should play in world politics. Regardless of the lack of military interest, it can be argued that South Africa has traditional ties to the West, is strongly capitalist, staunchly anti-Communist, and a loyal and dependable trading partner, while the Soviet Union, influential in Angola, Mozambique and among guerrilla groups in southern Africa, presents the gravest danger to American interests.

Soviet moves to control the strategic minerals and trade routes of southern Africa cannot be foreseen with certainty because of the difficulty of separating Marxist-Leninist revolutionary doctrine from the caution and pragmatism of day-to-day Soviet foreign policy. But we do know how Soviet leaders have behaved in the past under given circumstances, and this can tell us something about future actions.

Since Stalin, Soviet interests have been the centerpiece of Moscow's foreign policy, and are likely to remain so under General Secretary Mikhail Gorbachev. During the period of United States–Soviet détente, for example, President Leonid Brezhnev was negotiating trade policy and most-favored-nation status with the United States while America was deeply involved in war with Soviet-supported North Vietnam. Despite the loss of American influence in the Persian Gulf after the fall of the Shah of Iran,

---

*Chester A. Crocker, "Current and Projected Military Balances in Southern Africa," in Chester A. Crocker and Richard E. Bissell, eds., *South Africa in the Eighties* (Boulder, Colo.: Westview Press, 1979), p. 77.

Soviet leaders did not challenge American access to the Strait of Hormuz, which is much closer to their border than the Cape routes. It is unlikely that they would risk confronting the United States directly on any issue considered to be vital to American interests.

The fear of a Soviet stranglehold on the strategic resources of the West should be balanced by the realization that the United States and its allies have similar options on resources of strategic importance to Moscow, including the natural gas pipeline and American wheat shipments that are vital to the economy and stability of the Soviet system. Indeed, despite long-range ideological aims, Soviet foreign policy in southern Africa will probably be cautious in the next few years. Gorbachev must avoid being perceived in the West as adventuristic; instead, he must convey an image of prudent statesmanship in a bid to legitimize and consolidate his power.

A realistic approach to American foreign policy in South Africa suggests setting an agenda defined by American interests and recognizing the limits of United States influence and power. South Africa remains an area of strategic interest to the United States, but its significance will diminish over time as a strategic minerals policy is implemented.

The administration's policy of constructive engagement was designed to encourage incremental democratic change to dismantle the structure of apartheid. Despite the fact that this policy has proved ineffective, it is in the interest of regional stability that the United States continue to promote peaceful change. Clearly, in South Africa the environment is revolutionary. The United States cannot successfully pursue a policy that does not recognize this. While it serves no American interest to help topple the government of South Africa, it is not in the interest of the United States to intervene covertly or overtly to save Pretoria.

Despite our best intentions, the United States may not be able to stop what is in motion or to help Pretoria move more quickly toward institutional change. Americans must reflect realistically on the constraints imposed on United States foreign policy by the entrenched power and revolutionary challenge in South Africa. Nevertheless, United States policymakers must continue to seek just and workable solutions for all the people of South Africa, black and white, as they struggle for political power and survival.

GOODYEAR TOUGHS IT OUT[5]

In an oak-paneled conference room, Goodyear Tire & Rubber Co.'s international executive committee is facing a crowded agenda at its weekly meeting. Topics include a project to build tires for earthmovers in Luxembourg, a possible plant expansion in Taiwan, Argentina's economic problems—and a status report on Goodyear's operations in South Africa.

Goodyear, with a $100-million investment that accounts for almost 2,500 jobs, is among the top half-dozen American employers in South Africa. Recently, when riots were sweeping South Africa's townships, Goodyear let *Fortune* sit in on the committee session at the company's Akron headquarters. Goodyear also provided access to documents and key officials to help shed light on how a major corporation grapples with the thorny problem of operating in South Africa amid the rising clamor for sanctions and disinvestment.

The international policy meeting opens with good news. Despite South Africa's three-year recession and months of civil unrest, sales by Goodyear's subsidiary at Uitenhage in South Africa's East Cape rebounded in July, reports assistant controller H. Jay Elliott. The plant's managers and black workers appear to be coping with the turmoil and a government curfew that overlaps the factory's night shift; absenteeism at the plant has declined in the past three months from 30% to 6%. Joseph C. Graden, vice president in charge of international manufacturing, says that a $20-million expansion enabling the South African plant to produce radial truck tires will go into full operation ahead of schedule by year-end. Emmett H. Sellars, international vice president for tire sales, comments in passing that Goodyear's profit margins in South Africa have been among the best it achieves in any country.

Yet Goodyear's subsidiary isn't free of serious problems. The plunge of the South African currency, the rand, to record lows has depressed the division's earnings. Many workers are withdrawing contributions they had made to the company's pension fund, jeopardizing the retirement plan's viability. Those at the

[5]Article by *Fortune* reporter Felix Kessler. *Fortune.* 112:24+. S. 30, '85. Copyright © 1985 by Time Inc. All rights reserved. Reprinted by permission.

meeting speculate that a black boycott of white shopkeepers has boosted living costs for black employees, making it necessary for them to dip into savings.

One subject surprisingly *not* raised at the meeting: the notion that Goodyear should consider withdrawing from South Africa, as advocated by American foes of apartheid. Since Goodyear's top managers are in unanimous agreement, there's no need to debate the topic. "Who isn't against apartheid?" asks Robert E. Mercer, Goodyear's chairman. But he argues that a sudden pullout in response to pressure against the minority white government's harsh system of racial separation would only hurt blacks and stiffen the government's determination not to amend the racist laws.

Other officers and outside directors agree that Goodyear exerts a benevolent presence as a South African employer. "If the government were to emulate the kind of integrated microenvironment we have in that plant," says William R. Miller, a Goodyear vice president, "it would resolve most of the country's problems." Is staying in South Africa a vote for apartheid? "Definitely not," says W. Howard Fort, an Akron lawyer who recently retired after eight years on Goodyear's board. "Long before any pressures were applied, Goodyear was doing things contra to the apartheid laws because it thought it was the right thing to do." Miller and Fort, both black, have visited the Uitenhage plant and toured the East Cape region.

Goodyear has other compelling reasons for staying, such as profits and its high global visibility. "Because South Africa has always been profitable," says Jacques Sardas, Goodyear International's president, "we've never really considered leaving. Our presence there is good for our shareholders as well as South Africans—all of them."

With operations in 28 countries outside the U.S., from Argentina to Zaire, Goodyear does not want to set a negative precedent by giving in to pressure. "It would send a message to other countries that Goodyear is a company that folds its tent when things get hot," says Douglas F. Hill, Goodyear International's executive vice president. During the 1982 Falklands war, when such American companies as Exxon, Eastman Kodak, and Eli Lilly evacuated employees from Argentina, Goodyear left its five American managers in Buenos Aires. Goodyear employees who were recently pulled out of Colombia because of a suspected terrorist plot are chafing to return. "All I get three times a week is,

'When do we go back?'" says Hill, 52, himself a feisty ex-expatriate with 16 years' service in Africa and Latin America.

Goodyear, whose overseas operations contributed 33% of its $10.2 billion in sales last year, doesn't lightly abandon any subsidiary, especially one as lucrative as the one in South Africa. "For us, political risk is a relatively minor consideration," says Hill.

"You've got problems in Chile—and you can't just pull out of Chile. You've got problems in Argentina, in Peru. You can't leave every country with problems and export out of Akron, Ohio. It doesn't work that way."

Especially not in South Africa. Were Goodyear forced to sell its 1.1-million-square-foot plant suddenly, it would be stuck with whatever take-it-or-leave-it price a South African or European competitor like Dunlop might offer. And the protective trade barriers that have helped make South Africa such a profitable proposition would then effectively shut Goodyear out of the tire market there that it helped develop. It's a scenario Goodyear hardly relishes.

So Goodyear officials, out of either realism or fatalism, refuse to agonize over the "what if" prospects clouding South Africa. "Things would really have to deteriorate a lot more for us even to consider the possibility of selling out," says Sardas, an ebullient multilingual native of Egypt and a veteran of Goodyear's foreign legion. "But if there's a total collapse or revolution, we could make such a decision in a half-hour."

Goodyear began selling tires in South Africa in 1916 and started manufacturing there in 1947, the year before the Afrikaner government imposed apartheid on the already segregated nation. But Goodyear's big push commenced in the mid-1960s, says Clarence Alameda, a retired Goodyear vice president. "That was when we developed an aggressive marketing program aimed at selling to blacks, who'd been totally ignored until then."

That strategy coincided with a spurt of economic growth in South Africa. Job opportunities began opening for blacks, who had been restricted to mining or unskilled labor. Goodyear says it instituted an equal pay for equal jobs program before the Reverend Leon Sullivan promoted his voluntary nonsegregation code for U.S. companies in 1977 (*Fortune*, July 9, 1984). But Goodyear, one of the 12 charter subscribers to the Sullivan principles, candidly admits that it desegregated the company cafeteria and locker rooms only as a result of the code. Despite initial resistance, recalls John Purcell, Goodyear's former managing director for South Africa, desegregation "turned out to be not all that difficult."

Of 177 American companies conforming to the Sullivan code's amplified principles, Goodyear is one of the few that have always won top grades from Arthur D. Little, the Cambridge, Massachusetts, consulting firm that monitors corporate compliance with the code. IBM, Xerox, and a half-dozen other companies with outstanding records in South Africa weren't interested in being the subject of this article. Goodyear, by contrast, appears comfortable defending its South African presence at a time of rising shareholder pressure. Sullivan says he doesn't care whether American firms leave South Africa or remain—"but those that stay should be an active force for change." In a compliance form filed in mid-August, Goodyear affirms that its managing director "made several public calls on the government to eliminate apartheid laws," and that the company is supporting moderate black leaders attempting to win political rights. It is also proud that 34 of its 1,600 nonwhite employees supervise whites—still a rarity in South Africa.

To Goodyear, which has spent $6 million on nonwhite education and housing programs, all its social efforts constitute enlightened self-interest. Greater prosperity for South Africa's 23 million blacks, coupled with political stability, should boost the economy and spell higher tire sales—always the bottom line. "We would not be making tires there if we only thought of South Africa as having a market of 4.5 million whites," says Goodyear Chairman Mercer. Blacks and coloreds (South Africa's category for people of mixed race) own about 430,000 of the estimated three million cars in South Africa. If a company hesitates about making investments as a market develops and waits until everything settles down, says Mercer, "somebody else has the business."

What steams Mercer and other American firms in South Africa is the possibility that the U.S. may impose sanctions against technology transfers or new investments. "Sanctions would cripple us," says Mercer. "We're not going to run an operation down there that will put out questionable products because we can't keep our technology up to date." Moreover, sanctions might challenge the Afrikaner government to go it alone while punishing the best agents for change in South Africa, says another Goodyear executive. Adds Mercer: "We're doing more good through jobs, training, and pushing to eliminate apartheid than all the protesters and sign carriers that I've seen."

Goodyear officials and outside directors do not present a unified front in assessing U.S. policy toward South Africa. The Reagan Administration "wasted time and could have brought a lot more hard, steady pressure on the government for internal change," privately declares one Goodyear insider with deep knowledge of the region. Others, such as Mercer, feel that more U.S. pressure would simply reinforce the Afrikaner's bunker mentality.

About 3% of Goodyear's 107 million outstanding shares are held by universities or pension funds and financial institutions that might be swayed by calls for disinvestment. Some shareholders excoriate the company for selling tires to the police or military. Others accuse Goodyear of supporting apartheid by paying South African taxes and are threatening to boycott its products or dump its shares. But any disinvestment to date has been gradual, says Mark Blitstein, Goodyear's investor relations manager, and hasn't hurt the share price.

Pressure to get out of South Africa might reach a point at which Mercer would wonder whether the country's contribution of less than 1% to Goodyear's $411-million annual profits is worth the bother. So far the profit margin still outweighs the South African hassle factor. "But if it gets to be 20% of our troubles," Mercer says, "we'll have to reassess what we're doing." He hopes the time for reassessment—and withdrawal from a stricken nation—never arrives.

THE COSTS OF DISINVESTMENT[6]

The South African business community values its links with American companies active in South Africa and the role they have played in the country over many decades. Many American companies have been good corporate citizens, not only contribut-

[6]Article by Gavin Relly, chairman of the Anglo-American Corporation of South Africa, the country's largest corporation. *Foreign Policy*. 131+. Summer '86. Copyright 1986 by the Carnegie Endowment for International Peace. Reprinted by permission.

ing to general economic growth and development, but also actively promoting equal opportunities for all races, both in the work place and in society at large. Through this effort, much of it within the guidelines set by the Sullivan Principles of Fair Employment, they can claim some of the credit for the important erosion of apartheid that has taken place.

South African business leaders understand the enormous pressures brought against the continued presence of American business in South Africa as South African society undergoes the traumatic transition from the old apartheid era toward a yet undefined destination. They understand that such pressure has both economic and political components. As market conditions in South Africa have deteriorated during a prolonged recession, business profitability has declined, too. Businesses also are threatened by the tactics of antiapartheid activists, who have organized consumer boycotts against some U.S. firms both at home and abroad, and by the procurement bans imposed by a growing number of cities and states on companies that continue to have interests in South Africa.

Behind such activities lie two assertions: that foreign investment simply buttresses the apartheid state and that disinvestment and sanctions are the only ways left to pressure an intransigent white minority regime into dismantling apartheid before violent revolution becomes inevitable. On a moral, as opposed to instrumental or practical level, the argument also is often advanced that American democratic values simply make it impossible for U.S. citizens and corporations to be involved in any way with a racist system, irrespective of the consequences of withdrawal.

South African business leaders themselves are frustrated by the slow pace of change in South Africa and confronted by hard economic times and considerable social and political turbulence. Consequently, they cannot blame American companies if they take the view of Allen Born, president of AMAX, Inc., in Greenwich, Connecticut, who recently indicated that he was not interested in South Africa, or indeed the rest of Africa, for investment purposes because of political and economic turmoil.

South African executives can help their American counterparts resolve their political problems only by explaining their view of current South African reality, their long-term vision of a postapartheid society, and their own efforts toward structural change. In so doing, most would state clearly that the withdrawal of American and other foreign companies would damage irreparably the prospects for any viable postapartheid society emerging from the current stormy transitional period.

The fundamental principle that South African business leaders adhere to is the importance of individual freedoms and of a free enterprise economy. This view brings them into conflict with apartheid on both moral and pragmatic grounds. Apartheid, after all, seeks to restrict such fundamentals of the free enterprise system as labor mobility, the ability to choose where to live and educate one's family, and one's ability to participate freely in the country's political life.

Abundant evidence shows that apartheid and its associated economic policies have restricted the quantity as well as the quality of opportunity for all South Africans. This explains why business executives oppose restrictions, racial or otherwise, placed on these freedoms. Thus when South African business speaks of dismantling apartheid, it means the abolition of key apartheid laws. Major examples include the Population Registration Act, which classifies every individual South African according to race; the Group Areas Act, which designates residential areas according to race; and the pass laws, which restrict the mobility of black South Africans, forcing many to remain in rural homelands where opportunities are severely limited. (In April 1986 Pretoria announced that the pass laws will be scrapped effective immediately.) Just as important, many in the South African business community believe that the release of political prisoners and the "unbanning" of political parties are essential preconditions to free political processes.

Although South African business leaders are not unanimous on all these points, recent surveys conducted by the development economist Jill Nattrass of Natal University reveal that substantial majorities of white business executives drawn from all party and political backgrounds would support such measures.

But business leaders oppose apartheid for another important reason—it has become an ethnic, quasi-socialist system of government pursued by an Afrikaner oligarchy not hitherto imbued with free enterprise principles. In this respect, apartheid has incorporated some of the worst features of other centralized, bureaucratic, socialist systems. Fortunately, these central features of apartheid also have increasingly conflicted with an industrializing society's need for high economic growth. And the process of reform instituted in the late 1970s and pursued somewhat unevenly in the 1980s has resulted partly from the changing economic interests of the Afrikaner community and partly from domestic and international pressures.

What, then, can South African business (and its overseas counterparts) do to accelerate the dismantling of apartheid and to promote the kinds of fundamental political negotiations needed? Political negotiations among South African business leaders start with the assumptions that there can be no quick fixes, whatever the situation's urgency, and that a sweeping, business-led, efficiently managed transformation of society is not in the offing.

First, contrary to many foreign misperceptions, neither domestic nor foreign business can force the South African government to act against its will. One cannot simply assume, as many do, that because American business often can influence Washington in its favor, South African firms have the same power. Not only are the political issues in the two countries completely different—in South Africa, concerning the very nature of the state and the struggle for basic economic and political power—but the historical relationship between government and business has been completely different.

An Afrikaner Transformation

During the rise of Afrikaner nationalism in the early 20th century, and certainly since World War II, business—until recently, dominated by whites of English descent—has been cast in an adversarial role with respect to government. Afrikaners used their numerical preponderance among the white electorate to seize power and then, through essentially statist and socialist measures, redistributed wealth in favor of the Afrikaner community. Business had exceedingly limited influence over this process. In fact, after the Sharpeville tragedy of 1960, then Prime Minister Hendrik Verwoerd reacted angrily to urgings from English- and Afrikaans-speaking executives to end the system of reserving categories of jobs for whites. He refused to address a major gathering of business leaders, whom he charged with "paving the way for black domination." He also denounced as "traitors" the Associated Chambers of Commerce (ASSOCOM), the most liberal and vocal South African business organization. For some years, government departments refused to receive or even reply to correspondence from ASSOCOM officials. Even as late as 1976, when the ice had thawed, then Prime Minister John Vorster told an ASSOCOM convention that business leaders should keep out of politics, warning them that "efforts to use business organisations to bring about basic change in government policy will fail and cause unnecessary and harmful friction between the government and the private sector. You cannot ask me to implement policies rejected by the electorate and in which I do not believe."

As economic growth and successful political mobilization combined to transform the Afrikaner nation from a rural and blue-collar background into a modern Western people, a class of Afrikaner business leaders emerged whose interests increasingly clashed with apartheid. This class's influence was not unimportant in contributing to the erosion of apartheid in fields such as job assignments and trade union rights for blacks.

But on the central question of political power, the state—the very instrument of Afrikaner modernization—emerged as the key obstacle to political reform. More than 40 per cent of employable Afrikaners now work in the state sector, many having retreated there from the agricultural and mining sectors. Political reform threatens the livelihood of such people. The prospect of sharing power—with the inevitable loss of jobs in the state sector to black South Africans—let alone surrendering power, must look doubly unattractive when a deteriorating economy makes job alternatives hard to find.

The state sector has been the chief beneficiary of apartheid, and bureaucrats and nationalist politicians have been able, in most instances, to pass on the costs of apartheid policies to other groups. Where this has not been possible, these leaders sometimes have concluded that apartheid's costs are cheaper than submitting to pressures that they believe threaten their very security.

Many of the costs of disinvestment, increasing sanctions, and isolation can be passed on to others: black migrant workers from neighboring southern African states, black South Africans, and South African industry and commerce in the form of higher taxes, for example. Yet if sanctions continue to multiply, Pretoria probably will have been fully committed to a repressive and destructive siege by the time the government fully feels their adverse effects. This course of action will have been promoted by the polarizing effect of sanctions that could encourage black and white extremists and discourage those willing to negotiate.

These realities support the South African business view that there are no quick fixes for South Africa and that economic growth is essential to dispel notions of a zero-sum game, as well as to stimulate socioeconomic development. But any realistic assessment of black politics leads to the same conclusions.

Most South African business leaders vigorously oppose apartheid advocates' stress on ethnic divisions in South Africa, and many are campaigning actively for the principle of voluntary association. Nevertheless, the heterogeneous nature of the South African population is a troubling reality.

Undoubtedly, the banned African National Congress (ANC), the political group supported by the largest number of South African blacks, is an important political actor. Consequently, for practical as well as philosophical reasons, South African business advocates the release of the ANC's leadership and the "unbanning" of the organization—and indeed supports the same for all other detainees of conscience and banned organizations. Only when these individuals and groups are enabled to play their role in South Africa's political development will they become constructive forces able to move away from the politics of violence.

But the sad fact is that conflict and divisions among black and predominantly black political groupings based on ideology, interest, tribal identity, and sheer competition for influence are deepening. The black consciousness groups such as the Azanian People's Organization and the Pan-Africanist Congress have strong ideological differences with multiracial organizations and coalitions such as the ANC and the United Democratic Front, and have clashed violently with them in local conflicts. Zulu Chief Gatsha Buthelezi is regarded with intense suspicion by many black groups because of his participation in the homeland system and his opposition to sanctions. But much of this opposition reflects recognition that Buthelezi is a formidable contender for power. The Zulu Inkatha movement he heads is a disciplined mass political movement with a coherent set of principles.

Further complicating the situation are the homeland elites with their vested interests; uncontrolled, radical youth; and a wide range of trade unions that sometimes overtly support the above major groupings, but whose interests often differ importantly from theirs.

Whites should derive no comfort from these divisions because they simply make the whole inevitable process of reaching an accommodation in South Africa messier and more protracted, and the task of a postapartheid government more difficult. But they do exist, and only romantics and revolutionaries believe that they can be conjured out of existence or forcibly removed. Witness the history of Africa to the north of the republic.

Still, such difficulties and complexities in no way prevent South African business from constantly reiterating to government its view that only a process of negotiation with truly influential black leaders on issues of political power will make possible the final transition to a postapartheid society. And only such talks will remove the growing international political vote of no-confidence manifest in the disinvestment-sanctions movement. But rational persuasion obviously has its limits, and South African business leaders realize that constructive domestic and international pressures are essential.

A third reality that hampers rapid change in South Africa is the nature of the South African economy. Sooner or later, apartheid will go, and most of the problems associated with a modernizing, industrializing state with a peculiar mix of First and Third worlds will remain. As a result, the South African business community has focused on two overriding priorities: husbanding resources during the transition and trying to convince all major parties of the importance of wealth creation for the success of a postapartheid society.

In South Africa, as in every other country and in international society itself, the requirement for justice—meaning real equality of opportunity, not utopian egalitarianism—must be balanced with the need for order—meaning stable and effective government. Even during national crises, when the many who are suffering acutely regard anything other than the principle of justice as being of secondary importance, the country's long-term well-being demands that balance be borne in mind.

All South Africans need to be acutely aware of the limited resources available to government and the importance of maintaining and, if possible, increasing resources in the interests of postapartheid society. This is a long-term commitment requiring steady adherence to free enterprise principles and a proper appreciation of the South African economy's real nature.

As a trading country, South Africa can preserve its mining and manufacturing base only if it retains its membership in the Western-dominated international economic system. South Africa must therefore both maintain and expand the capital and technology inflows essential to an industrializing society, and also maintain an ability to compete in international markets.

But South Africa has to run harder than its widespread image in the West as an industrialized country might suggest. Despite all its minerals and diamonds, South Africa is wealthy only in comparison with its less fortunate African neighbors: Its gross national product (GNP) per capita in 1982, when its population was estimated at 30 million, was two and one-half times larger than the average for its 20 subequatorial African neighbors, but only 25 per cent of Canada's.

Further, South Africa has an annual population growth rate of 2.7 per cent and a typical Third World population profile—more than one-half of the population is under the age of 20. Fulfilling even the basic needs of a growing population, such as health, education, employment, and general contentment, is very difficult. Currently, an annual average economic growth rate of 6 per cent is required to create employment for more than 300,000 new job seekers every year. Yet not even this growth rate will help the existing pool of unemployed, estimated at up to 25 per cent of those blacks able to work.

Without foreign capital inflows, the South African economy can grow at little more than 3.5 per cent per annum. In fact, recent growth has been even lower, averaging only 2.5 per cent during the last decade and a shocking 1.1 per cent during the last 5 years. Contributing to these dismal statistics have been the cessation of capital inflows over the last decade and the increase of outflows recently. Economic growth is not in itself sufficient to transform the present order into a more just and stable society, but the above statistics amply demonstrate that it is necessary.

Without international development capital, dismantling apartheid will present both serious problems and major opportunities. Unproductively used or wasted resources will be released by several imminent reforms: The abolition of influx control set for mid-1986 by President P. W. Botha, and now confirmed with immediate effect, will remove one of the fundamental impediments to the creation of a free enterprise economy—namely, the absence of labor mobility.

The accelerated deregulation of the mass of red tape inhibiting small-business activity, if accompanied by labor-intensive housing schemes aimed at reducing the housing backlog in urban areas, will boost the domestic economy and have important multiplier effects throughout the economy and society. Increased urbanization and modernization will be the best form of birth control. As is the case everywhere in the world, urban families in South Africa already are significantly smaller than families in impoverished rural areas. The abandonment of forced population removals, one of the most abhorrent apartheid policies, and of totally unproductive homeland consolidation measures will save enormous human and financial resources.

Among potential dangers, even during the current transition period, satisfying the black population's pent-up socioeconomic demands is requiring ever greater wealth. Black expectations are constantly rising and will no doubt continue to do so when blacks have access to political power.

Meeting those expectations will require development capital as well as transformed business and government policies. Such development capital cannot come solely from South African sources, whatever the economically liberating effect of dismantling apartheid. Currently, government spending stands at a very high 27 per cent of the GNP. But that spending has gone to civil service salaries rather than to essential infrastructure, thereby gravely inhibiting economic growth. Moreover, higher individual and corporate taxes have diminished available investment capital. Similarly, private savings have dropped, exacerbating a vicious circle. Not only will remedying all these shortcomings still leave South Africa short of investment capital, but transformations in South African politics surely will introduce new constraints on the economy.

New Initiatives

Concerning its own policies, South African business is coming to the conclusion that it cannot adapt itself to the new South Africa by carrying on much as it has in the past. The drive to achieve a more representative complexion among employees at all levels will require a range of affirmative action programs much more ambitious than the few in place today. Greater worker participation in business, not just through trade unions but also through shareholding programs and other mechanisms, is likely.

Above and beyond these measures black small business must be encouraged by a variety of means, some similar to well-known minority business schemes in the United States. As Americans themselves understand from hard experience, such programs and initiatives will be controversial and not always successful. Although corporate executives may take progressive stances, their work forces may be resistant to change and imbued with traditional attitudes. What is clear is that the complexion of South African business will in many respects be transformed, though the fundamental principles of private ownership of property will perforce have to remain.

Specifically, my company, Anglo American Corporation of South Africa, is following three important strategies. They all reflect our general belief that what we do now will determine whether we are seen as a credible, nonracial organization in a free enterprise society. First, Anglo American is making a determined effort to visualize what "credible" will mean in 10 or 15 years. It certainly will not mean a simple linear projection of current practices, however progressive our manning and industrial relations policies may be. Credibility will require an absolute, mind-wrenching effort to grasp the future and translate it back to the real action we should be taking now.

Second, we must support and nurture effective and responsible trade union activity. It is impossible to face the future in industrial affairs if we have no one to talk to. We see that this will be a difficult and bumpy road, but we also know that we must move along it, and hope that the trade unions will develop a genuine management role in human and social affairs. This effort will require very careful analysis of the future relationship between management and unions, as it will undoubtedly mature into some much greater form of worker participation.

Labor-management relations must evolve in this direction in order to stave off the kinds of extreme left-wing measures that have ruined so much of the rest of Africa. This prospect also allows hope that intelligent self-interest in the trade unions developing from this greater responsibility and involvement ultimately will offset pressures for purely political solutions.

Third, the company must be a stalwart advocate of the free enterprise theme, with the important obligation that we position ourselves to be seen both practicing and encouraging free enterprise. As a very large corporation, Anglo American naturally has the capitalist label hung around its neck. It will be deeds, rather than words, however, that determine whether we are acceptable to a society that, with the best intentions in the world, will have simplistic views about wealth.

Business operates on a long-term basis. Anglo American needs to plan for a long-term future to encourage industrial and economic growth. If we can show that we are taking a long-term view of the future of South Africa, organizations like the ANC and the trade unions will be encouraged to do the same. It is important to think about the best ways to change mindsets to achieve a democratic South Africa. Business can be at the cutting edge without resorting, as is sometimes advocated, to measures such as not paying taxes. Apart from eliciting the same kinds of counter-productive responses from government that foreign sanctions evoke, such moves would only further undermine respect for the rule of law.

Business leaders realize that the form of the state will have to change just as dramatically as the shape of their businesses. But for all their specificity and agreement on the steps needed to dismantle apartheid, executives seem less united and articulate on what constitutional structure should replace the current system. This matter will have to be negotiated, and business leaders' roles will in one sense be confined to mediating among various political forces. But they can advise on economic structures and, in their long-term commitment to free enterprise, and to the idea of wealth creation, encourage political organizations to take a similar long-term view.

In regard to appropriate political systems, some business voices favor the federal option. It seems to provide the most scope for devolving and sharing power in a way that reflects South African social diversity, and to be most conducive to ensuring the survival of individual freedoms and free enterprise.

Many, to be sure, fondly imagine that federalism can serve as a device to ensure continued white domination; the ruling National party's constitutional vision of an ethnic confederation or federation certainly qualifies as an example. No thinking business leader, however, believes that this is a viable political goal for white South Africans any longer.

At the same time, devices to ensure the protection of individuals and, possibly, minorities—for example, bills of rights and systems of voting such as proportional representation—reflect genuine and valid concerns. Indeed, the adoption of a bill of rights, now widely advocated in liberal and business circles in

South Africa (witness the important business charter published
by the Federated Chamber of Industries), is one way of helping
to restore the classic Western democratic concept of the rule of
law so tragically eroded during the apartheid era. A bill of rights
would not be worth the paper it was written on unless it was supported by the majority of the population of South Africa. Yet one
of the most positive and exciting developments in South Africa
currently is the effort being made by many, including prominent
business leaders, to find common ground in the area of commitment to various freedoms and common-law principles as a prelim-
inary to getting a real negotiating process off the ground.

Realistically, it would be foolish not to expect that at least a
measure of social welfarism will be present in postapartheid society; that the state—just like its Afrikaner predecessor—will try
to redistribute wealth; and that some centralization and
bureaucratization will ensue. What business can and must do is
constantly stress the importance of maintaining a wealth-
generating private sector, hampered as little as possible and able
to compete in both domestic and international markets.

Whatever one's political persuasion, one lesson from the first
25 years of independence in African countries has been absolutely clear: Massive state intervention in the economy through nationalization, through the creation of parastatal enterprises, and
through the building of vast bureaucracies that ignored the interest of agriculture and the bulk of the rural population has been
uniformly disastrous. The 1980s have seen a growing realization
of the inappropriateness, not to say destructiveness, of such policies, and country after country, even if ostensibly maintaining a
socialist line, has moved to stimulate or reestablish its private sector: Mozambique, Tanzania, and Zambia are three examples
close to South Africa. The pragmatic economic policy thus far
pursued by the impeccably socialist Prime Minister Robert Mugabe of Zimbabwe owes much to the advice of Mozambican President Samora Machel, who exhorted Mugabe not to repeat
Mozambique's mistakes, to retain skilled whites, and to stimulate
agricultural production.

It is to be hoped that African leaders will exert similar influence on black South Africans who will be important in the new
South Africa. Indeed, leaders of black southern African states
know that a vibrant South African economy is necessary if their
own economies are to grow adequately. Business has a duty not

to leave this to chance. Of course, South African companies must live out their free enterprise faith in South Africa, pressure government to create circumstances in which all South Africans are free to participate in the capitalist system, and involve themselves in all of the affirmative action programs mentioned above. But they must also engage black political groups in a dialogue about the economic future of South Africa. That was one of the key motivations behind the visit by a group of seven South African business leaders that I led last year to the ANC in Zambia.

The ANC's freedom charter, however admirable it may be in many respects, is a distinctly vague and woolly document on economic matters. Conceived in the circumstances of the mid-1950s, when South Africa was a vastly different place politically and economically, the charter asserts that "the mineral wealth beneath the soil, the banks and monopoly industry shall be transferred to the ownership of the people as a whole: all other industry and trade shall be controlled to assist the well-being of the people."

Yet the goal of continued competition in the international economy is incompatible with nationalization: Large and sophisticated organizations where efficiency is at a premium are rendered less efficient by state intervention, and in the international marketplace, that is their death knell. Even attempts to break down the allegedly monopolistic large companies in South Africa are entirely misguided. Small, open economies like South Africa's benefit from the international operations of large companies. A corporation like Anglo American, employing some 300,000 South Africans, can finance very large projects that generate jobs at home and much needed foreign earnings from sales abroad. It also prides itself on its expertise and efficiency.

Some U.S. companies present in South Africa already have launched innovative efforts, placing considerable development capital in areas such as education, training, and housing. The best American companies are living out their nonracial faith, not just in words, but in deeds. Although they are not breaking the law in South Africa (problematical in a country that needs more respect for the concept of the rule of law), American companies are nevertheless finding ways of challenging existing apartheid legislation that sometimes catalyze the slow process of reform. Thus Americans have helped break down still existing separation of amenities, such as the reservation of certain beaches for certain racial groups, and some are planning to build racially integrated residential areas for their employees as an exception to the Group Areas Act. Such moves do not dramatically sweep apartheid aside. But they do serve a pioneering or path-breaking function that helps government and the rest of the community follow in their footsteps.

Apart from their own initiatives, American companies also can participate in South African–led initiatives. The Urban Foundation, for example, which has done much to spearhead socioeconomic reform in South Africa in the last decade, is leading a great coalition of South African employer groups, black and white, to form a Private Sector Council on Urbanisation. This body will help manage and increase the economic opportunities created by the urbanization process. In the field of education there are private-sector and community projects worthy of support at all levels ranging from primary through technical and university.

South Africa is not a country for the fainthearted. It presents immense challenges but also immense opportunities, as well as the excitement of involvement in one of the great historical processes of change seen in the 20th century. South African business is rapidly adapting, planning, and mobilizing to participate in that great experiment, but it knows that its resources, even when combined with the economic forces liberated by the abolition of apartheid, will be inadequate to the challenge. The American counterparts of South African executives therefore face an awesome responsibility. Many have made good profits in South Africa for decades. But faced with lean times and a host of pressures, they are attracted to the easy option of withdrawal, especially if the ignorance, mischief making, and mythology underlying those pressures are ignored. Greater participation in South Africa and the structural reform initiatives proposed by South African business are much harder roads to walk. But they may also be in one of business's best and most prominent traditions—business risk taking.

BIBLIOGRAPHY

An asterisk (*) preceding a reference indicates that the article or part of it has been reprinted in this book.

BOOKS AND PAMPHLETS

Adam, Heribert and Moodley, Kogila. South Africa without apartheid: dismantling racial domination. University of California Press. '86.

*Amnesty International. South Africa briefing. Amnesty International Publications. '86.

Brewer, John D. After Soweto: an unfinished journey. Clarendon Press. '86.

Breytenbach, Breyten. End papers: essays, letters, articles of faith, workbook notes. Farrar, Straus, Giroux. '86.

Breytenbach, Breyten. The true confessions of an albino terrorist. Farrar, Straus, Giroux. '85.

Brink, Andre Philippus. Writing in a state of siege: essays on politics and literature. Summit Books. '86.

Coker, Christopher. The United States and South Africa, 1968-1985: constructive engagement and its critics. Duke University Press. '86.

Crapanzano, Vincent. Waiting: the whites of South Africa. Vintage Books. '86.

De Gruchy, John W. The church struggle in South Africa. W. B. Eerdmans. '86. (2nd ed.)

Finnegan, William. Crossing the line: a year in the land of apartheid. Harper & Row. '86.

Giliomee, Hermann Buhr and Schlemmer, Lawrence. Up against the fences: poverty, passes, and privilege in South Africa. St. Martin's Press. '85.

Gordimer, Nadine and Goldblatt, David. Lifetimes: under apartheid. Knopf. '86.

Grundy, Kenneth W. The militarization of South African politics. Indiana University Press. '86.

Ingham, Kenneth. Jan Christian Smuts: the conscience of a South African. St. Martin's Press. '86.

Jarvie, Grant. Class, race, and sport in South Africa's political economy. Routledge & Kegan Paul. '85.

Jones, Toeckey. Skindeep. Harper & Row. '86.

Leach, Graham. South Africa: no easy path to peace. Routledge & Kegan Paul. '86.

Leape, Jonathan, Baskin, Bo and Underhill, Stefan. Business in the shadow of apartheid: U.S. firms in South Africa. Lexington Books. '85.

Lelyveld, Joseph. Move your shadow: South Africa black, and white. Penguin Books. '86.

Lipton, Merle. Capitalism and apartheid, South Africa, 1910–84. Rowman & Allanheld. '85.

Love, Janice. The U.S. anti-apartheid movement: local activism in global politics. Praeger. '85.

Mandela, Winnie, Benjamin, Anne and Benson, Mary. Part of my soul went with him. Norton. '85.

Mathabane, Mark. Kaffir boy: the true story of a black youth's coming of age in apartheid South Africa. Macmillan. '86.

Meyer, Carolyn. Voices of South Africa: growing up in a troubled land. Harcourt Brace Jovanovich. '86.

Morris, Michael Spence Lowdell. Soapy water and cabinda: a 1985 rollercoaster through myth and fact in South African political violence. Terrorism Research Associates. '85.

Naidoo, Beverley. Journey to Jo'burg: a South African story. J. B. Lippincott. '85.

Neuhaus, Richard John. Dispensations: the future of South Africa as South Africans see it. W. B. Eerdmans Pub. Co. '86.

North, James. Freedom rising. North American Library. '86.

*Omond, Roger. The apartheid handbook. Penguin Books. '85.

Peace, Judy Boppell. The boy child is dying: a South African experience. Harper & Row. '86.

Razis, Vincent Victor. The American connection: the influence of U.S. business on South Africa. St. Martin's Press. '86.

Rotberg, Robert I. South Africa and its neighbors: regional security and self-interest. Lexington Books. '85.

Smith, Wilbur A. Power of the sword. Little, Brown. '86.

Stadler, Alfred William. South Africa: the political economy of apartheid. St. Martin's Press. '87.

Thompson, Leonard Monteath. The political mythology of apartheid. Yale University Press. '85.

Uhlig, Mark A. Apartheid in crisis. Vintage Books. '86.

Venter, C. The Great Trek. D. Nelson. '85.

Wheatcroft, Geoffrey. The Randlords. Atheneum. '86.

Wilson, Francis and Badsha, Omar. South Africa: the cordoned heart. W. W. Norton & Co. '86.

Woods, Donald. South African dispatches: letters to my countrymen. H. Holt. '87.

PERIODICALS

AFRIKANERS

South Africa: defending the laager. Hale, Frederick. Current History. 84:155-8+. Ap. '85.

My traitor's heart. Malan, Rian. Esquire. 104:75-8+. N. '85.

The Boers' war. Rush, Norman. Harper's. 273:22-4. Ag. '86.

*Tales of Afrikaners. Coetzee, J. M. The New York Times Magazine. 19-22+. Mr. 9, '86.

How the Afrikaners' past shapes their decisions today. Rose, Jonathan. Scholastic Update (Teachers' edition). 118:9-11. Ja. 10, '86.

No from the right in South Africa. Knight, Robin. U.S. News & World Report. 100:30-1. Je. 9, '86.

The white tribe. Coetzee, J. M. Vogue. 176:490-1+. Mr. '86.

South Africa's new dissenters (dissent within Afrikaner ranks). World Press Review. 32:47-8. D. '85.

APARTHEID

*Laboring under apartheid. Belknap, Timothy. Africa Report. 30:57+. My.-Je. '85.

*The year of the amabuthu. Lodge, Tom and Swilling, Mark. Africa Report. 31:4. Mr.-Ap. '86.

South Africa: the hard questions (special section; with editorial comment by George W. Hunt). America. 153: inside cover, 45-63. Ag. 3-10, '85.

Amandla! The rallying cry against apartheid. Brown, Frank Dexter. Black Enterprise. 15:58-61. Ap. '85.

Mogopa: death of a South African village (homelands policy). Browne, F. H. The Christian Century. 101:366-8. Ap. 11, '84.

What is the solution to South Africa's racial problems? (interview with L. H. Sullivan). Christianity Today. 29:56-8+. O. 4, '85.

The race for South Africa. Johnson, Paul. Commentary. 80:27-32. S. '85.

Fighting with bare hands (homelands policy). Mariechild, Jenna. Commonweal. 113:104-7. F. 28, '86.

Race politics in South Africa: change and revolt. Grundy, Kenneth W. Current History. 85:197-200+. My. '86.

U.S. response to apartheid in South Africa (statement, April 17, 1985). Crocker, Chester A. Department of State Bulletin. 85:38-40. Je. '85.

Ending apartheid in South Africa (special section). Department of State Bulletin. 86:1-17. S. '86.

The case against South Africa. Ebony. 40:132-4+. My. '85.

Facing up to apartheid. Baker, Pauline H. Foreign Policy. 64:37-62. Fall '86.

Revolt on the veldt (African National Congress). Douglis, Carole A. and Davis, Stephen M. Harper's. 267:30-41. D. '83.

*Diamonds and migrant labour in South Africa, 1869-1910. Turrell, Rob. History Today. 36:45-9. My. '86.

A man with no way out (S. Mali). Whipple, Christopher. Life. 8:101-6+. Je. '85.

Mother of revolt (W. Mandela). Whipple, Christopher. Life. 9:30-2+. Ag. '86.

South Africa under siege (special section; with editorial comment by Kevin Doyle). Maclean's. 98:2, 18-25. Ag. 5, '85.

*Green is detained. Yellow is missing. Red is confirmed dead. Hochschild, Adam. Mother Jones. 11:14+. S. '86.

Crucibles of the black rebellion. Rieder, Eric. The Nation. 241:169-72. S. 7, '85.

The black agenda for South Africa. Calabrese, Mike and Kendall, Mike. The Nation. 241:393+. O. 26, '85.

After apartheid. Horowitz, Donald L. The New Republic. 193:19-23. N. 4, '85.

The South African wasteland. Breytenbach, Breyten. The New Republic. 193:32-8. N. 4, '85.

Life in Crossroads (squatter camps). Waldorf, Lars. The New Republic. 195:17-19. Ag. 25, '86.

Who is the ANC? (African National Congress). Mufson, Steven. The New Republic. 195:20-2+. Ag. 25, '86.

The coming struggle for power. Uhlig, Mark A. The New York Review of Books. 31:27-31. F. 2, '84.

Waiting for Mandela. Coetzee, J. M. The New York Review of Books. 33:3+. My. 8, '86.

Into the dark chamber: the novelist and South Africa (depiction of torture). Coetzee, J. M. The New York Times Book Review. 91:13+. Ja. 12, '86.

Oppenheimer of South Africa. Lelyveld, Joseph. The New York Times Magazine. 32-5+. My. 8, '83.

Misery in a South African homeland (Ciskei). Lelyveld, Joseph. The New York Times Magazine. 36-9+. S. 25, '83.

Exiles in their native land (new Constitution). Klaaste, Aggrey. The New York Times Magazine. 34-5+. Je. 24, '84.

Defiance in South Africa. Cowell, Alan. The New York Times Magazine. 30-6+. Ap. 14, '85.

A rare talk with Nelson Mandela. Dash, Samuel. The New York Times Magazine. 20-2. Jl. 7, '85.

Guarding the gates of paradise. Gordimer, Nadine. The New York Times Magazine. 34-9+. S. 8, '85.

South Africa: dream and reality. Lelyveld, Joseph. The New York Times Magazine. 40-3+. S. 22, '85.

Notes and comment (anti-apartheid protests in U.S.). The New Yorker. 60:17-19. D. 31, '84.

Waiting (I). Crapanzano, Vincent. The New Yorker. 61:50-2+. Mr. 18, '85.

Waiting (II). Crapanzano, Vincent. The New Yorker. 61:52-4+. Mr. 25, '85.

Notes and comment (differences between current anti-apartheid protests and the protests of the 1960s). The New Yorker. 61:35-6. My. 6, '85.

Notes and comment (National Public Radio's interview with Louis Le Grange, Law and Order Minister). The New Yorker. 62:27-8. S. 8, '86.

Apartheid's harsh grip. Treen, Joseph. Newsweek. 101:31-2+. Mr. 28, '83.

Dealing with apartheid (special section). Newsweek. 105:28-36+. Mr. 11, '85.

Can South Africa save itself? (special section). Newsweek. 106:14-20+. Ag. 19, '85.

Mandela: battling apartheid's rules (W. Mandela). Whitaker, Mark. Newsweek. 106:34-6. D. 16, '85.

Blacks at war (violence directed toward each other). Whitaker, Mark. Newsweek. 107:32-5. Je. 2, '86.

South Africa's civil war (special section). Newsweek. 107:34-43. Je. 23, '86.

Swirling shades of gray (race discrimination in South Africa). Gammon, Clive. Sports Illustrated. 58:78-84+. My. 16, '83.

The fires of anger. Iyer, Pico. Time. 125:40-1+. Ap. 8, '85.

Black rage, white fist (declaration of state of emergency). Smith, William E. Time. 126:24-32. Ag. 5, '85.

Gathering hints of change (special section). Time. 126:22-6. Ag. 19, '85.

Can South Africa avoid race war? (special section). U. S. News & World Report. 99:20-4. Ag. 26, '85.

South Africa teeters on a knife-edge. Knight, Robin. U. S. News & World Report. 99:27-31. S. 2, '85.

Multi-part resolution on South African apartheid. UN Chronicle. 20:34-6. F. '83.

Assembly approves three global meetings on Southern Africa issues; adopts International Convention against Apartheid in Sports. UN Chronicle. 23:16-25. F. '86.

South Africa (address, March 30, 1983). Oppenheimer, Harry Frederick. Vital Speeches of the Day. 49:648-52. Ag. 15, '83.

South Africa's agony (special section). World Press Review. 32:37-42. Je. '85.

South Africa (special section). World Press Review. 32:35-40. N. '85.

SOUTH AFRICA AND THE UNITED STATES

*Standing for sanctions. Gray, William H., III. Africa Report. 31:27. Mr.-Ap. '86.

The churches and investment in South Africa. Sincere, Richard E. America. 150:145-9. Mr. 3, '84.

The screws are tightening on U.S. companies. Miller, Frederic A., Arnold, Bob and Jones, Jim. Business Week. 38-40. F. 11, '85.

Leaving South Africa (U.S. business). Kapstein, Jonathan, Hoerr, John and Weiner, Elizabeth. Business Week. 104-7+. S. 23, '85.

The ethics of disinvestment. Pohl, Keith I. The Christian Century. 102:759-60. Ag. 28-S. 4, '85.

Falwell raises a stir by opposing sanctions against South Africa. Spring, Beth. Christianity Today. 29:52-4+. O. 4, '85.

U.S. policy toward South Africa. Congressional Digest. 64:225-56. O. '85.

*The United States and South Africa: the strategic connection. Rhoda Plotkin. Current History. 85:201+. My. '86.

*South Africa: why constructive engagement failed. Ungar, Sanford J. and Vale, Peter. Foreign Affairs. 64:234-58. Winter '85/'86.

Beyond constructive engagement. Clough, Michael. Foreign Policy. 61:3-24. Winter '85/'86.

*The costs of disinvestment. Relly, Gavin. Foreign Policy. 63:131-46. Summer '86.

Scoring corporate conduct in South Africa (Sullivan Code). Sherman, Stratford P. Fortune. 110:168-72. Jl. 9, '84.

Time to quit South Africa? (U.S. companies). Nielsen, John. Fortune. 112:18-23. S. 30, '85.

*Goodyear toughs it out (South African investment). Kessler, Felix. Fortune. 112:24-6. S. 30, '85.

South Africa: time to stay—or go? Smith, Lee. Fortune. 114:46-8. Ag. 4, '86.

Britain's goodbye? (refusal to join Commonwealth in imposing economic sanctions on South Africa; special section; with editorial comment by Kevin Doyle). Maclean's. 99:2, 14–22. Ag. 18, '86.

Divestment stirs a new generation (anti-apartheid protests). Gitlin, Todd. The Nation. 240:585–7. My. 18, '85.

Reagan's real aims in South Africa. Downey, Thomas J. The Nation. 242:138–40. F. 8, '86.

Students, stocks and shanties (campus divestment movement). Wiener, Jon. The Nation. 243:337–40. O. 11, '86.

Reagan and South Africa: the case for urgent understanding. Hutchinson, John. National Review. 37:25–6+. N. 1, '85.

Divestment imperative. North, James. The New Republic. 192:10–12. Mr. 25, '85.

South Africa's lobbyists. Ungar, Sanford J. The New York Times Magazine. 30+. O. 13, '85.

What America should do about South Africa (why sanctions would hurt blacks most of all). Suzman, Helen. The New York Times Magazine. 14–17. Ag. 3, '86.

The friends of Mr. Botha (American conservatives). Watson, Russell. Newsweek. 106:30–2. S. 2, '85.

Falling short (reaction to R. Reagan's speech on South Africa: special section). Time. 128:12–16+. Ag. 4, '86.

South African reforms and U.S. foreign policy. Williams, Franklin H. USA Today (Periodical). 113:32–5. Jl. '84.

*U.S. economic relations with South Africa: apartheid, some solutions (address, July 22, 1986). Reagan, Ronald. Vital Speeches of the Day. 52:642–5. Ag. 15, '86.

SOUTH AFRICAN POLITICS

What can become of South Africa? O'Brien, Conor Cruise. The Atlantic. 257:41–50+. Mr. '86.

*Is reconciliation possible in South Africa? An interview with Allan Boesak. Hoekema, David A. The Christian Century. 101:546–50. My. 23, '84.

South Africa's domestic strategy. Grundy, Kenneth W. Current History. 82:110–14+. Mr. '83.

South Africa: no new political dispensation. O'Meara, Patrick. Current History. 83:105–8+. Mr. '84.

Revolution in the making: black politics in South Africa. Karis, Thomas G. Foreign Affairs. 62:378–406. Winter '83/'84.

South Africa digs in for a long stay. Goodman, David L. The Nation. 240:545+. My. 11, '85.

Pax Pretoriana. De St. Jorre, John. The New Republic. 190:20-3. Ap. 2, '84.

The struggle: power and politics in South Africa's black trade unions. Cowell, Alan. The New York Times Magazine. 14-27. Je. 15, '86.

*Inside the African National Congress. Uhlig, Mark A. The New York Times Magazine. 20-1+. O. 12, '86.

Politics of the laager. Whitaker, Mark. Newsweek. 106:36-8. Ag. 12, '85.

South Africa: will white rule end? Reed, David. Reader's Digest. 128:146-53. F. '86.

*An interview with Bishop Desmond Tutu. Cooper, Marc and Goldin, Greg. Rolling Stone. 29-30+. N. 21, '85.

Regional stability in Southern Africa: no cause for optimism. Wolpe, Howard. USA Today (Periodical). 113:23-4. Mr. '85.